Torah Revealed, Torah Fulfilled

Torah Revealed, Torah Fulfilled

SCRIPTURAL LAWS IN FORMATIVE JUDAISM AND EARLIEST CHRISTIANITY

Jacob Neusner
Bruce D. Chilton
Baruch A. Levine

NEW YORK • LONDON

2008

T&T Clark International, 80 Maiden Lane, New York, NY 10038

T&T Clark International, The Tower Building, 11 York Road, London SE1 7NX

T&T Clark International is a Continuum imprint.

www.continuumbooks.com

tandtclarkblog.com

Copyright © 2008 by Jacob Neusner, Bruce D. Chilton, and Baruch A. Levine

Scripture translations are by the authors unless otherwise indicated.

All rights reserved. No part of this book may be reproduced, stored in a retrieval system, or transmitted, in any form or by any means, electronic, mechanical, photocopying, recording, or otherwise, without the written permission of the publishers.

Library of Congress Cataloging-in-Publication Data

Neusner, Jacob, 1932-
  Torah revealed, Torah fulfilled : scriptural laws in formative Judaism and earliest Christianity / Jacob Neusner, Bruce D. Chilton, Baruch A. Levine.
    p. cm.
  Includes bibliographical references and index.
  ISBN-13: 978-0-567-02739-9 (hardcover : alk. paper)
  ISBN-10: 0-567-02739-2 (hardcover : alk. paper) 1. Bible. O.T. Pentateuch—Criticism, interpretation, etc. 2. Bible—Criticism, interpretation, etc. I. Chilton, Bruce. II. Levine, Baruch A. III. Title.

BS1225.52.N49 2008
220.6—dc22

2008025362

Printed in the United States of America

For

Joseph Cardinal Ratzinger
Benedict XVI

Contents

Preface ix

Part One: Idolatry and Paganism

1. Scripture's Account: Idolatry and Paganism
   Baruch A. Levine 3
2. Rabbinic Reading: Idolatry and Paganism
   Jacob Neusner 25
3. Early Christian Interpretation: The Case of Justin Martyr
   Bruce D. Chilton 33

Part Two: The Nazirite

4. Scripture's Account: The Nazirite
   Baruch A. Levine 45
5. Rabbinic Reading: The Nazirite
   Jacob Neusner 56
6. The New Testament's Interpretation:
   The Nazirite Vow and the Brother of Jesus
   Bruce D. Chilton 63

Part Three: The Sabbath

7. Scripture's Account: The Sabbath
   Baruch A. Levine 77
8. Rabbinic Reading: The Sabbath
   Jacob Neusner 89
9. Early Christian Interpretation:
   Sunday in the New Testament
   Bruce D. Chilton 104

Part Four: Dietary Purity

10. Scripture's Account: Dietary Purity
    Baruch A. Levine — 113
11. Rabbinic Reading: Clean and Unclean Foods
    Jacob Neusner — 124
12. The New Testament's Interpretation:
    Eucharist as Holy Food, Mimesis of Sacrifice
    Bruce D. Chilton — 131

Part Five: Sexual Purity

13. Scripture's Account: Sexual Purity
    Baruch A. Levine — 143
14. Rabbinic Reading: Sexual Purity
    Jacob Neusner — 160
15. Christian Interpretation:
    Sexuality and Family in Christianity
    Bruce D. Chilton — 173

Part Six: Lex Talionis

16. Scripture's Account: Lex Talionis
    Baruch A. Levine — 187
17. An Eye for an Eye: Lex Talionis in Talmudic Law
    Baruch A. Levine — 204
18. The New Testament's Interpretation: Jesus' Lex Talionis
    Bruce D. Chilton — 217

Notes — 229

Index — 237

Preface

Each party to the millennial disputation between Judaisms and Christianities lays claim to articulate the true meaning of the Torah of Sinai. Most Judaisms from antiquity to modern times claim in their postscriptural formulations to set forth the message of the Torah of Sinai and validate their respective ways of life and worldview by appeal to the Torah. The theology of rabbinic Judaism forms one powerful example of that fact, with its reading of Israelite history as a recapitulation of the history of Adam and Eve. But other Judaisms made the same case for themselves; the *Serakhim*—episodic exegeses of passages of Israelite Scripture found in the Dead Sea Library—are an excellent example.

Not to be outdone, Christianities claim that with Christ the promises of Israelite prophecy were kept. Catholic and orthodox Christianity therefore affirmed the Hebrew Scriptures as the Old Testament, precursor of the New. Even Christian gnostics had to come to grips, if in a negative way, with the Creator-God made known in the Hebrew Scriptures. So from rabbinic Judaism on the one side, through normative and catholic Christianity in the middle, to gnostic Christianity on the other side—all these parties appealed to the common heritage of Israelite Scripture.

One important area at which the competing traditions intersect is scriptural law. The Torah expounds the imperatives of the Sabbath, for example, and rabbinic Judaism articulates those imperatives in a vast exercise of extension and amplification. The Gospels attribute to Jesus important expositions and alterations of the Sabbath rules in light of his own authority. Here is a topic where classical Christianity and rabbinic Judaism intersect, and we may compare and contrast the outcomes. In these pages we expound six components of the Torah's law, spelling out how, in their classic canonical statements, a particular community of Judaism, rabbinic Judaism, and a distinct community of Christianity, the catholic and orthodox church, each received and handed on the Scriptural heritage. Stated simply, the comparison and contrast on a common agendum reveal choices each community selected within a program that Scripture made available to all. These are topics of scriptural law taken up in the writings of the Judaism represented by the rabbinic canon from the Mishnah through the Talmud of Babylonia, and in the writings of the Christianity represented by the Gospels and Paul's Letters and the interpretation of the catholic fathers of the church.

The particular Judaism that speaks here in its response to Scripture's laws is represented by legal and exegetical writings, specifically, four ancient law codes and a dozen compilations of exegesis of Scripture produced in the first six centuries CE by sages bearing the title "rabbi," meaning, "my lord." The Halakhic documents are the Mishnah, around 200 CE; the Tosefta, a supplement, around 250–300 CE; two commentaries to the Mishnah as amplified by the Tosefta; the Talmud of the Land of Israel, known as the Yerushalmi, about 400 CE; and the Talmud of Babylonia, known as the Bavli, ca. 600 C.E. The Haggadic documents present commentaries to Genesis, Exodus, Leviticus, Numbers, and Deuteronomy—the Pentateuch, privileged in rabbinic Judaism; as well as Song of Songs, Lamentations, Ruth, and Esther. The Bavli also contains a large component of Haggadic writing. These documents, all together forming the canon of formative rabbinic Judaism, preserve the state of the rabbinic system from the first through the seventh centuries CE and in continuator-writings define the norms of a single, uniform, universal Judaism from then to modern times.

The New Testament was produced in primitive communities of Christians to prepare people for baptism, to order worship, to resolve disputes, to encourage faith, and for similar communal purposes. As a whole, it is a collective document of primitive Christianity. Its purpose is to call out and order true Israel in response to the triumphant news of Jesus' preaching, activity, death, and resurrection. The New Testament provided the church with the means of accessing the Spirit spoken of in the Scriptures of Israel. Once the New Testament was formed, it was natural to refer to the Scriptures of Israel as the "Old Testament." Early Christianity (between the second and fourth centuries CE) designates the period during which the church founded theology on the basis of the Scriptures. From thinkers as different from one another as Bishop Irenaeus in France and Origen, the speculative teacher active first in Egypt and then in Palestine, a common Christian philosophy began to emerge. The diversity involved inevitably produced disputes, notably between those theologians called "catholic" and those called "gnostic." Early Christianity cannot be understood in its history without reference to gnostic thought; but for the purpose of comparison with the thought of ancient Israel and the rabbis, an obvious Christian counterpart is the catholic and orthodox church, which embraced—in opposition to clearly stated gnostic denials—both the Hebrew Scriptures and the biblical claim that God may be known through his creation of a basically good earth.

We seek to identify the recurrent tensions, the blatant points of emphasis, the recurring indications of conflict and polemic. Framing the issue of the disposition of the scriptural heritage in broad terms, we describe what characterizes the Gospels and the Mishnah, the letters of Paul and the Tosefta. In other words, if we take whole and complete the writings of first- and second-century people claiming to form the contemporary embodiment of Scripture's Israel and ask what they all stress as a single point of insistence, the answer is self-evident. Nearly every Christianity and nearly all known Judaisms appeal for validation to the Scriptures of ancient Israel, their laws and narratives, their prophecies and visions. All parties appeal to Scripture—but not to the same verses of Scripture. In Scripture, all participants in the common Israelite culture propose to find validation—but not for a common theological program subject to diverse interpretation. From Scripture, every community of Judaism and Christianity takes away what it will, but not with the assent of all the others.

Why do we select the ancient Israelite Scripture in particular and in common?

Open any ancient Judaic religious text, and what do you find if not a systematic response to Scripture, its law, narratives, and prophecies? The rabbinic literature of the formative age focuses not only on the amplification of Scripture's laws but also on the recapitulation of its narratives. The ancient rabbis composed a massive demonstration that their law and doctrine simply replicated those of Scripture; that forms the single pervasive proposition of the rabbinic canon. For their part, the Gospels find the meaning of Jesus' words and deeds in the context of Scripture, and there is no understanding Rabbi Jesus (in the elegant formulation of Professor Chilton) without constant reference to the Torah and Prophets. The Letters of Paul, the Pastoral Epistles, the Letter to the Hebrews—all conduct a dialogue with Scripture. The systematic citation of proof texts of Scripture by rabbinic Judaism and orthodox, catholic Christianity forms an indicator of this deeper conviction, characteristic of each party: here is fulfilled the intent of God's instruction to Moses and to the prophets.

Our purpose is both academic and theological. In these exercises we contribute to the academic study of religion, particularly comparative religions, seeking perspective through contrasting the presentation of common topics. We contribute to the theological conversation between Judaism and Christianity. A program of sharing Scripture and contesting its intent and meaning allows ample space for each party to establish a position it deems valid by the criteria of truth accepted by all participants: a true argument. To begin with, what emerges is an exchange of information—not to be gainsaid. But in time the range of choices facing the formative generations of Christianity and Judaism will register, and Judaisms and Christianities will come into a common focus: facing a common set of propositions, each heir of Scripture made its choices. And that brings us to our distinctive contribution: the specification of ways taken and ways not taken.

Topic by topic comes the Torah's original statement, as expounded by Professor Levine. What follows is a two-part exposition: the rabbinic-Judaic and Christian formulation of the same topic, spelled out by Professors Neusner and Chilton, respectively. These three elements form the shank of each part. All together, they afford perspective on the distinct viewpoints that animate important components of ancient Judaism and ancient Christianity.

PART ONE

Idolatry and Paganism

1

Scripture's Account

Idolatry and Paganism

Baruch A. Levine

The principal mandate of biblical religion is the exclusive worship of the God of Israel, whose name is written with four Hebrew consonants, *Yod-Heh-Waw-Heh* (= *YHWH*), the Tetragrammaton. "Yahweh" has become the conventional pronunciation of this divine name in modern scholarship. The exclusive worship of Yahweh is specifically ordained in the second commandment of the Decalogue. It is introduced by the first commandment, which is more precisely a declaration: "I am Yahweh, your God, who brought you out of the land of Egypt, out of the house of bondage" (Exod 20:2; Deut 5:6). And so it is written in Deut 6:4: "*Šĕmaʿ Yiśrāʾēl*—Give heed, oh Israel! Yahweh is our God, Yahweh is (the only) one." The opening affirmation of the Decalogue generates the negation of polytheism, which follows immediately in the opening words of the second commandment: "You shall have no other gods in my presence" (literally, "facing my countenance," Hebrew: ʿ*al-pānāy*, Exod 20:3; Deut 5:7).

Like any number of biblical statements on the subject of proper worship, the Decalogue acknowledges that "other gods" indeed exist, while emphatically prohibiting Israelites from worshipping them. Accordingly, the belief system underlying the Decalogue is best defined as henotheism, the worship of one national god, rather than universal monotheism, which negates the very existence of the "gods" worshipped by other nations. The conception of Yahweh as God of all nations was to emerge at a later stage in biblical religion, and it is expressed in unequivocal statements. An example is the exilic Deutero-Isaiah (45:5): "I am Yahweh, and there is none other; except for me, there is no god!" This stands in bold contrast to the epic tradition, epitomized in Exod 15:11: "Who is like you among the gods, Yahweh?"

After outlawing the worship of other gods, the second commandment continues with the prohibition of idolatry, which is defined as the worship of cult images thought to represent, or symbolize, divine beings:

4 Idolatry and Paganism

You shall not fashion for yourself a sculptured image, nor any likeness of what is in the heavens above, or of what is on the earth below, or of what is in the waters under the earth. You shall not bow down to them nor worship them. For I, Yahweh, am your God; an impassioned god [ʾēl qannāʾ], who visits the guilt of fathers on sons, and on children of the third and fourth generations of those who hate me, but who acts with kindness to the thousandth generation of those who love me, and keep my commandments. (Exod 20:3–6; Deut 5:7–10)

In sequence, the ban on idolatry is a corollary of the prohibition of polytheism; it prescribes a means of eliminating polytheism from the midst of the people of Israel. This is the ultimate objective of the second commandment. Although not all ancient Near Eastern cults were iconic, most were, by far, so that if Israelites were to avoid fashioning images and bowing down to them, so the thinking goes, they would predictably avoid worshipping "other gods" in the process. Understood in this way, the ban on idolatry does not constitute a separate commandment.

To put it in graphic terms, the Decalogue warns that Yahweh will not share the stage with other deities, which is what "facing my countenance [ʿal-pānāy]" connotes. Consequently, cult images of other deities were not to be installed in Yahweh's sacred spaces, facing him, as was characteristic of the cultic scene in ancient Canaan and elsewhere. Normally, a cult installation, whether an open-air bāmâ (platform/high place) or an enclosed sanctuary, contained an assemblage of images, one usually representing the national god, who is joined by images of other deities, including a consort goddess. We know this, for example, from the contemporary Edomite cult site at Qitmit in the southern Negev, where the Edomites' national god, Qaus, did share the stage with other deities. Yahweh will not countenance this sort of cultic choreography; he will punish idolaters and their descendants. This stipulation begins in the Decalogue as a prohibition affecting only Israelite cult sites where Yahweh was worshipped; in time it became territorial, so that idolatrous cults were banned from the entire land, no matter who the worshippers were. This expanded horizon is most clearly reflected in Deuteronomy, especially in the writings of the Deuteronomist, and subsequently, in the priestly literature of the Torah. It is also an essential, prophetic doctrine.

The contextual exegesis of the second commandment raises critical questions at the outset: If, indeed, the image ban was directed at representations of "other gods," where, if at all, does the Hebrew Bible explicitly prohibit fashioning images of Yahweh himself? Do we have evidence of the utilization of images of Yahweh in ancient Israel? There is every indication that the proper cult of Yahweh was aniconic from the very outset. For this reason, most likely, we lack a clear, biblical statement banning images of Yahweh; such a statement was deemed unnecessary!

Most modern scholars have read the second commandment differently, however, and have concluded that the Decalogue's ban applied as well to images of Yahweh by inference, or a fortiori. That interpretation of the second commandment collides with the tone of biblical pronouncements on the subject of idolatry, as we shall see. What is more, it impacts our understanding of official attitudes toward idolatry in biblical Israel by implying that polytheism is sinful because it is idolatrous. The converse is closer to the mark: Idolatry is sinful because it is intimately associated with polytheism. It is the eradication of polytheism, with its mythological conceptions of the divine, that is, after all, the principal religious challenge addressed in the Hebrew Bible. As the political horizon expanded beyond native Canaanites and neighboring peoples, idolatry came to symbolize, as well, the threatening power of the idolatrous empires of the world, especially the Egyptians, Assyrians, and Babylonians. At that point Israelite prophets began to expound the doctrine that Yahweh, the God of Israel, is the only deity who truly exists and exercises power.

Because idolatry was a prevalent feature of polytheism, its meaning and practice cannot be discussed in detachment from polytheism. And yet, it would carry us beyond the extent of the present inquiry to engage the protracted struggle against polytheism in all of its aspects. Consequently, we will limit ourselves to biblical sources that relate explicitly to idolatry, while remaining aware that much more could be said about the varieties of worship in ancient Israel. The selected sources are of several types, ranging from laws and rituals, to etiological narratives and prophetic polemic.

The Ban on Cult Images: Iconoclasm in the Service of Cultic Exclusivity

Prohibitions and Admonitions in the Torah

In Torah literature, the closest we come to an implied prohibition of images of Yahweh is in the Deuteronomist's recollection of the theophany at Mount Sinai/Horeb. Thus, Deut 4:12, 15–20:

> Then Yahweh spoke to you out of the fire; you heard the sound of words but perceived no pictorial form [těmûnâ]—nothing but a voice.
>
> Exercise great care for yourselves—since you beheld no pictorial form on the day Yahweh spoke to you at Horeb from the midst of the fire—lest you act wickedly by fashioning the form of any symbol for yourselves, a design [tabnît], either male or female. [Or] the design of any animal on the earth, or the design of any winged bird that flies in the heavens, or the design of any creeping creature on the ground, or the design of any fish that is in the waters under the earth. And [this is] lest you lift your eyes heavenward and behold the sun and the moon and the stars, the entire host of heaven, and you are lured away into bowing down to them and worshipping them, those that Yahweh has apportioned to all the peoples under the heavens. But Yahweh adopted you, and brought you out of the

iron blast furnace, from Egypt, to become his land-possessing people as of today. [cf. Deut 4:23, 25]

The main thrust of this statement is surely the prohibition of polytheism, not merely of idolatry, strictly speaking. As a matter of fact, some astral cults of the kind alluded to here were aniconic. A prime example is the Egyptian cult of Aten, in which Raʿ, the sun god, was worshipped exclusively. The House of the Aten in Tell el-Amarna contained no cult images, only a stela representing the Pharaoh and his queen worshipping the Aten. The Aten temples were open to the sky so as to ensure that the sun in the heavens would be worshipped, not some emblem symbolizing the sun.

And yet, the wording of the Deuteronomist presumes an expectation on the part of the Israelites that a proper deity would have manifested his presence in an image or pictorial representation. The message is clear: Yahweh has no desire to be represented morphically. Rather, he made his presence felt by means of words spoken in a resounding voice emerging from mighty flames, and by his mighty acts of liberation, which the Israelites had experienced. More will be said on this subject when we discuss idolatry as a phenomenon (below).

The rest of Torah literature is consistent regarding the ban on cult images to be directed at representations of "other gods," not toward prohibiting images of Yahweh. We begin with Exod 20:19b-20, in the introduction to the Book of the Covenant:

You have seen for yourselves how I spoke with you from the heavens. Therefore, you shall not fashion gods of silver with me [ʾittî], nor shall you fashion gods of gold for yourselves.

The force of prepositional phrase ʾittî, "with me," is graphic: "near me, alongside me." This formulation reflects the description of the cultic scene, as it has been described above. See further, in Exod 23:24; 34:14, 17:

You shall not bow down to their gods nor worship them, nor fashion objects like theirs. Rather shall you surely tear these down, and smash their cultic stelae.
For you shall not bow down to any other deity, for Yahweh is named "the impassioned one." He is truly an impassioned God.
You shall not fashion for yourselves molten gods.

Clearly resonating with the Decalogue, these statements equate *images* with *gods* by metonymy, so that the worship of "other gods" is expressed as bowing down to the idols that represent them. Furthermore, these statements are also Deuteronomist in tone, as is brought out by a passage in the introduction to the Deuteronomic Code, in Deut 12:2–3:

> You must utterly destroy all of the cult sites where the nations you are about to dispossess used to worship their gods, atop high mountains and on the hills and under every luxuriant tree. You must tear down their altars, smash their cultic stelae, and their Asherim burn in flames, and cut down the statues of their gods, so that you obliterate their name from that site.

This aggressive policy, couched in the context of the Israelite conquest of Canaan, is preceded by other, similar statements in Deut 7:5, 25; 9:12, 16. The same theme also informs the covenant curses in 27:15; 28:36, 64 and the admonition of 29:15–17. The Deuteronomic Code itself (roughly 12:4–26:19, with interpolations), addresses the issue of polytheism in a prominent way (12:29–31; 13:7–19), but hardly, if ever, refers explicitly to idolatry in that context.

The priestly source in Torah literature, in the Holiness Code of Leviticus, contains a statement explicitly prohibiting idolatry: "Do not turn toward idols or fashion for yourselves molten gods (Lev 19:4). The idiomatic *pānâ ʾel-*, "to turn toward," used in this verse, connotes both reliance upon and deference toward the object of the act, in this case the idols representing other gods. Further on, Lev 19:31 employs the same idiom in prohibiting certain kinds of divination. In what appears to be a postscript to the Holiness Code, Lev 26:1 prohibits fashioning and installing various cult objects:

> Do not fashion for yourselves idols, nor erect for yourselves any image or cult stela, nor install in your land any figuratively decorated stone upon which to bow down; for I, Yahweh, am your God.

A passing reference to idolatry comes in Lev 26:30, in the curse section of the epilogue to the Holiness Code. Yahweh threatens to destroy the Israelite cult platforms, where forbidden idols had been installed. Finally, in Num 33:52 we read Moses' words to the Israelites in the steppes of Moab, as they prepare to enter the promised land:

> You must drive out all of the inhabitants of the land from your presence. You shall ruin all of their figurative objects, and all of their molten images shall you ruin, and all of their cult platforms shall you destroy.

In summary, the commandments, laws, and admonitions of the Torah, often resonating with the diction of the Deuteronomist, were aimed at preventing the worship of other gods on the part of Israelites; they do not directly address the use of images of Yahweh as an issue. At the most, the Deuteronomist conveys an awareness of the appeal of idolatry, urges resistance to it, and reminds the people that at their pristine theophany, they had not seen any morphic representation of Yahweh. As we close the book on Torah literature, the image ban has become territorial, prohibiting all those who inhabit the promised land, Israelites and others, from practicing idolatry.

8   *Idolatry and Paganism*

Etiological Narratives Related to Northern Israelite Cults

In the search for indications that images of Yahweh, as distinguished from those representing other deities, may have been in use in ancient Israel, some have pointed to various biblical narratives that relate to cultic activity in northern Israel. First to appear in biblical literature, and set at the time of the Exodus, is the episode of the golden bull-calf, related in Exod 32 (and recollected in Deut 9:16). Then there are the narratives about the idols possessed by Micaiah/Micah, preserved in Judg 17–18. We also find cryptic references to an Israelite bull cult in Hosea's prophetic condemnations (8:5; 10:5), and Judg 6 preserves a narrative relating how the charismatic leader Gideon/Jerubbaal affirmed his loyalty to Yahweh.

The episode of the golden bull-calf would allow us to conclude that Yahweh was depicted in image form only if the golden bull-calf was intended to represent Yahweh. Historically, this narrative is associated with the sin of Jeroboam I, king of northern Israel in the latter part of the 10th century BCE. He is condemned for having installed bull calves at Dan and Bethel (1 Kgs 12:28–33; 2 Kgs 10:29; 2 Chr 11:15; 13:8). If, however, the image of the golden bull-calf represented, for example, the Syro-Canaanite deity El, often depicted as a bull, and who bore the epithet $tr\ il$, "the Bull, Ilu," in Ugaritic mythology, then its fashioning would not indicate that images of Yahweh himself were employed as objects of worship by Israelites. Similarly, the discovery of statues of bulls at ancient sites in the land of Israel does not mean that such artifacts represented Yahweh.

The account of the golden bull-calf is admittedly ambiguous and sends a double message regarding the character of worship in ancient Israel. It appears that, like most etiological texts of this sort, it has undergone extensive redaction, responding to developments in Israelite religion. On the one hand, we read that Aaron identified the image of the bull-calf as "your god, O Israel, who brought you out of the land of Egypt" (Exod 32:4; cf. v. 8). This resonates with and yet directly contravenes the first commandment of the Decalogue. It is as if to say, "This image, not Yahweh, is your god." On the other hand, we read in Exod 32:5 that Aaron announced a festival to Yahweh when the image of the bull-calf had been installed, thereby implying that it did, indeed, represent the God of Israel. There are, however, good reasons to conclude that the original import of the episode was to condemn El worship, to outlaw what may be termed "cultic regression," a reversion to earlier practices. None other than the patriarchs, themselves, had worshipped El (e.g., Gen 31:13), but at a later time, so we are told, Moses was informed that it was Yahweh, not El, who had revealed himself to the Patriarchs (Exod 6:2–9). If this analysis of the episode of the golden bull-calf is correct, it cannot be adduced as evidence that Israelites utilized images of Yahweh and that the second commandment is targeting this practice.

Like the account of the golden bull-calf in Exod 32, the narratives preserved in Judg 17–18 have been taken to mean that Israelites at one time utilized cult images of Yahweh. In the book of Judges, as it has been edited, we first read in Judg 17:1–6 of a certain resident of the Ephraimite hill country named Micaihu (Micah), who possesses two idols and keeps them in his house. These objects are described as *pesel ûmassēkâ*, "a sculpted image and a molten image" (17:3). This is a rare combination of terms, occurring elsewhere only in the covenant curse of Deut 27:15: "Cursed be the person who fashions a sculptured image or a molten image, which is an abomination to Yahweh, and stores it in a secret place." That Torah statement clearly refers to the clandestine worship of other gods. In effect, Micaihu is doing precisely what Deut 27:15 prohibits!

Now, both Micaihu and his mother pronounce blessings in the name of Yahweh, while at the same time having private recourse to images of other gods in their homes, not in public. This detail is significant because Micaihu himself operates a local temple (Jud 17:5). It reveals the mentality of the author, who projects a pattern of worshipping other gods alongside Yahweh. Judges 17:7–13 carries the tale further, relating how a certain Micah (the same person, with his name spelled differently) secures the services of an itinerant Judean Levite as a priest to officiate at his temple. Once again, we read of Micah's home, which is fast becoming a meeting place for travelers. So now Micah has cult images and also a trained priest, who extends the ambiguity of this tale by expressing gratitude to Yahweh for his professional good fortune.

Enter the migrating Danites, whose adventures are told in Judg 18, which is the primary text. The Danites send spies from their settlement in Zorah and Eshtaol to reconnoiter the land to the north, and on the way, these men lodge at the home of Micah. They request the young priest whom Micah has appointed to make oracular inquiry on their behalf to Yahweh, which he does. The priest tells the Danites that Yahweh is with them in their search for a new territory (Judg 18:2–6). The Danite spies proceed to Laish in Upper Galilee, then report back to their base with encouraging news. The Danites then dispatch a military force to conquer that northern area, again passing through Micah's town. They not only lure away Micah's priest but also steal his cultic paraphernalia to boot, as specified in Judg 18:16–17: the sculpted image and the molten image, about which we have read, and also the ephod and teraphim. This list of cult objects is repeated with variations.

Two postscripts were tacked on to Judg 18, in verses 30–31, as if to correct for some omissions: They chronicle what has happened to Micah's *pesel* in the course of time. First, we are told that the Danites installed Micah's idol at the cult site of Dan, and that it was served by a named priestly family until the northern Israelites were deported (721 BCE). A later editor added a qualification: That same image had been installed at Shiloh, where it stood as long as the temple lasted there, after which it was presumably relocated in Dan. The point is inescapable: The northern Israelites had been idolatrous from the start!

The Role of the Image Ban in Advancing the Yahwist Movement

The Hebrew Bible, if read closely, tells of a protracted struggle within the Israelite societies over the exclusivity of the cult of Yahweh. The Yahwist movement sought to break free of the older pattern of worshipping the God of Israel alongside other gods and goddesses of the regional, West-Semitic pantheon—El, Baal,

Ashtoreth, Asherah, and others. Goddesses were apparently the first to be targeted, and they were followed by the rejection of Baal. The fate of El was quite different. Against the background of a tradition of El worship by the patriarchs, and notwithstanding limited polemics against El worship, El was eventually synthesized with Yahweh, so that his separate identity was submerged. In the context of this religious conflict, the banning of images served as a way of promoting the exclusive worship of Yahweh.

The historical books of the Bible, from Joshua through Kings, pursue several agendas, one of which is to identify the persistent heterodoxy of the Israelites as the underlying cause of defeat and ruin. Both historiographers and redactors preached the doctrine that to deserve all good things—victory, prosperity, peace, and security—required the total abandonment of idolatry as a feature of polytheism. Whereas the narratives of Judg 17–18 were aimed against El worship, the historical books, taken as a whole, focus more on the Baal cults of northern Israel, and to an extent on the cult of Asherah. We periodically encounter the command to eliminate other gods, which functionally translates into casting away the images that represent or symbolize them. Observe examples as in Joshua's farewell instructions to the Israelites (Josh 24:14):

> Now, then, fear Yahweh and worship him with sincere truthfulness, and remove the gods whom your ancestors worshipped in Cis-Euphrates and in Egypt, and instead worship Yahweh. [cf. 24:23]

And in Samuel's words to the Israelites, who sought relief from the Philistines (1 Sam 7:3–4):

> Then Samuel spoke to the entire house of Israel as follows: If with all of your heart you intend to return to Yahweh, remove the alien gods from your midst, and the Ashtoreth-goddesses, and commit yourselves to Yahweh. Worship him alone, and he will rescue you from the power of the Philistines. So the Israelites removed the Baal-gods and the Ashtoreth-goddesses and worshipped Yahweh exclusively.

In the above passages, reference is certainly to the removal of images of other gods. There are numerous further expressions of the "removal" typology (1 Sam 28:3; 1 Kgs 15:12; 2 Kgs 3:2; 2 Chr 14:3; 33:15; 34:33; and cf. Gen 35:2). First and Second Kings preserve routine condemnations of polytheism, classified as the worship of divine images. These are usually to be found in retrospective criticisms of the kings of Judah and northern Israel, blaming them for the fate of the two kingdoms. An example is 1 Kgs 14:9, within a prophetic address to the wife of Jeroboam on the subject of her husband's sins:

> You have done worse things than all who preceded you. You went about fashioning other gods and molten images so as to anger me; but as for me, you have cast me behind your back.

Jeroboam I epitomized the heterodoxy of the kings of northern Israel, because he had sponsored the bull cults at Dan and Bethel and had altered the cultic calendar (1 Kgs 11–13; and cf. 2 Kgs 17:22–23; 23:15). In effect, the breakup of the united monarchy after the death of Solomon, as well as the Assyrian annexation of the northern kingdom of Israel in 721 BCE, are blamed on Jeroboam's idolatry. His name is further evoked in redactional references to "the sins of Jeroboam" as the issue of the *bāmâ* platforms comes to the fore in Second Kings. In a parallel manner, 2 Kgs 21 recounts the cultic sins of Manasseh, king of Judah, whose heterodoxy is similarly blamed for the ultimate downfall of the southern kingdom at the hands of the Babylonians.

It would be well to step back at this point so as to examine some pivotal episodes related in the historical books, where iconoclasm figures in the ascendancy and eventual dominance of the Yahwist movement. We begin with Judg 6, the story of Gideon, whose real name was Jerubbaal, one of the biblical "judges," a charismatic leader from northern Israel. After sacrificing to Yahweh, whose messenger had appeared to him amid signs, Gideon was ordered to tear down the Baal altar and the wooden Asherah maintained by his father, which he did, and to offer sacrifice to Yahweh. At one point, the wording of the text is cryptic. The strange reference to *par haššôr*, "the young bull of the bull" (Judg 6:25; cf. 6:28), has been taken as an allusion to a statue of a bull associated with the Baal altar, a statue presumably to be destroyed along with the Asherah. On this basis we would translate: "the young bull for the bull image." In any event, the clear message of this narrative is that Yahweh, not Baal of the regional pantheon, is the deity who alone should be worshipped. Not only did Yahweh liberate the Israelites from Egypt in the past, something that Gideon had known before his assignment as leader of the people, but he also is the deity who would now grant them sovereignty over the promised land and victory over their current enemies.

Iconoclasm also figured in Jehu's overthrow of the Omride dynasty in the latter half of the ninth century BCE. In 2 Kgs 9–10 we read that this Transjordanian usurper first killed off the descendants of the house of Ahab and then proceeded to lure all of the Baal priests into the Baal temple, which stood either inside the capital of Samaria or on its outskirts. It is in the course of reading about that event that we encounter references to iconoclasm, as in 2 Kgs 10:26–28:

> They took out the stelae of the temple of Baal and burned it. They tore down the Baal stelae, and tore down the temple of Baal and made it into latrines, to this very day. Thus Jehu eradicated the Baal cult from Israel.

The only cult objects explicitly mentioned are the Baal stelae, but it is to be assumed that the Baal temple contained any number of images, and its razing effectively destroyed them. As the text states, these actions eliminated the worship of Baal, or at least struck it a major blow. Jehu's actions on behalf of the cult of Yahweh and against Baal worship, set in an early period, are reenacted, albeit in a quite different manner, by Josiah, King of Judah, in 622 BCE, as recounted in 2 Kgs 22–23. Along with initiating reforms in the manner of Israelite worship, and tearing down the local *bāmâ* platforms, Josiah set out to purge the Jerusalem temple and to destroy idolatrous cult sites in Jerusalem's environs. He decommissioned the necropolis of Bethel by defiling it permanently. Among other things, he ground to dust the Asherah idol that Manasseh had installed in the Jerusalem temple. What we have is a typology of iconoclasm undertaken by committed Yahwist kings to combat the tendency within Israelite society to worship other gods alongside Yahweh, God of Israel. Reading 2 Kgs 23 brings us back to the second commandment of the Decalogue. According to the text, in Jerusalem and Judah the very prohibitions specified in the Decalogue had been violated.

Biblical scholarship has found it difficult to account for Josiah's activities, which seem to reflect two distinct agendas: (1) The centralization of the cult of Yahweh in the Jerusalem temple and the consequent banning of the *bāmâ* platforms, and (2) the purification of the temple and priesthood and the elimination of idolatry, as it involved the worship of other gods. It is reasonable, however, to regard both of these agendas as part of the same, overall struggle to advance strict Yahwism in preexilic Judah. Cult centralization was not a separate issue, practically speaking, but in large part an effort to control Israelite worship by restricting its venue. Its aim was to eliminate forms of worship, current at local cult sites and even in the Jerusalem temple, where Israelites tended to worship Yahweh alongside Baal and Asherah and other West Semitic deities. In the same vein, it is legitimate to include as examples the many references in First and Second Kings to the sins of Judean and northern Israelite kings in sponsoring the worship of other gods for the benefit of their foreign wives. Normally, such references are to be found in redactional entries, which employ terms taken from the vocabulary of idolatry.

The postexilic historical books, Ezra-Nehemiah and Chronicles, add little to what we know of the role of the image ban in advancing strict Yahwism. References to idolatry in Chronicles occur mostly in restatements of verses from First and Second Kings. In some respects, the struggle against polytheism was over by the time Chronicles was written, and other concerns dominated the agenda. In a romanticized narrative of piety, Daniel 3 extols the virtues of the Judean exiles in Babylonia, who refused to bow down to a cult image erected by Nebuchadnezzar.

Idolatry as a Target of the Prophetic Movement

All of the biblical prophets, both literary and nonliterary, sought to eliminate polytheism. And yet they varied greatly in the extent of their specific attacks on idolatry, as a prime feature of polytheism. We begin with the earliest of the literary prophets: Hosea, Amos, Micah, and First Isaiah. For the most part we encounter in their writings prophetic teachings that were current during the eighth century BCE, both in Judah and in northern Israel, and we again observe a disproportionate focus on northern Israelite heterodoxy. Thus Hosea (4:17) of northern Israel says: "Ephraim is addicted to images. Count him out!"

This statement is part of a larger prophecy of rebuke, which takes up all of Hosea, chapter 4. The people of northern Israel, in the years leading up to the

Assyrian annexation, are described as "hooked" on idolatry, unable to give it up. Truth be told, they had been worshipping Baal since the time of the Exodus from Egypt (Hos 11:1–2; 13:1–2). The same thought is expressed in 8:3–6, a cryptic passage already noted for its reference to a northern Israelite bull cult in Samaria. Thus Hos 8:4b–6 declares:

> Of their silver and gold they have made themselves idols,
> For this reason they will be banished.
> I reject your bull-calf, Samaria! I am furious with them!
> How long will they be unworthy of exoneration?
> For it was Israel's doing!
> For it [the bull-calf] was made by a craftsman; it is not a god!
> For surely, the bull-calf of Samaria shall be reduced to splinters!

Further on, in Hos 10:5–6, the prophet predicts that the famous idol of Samaria will be carried away to Assyria, along with the Israelite deportees. The theme of idols being carried away by conquerors occurs again in a condemnation of the royally sponsored temple at Bethel by the prophet Amos (5:26–27), who mentions emblems of Saturn used in a forbidden astral cult. For his part, Micah (1:7) predicts the destruction of Samaria and states that its idols will likewise be destroyed. The prophet derides those cult objects by saying that they were paid for from the harlot's hire, an arrangement specifically forbidden in Deut 23:19. Further on, Micah (5:12–14) prophesies that Yahweh, in destroying the land, will bring an end to sorcery and divination among the Israelites, and to idolatry as well.

Before leaving the eighth-century prophets, it is worth mentioning that the book of Hosea preserves a rare prophecy of repentance, which will bring an end to idolatry in Israel. In addressing the Israelites of the northern Kingdom before its downfall, soon after middle of the eighth century BCE, the prophet envisions the people abandoning idolatry willingly. As part of a larger commitment not to rely on treaties with either Egypt (signified by the reference to horses) or with Assyria, they also pledge to worship Yahweh exclusively. Thus Hosea 14:4 and 9, part of a projected dialogue between the Northern Israelites and Yahweh, declares:

> Assyria shall not save us; no longer will we ride on horses.
> No longer will we call our handiwork our god.
> For by you [alone] will the orphan be shown love. . . .
> Ephraim [shall ask]: "What further need do I have of idols?"
> Beholding him, I [Yahweh] replied:
> "I am like a verdant cypress tree.
> Your fruit is available from me."

Turning to the most extensive of the early prophets, First Isaiah of Jerusalem, one is surprised by the paucity of specific references to Israelite idolatry. The prophet is clearly aware of the presence of idolatry in Judah and Jerusalem (Isa 2:8, 18–20), a reality further implied by the words he puts into the mouth of the king of

Assyria. That powerful ruler boasts that he has conquered capitals with more idols than Samaria and Jerusalem (Isa 10:10). In this very statement, the prophet introduces a new category, *mamlĕkōt hāʾĕlîl*, "the idolatrous kingdoms," a thought later resonated by the prophet Jeremiah (50:38) in describing the devastation of Babylonia: "For it is a land of idols, and they revel in evil spirits."

First Isaiah denies the very existence of other gods. As a result, the scope of his polemic against idolatry shifts from endorsing an internal cultic policy of exclusivity, to formulating a global ideology in response to the Assyrian threat. This shift has been already seen in Hos 14, and in the same vein the prophet Nahum (1:14), prophesying at the time of Nineveh's downfall near the end of the seventh century BCE, foresees that Yahweh will eliminate all of the enemy's idols from their temples.

Jeremiah and Deutero-Isaiah carried the attack further. The practice of idolatry is an indication that the nations of the world are stupid, or else they would surely realize that idols are powerless. This theme is also expressed by Habakkuk (2:19), speaking at the time of the Babylonian destruction of Jerusalem. He chides the Judeans for having placed their trust in idols, in effect portraying his own people as being as stupid as the nations:

Ah, you who say: "Wake up!" to wood, "Awaken!" to inert stone.
Can it provide [oracular] instruction?
It is encased in gold and silver, and there is no breath in it at all.

Prophetic diatribes against idolatry emphasize above all else that idols are the products of human manufacture. In discussing idolatry as a phenomenon (below), we will have occasion to shed light on the serious implications of this typology, which receives its fullest expression in Jer 10 and in Deutero-Isaiah, chapters 40; 44; and 46. Except for later interpolations, these writings range from the near-exilic period of the late seventh century to the conclusion of the exile during the third quarter of the sixth century BCE. The several parodies exhibit many similarities, suggesting that there was a typology of parodies on idolatry. Let us turn first to Jer 10:3b–10 (with omissions):

For it [the idol] comes from a tree of the forest,
That a craftsman fashioned, having felled it with an ax.
He adorns it with silver and gold; he fastens it with nails,
Using a hammer, so that it will not come apart.
Such objects are like a scarecrow in a cucumber patch.
They cannot speak, and are carried about, being unable to walk.
Have no fear of them, for they can do no harm,
Nor is it in them to do any good. . . .
It is a piece of wood.
Worked silver is imported from Tarshish, and gold from Uphaz.
It is the product of a craftsman, and of a goldsmith's hands.

> Their clothing is blue and purple; all of them are the product of
>   skilled men.
> But Yahweh is the true God; he is a living God, an eternal King.

Verses 6–7 and the concluding verses 9–10 cast the detailed descriptions of idol manufacture in theological perspective. They contrast the grandeur of Israel's God with the absurdity of idolatry. In Jeremiah's later prophecy on how Babylon will fall at the hands of Cyrus, which brought an end to the Judean exile, we find a triple equation: idols = the gods they represent = the nations who worship them: The defeat of a nation is the defeat of its false gods. Thus Jer 50:2 urges:

> Tell it among the nations and proclaim!
> Raise a banner, and proclaim!
> Withhold nothing. Declare:
> Babylon is captured, Bel is shamed, Marduk is shamed!
> Her idols are shamed, her abominable objects are shamed.
> [cf. Jer 51:52; Isa 19:1–3]

The exilic prophet known as Deutero-Isaiah is credited with three further denunciations of idolatry, similar in tone to those of Jeremiah, in which the manufacture of idols by humans is held up as a demonstration of their powerlessness and the absurdity of worshipping them. After extolling Yahweh's cosmic power, the prophet poses a rhetorical question:

> To whom, then, can you compare the Deity?
> Which likeness can you set up to represent him?
> As for the idol—a woodcutter shaped it,
> And a smith overlaid it with gold, forging links of silver.
> One who would *shape a pictorial image*
> Chooses wood that does not rot, and seeks out a skilled woodcutter,
> To erect for him an idol that will not topple. [emendation yields:
>   *hamměnassēk těmûnâ* (Isa 40:18–20)

A second and even more graphic diatribe against idolatry appears in Isa 44:9–17 (with omissions). Speaking of the cult image and its manufacturers, the prophet says:

> Those who fashion idols act aimlessly;
> For their treasured products are useless.
> As they themselves can testify, those [objects] cannot see or know.
> For this, those [craftsmen] shall be shamed.
> For who would fashion a god, or cast a statue, that is of no
>   benefit? . . .
> The craftsman in iron, with his tools,
> Works it over charcoal, and fashions it by hammering. . . .

16   *Idolatry and Paganism*

> The craftsman in wood measures with a line,
> And traces a shape with a stylus.
> He forms it with scraping tools, marking it out with a compass.
> He gives it a human form, the beauty of a man, to dwell in a temple.
> He fells cedars for his use, and selects plane trees and oaks. . . .
> All this serves man for fuel: he takes some of these to warm himself.
> He builds a fire and bakes bread,
> At the same time, he makes a god of it, and worships it;
> Fashions an idol and bows down to it.
> Half of it he burns in fire; on that half of it he roasts meat.
> He consumes the roast and is sated. . . .
> The rest of it he fashions into a god.
> He worships it, and prays to it, saying:
> "Save me, for you are my god!"

Yet another diatribe against Babylonian idolatry is preserved in Isa 46:5–7, against the background of a prophecy of the downfall of Babylon, conveyed in the opening verses of the chapter:

> Bel is fallen, Nebo has collapsed,
> Their images have become a burden for beasts and cattle.
> Those you carried aloft are now loaded up, an exhausting burden.
> The [people], too, have fallen collapsing; unable to carry off the
>   burden,
> As they themselves went into captivity. (46:1–2)
> But to whom can you depict me by resemblance?
> To whom can you liken me by comparison?
> Those who squander gold from the purse,
> Weigh out silver on the balance of the scale.
> They hire a metal smith to fashion it into a god,
> To which they then bow down and prostrate themselves. . . .
> Moreover, if one cries out to it, it will not answer;
> It will not rescue him from his distress. (46:5–9, with omissions)

Perhaps this is the place to take note of the theme of idolatry in the Psalms, where we mostly encounter proverbial recollections of Israel's past sins (78:58; 96:5; 97:7; 106:36–39). More specific is the didactic parody of 115:2–8, paralleled in 135:15–18. Both texts are late compositions, which resonate with the parodies in Jeremiah and Deutero-Isaiah just cited.

> How can the nations say: "Where is their God?"
> For our God is in heaven, and he accomplishes all that he desires.
> Their idols are of silver and gold, the product of human
>   manufacture.
> They have mouths but cannot speak, eyes but cannot see;

They have ears but cannot hear, noses but cannot smell;
They have hands but cannot touch, feet but cannot walk;
They can make no sound in their throat.
May those who fashion them become like them,
All who place their trust in them! (115:2–8)

It would be well at this point to survey Ezekiel's condemnations of idolatry. His prophecies begin before the destruction of the first Israelite temple of Jerusalem and continue well into the years of the exile in Babylonia, where he lived among his fellow Judeans. He was fairly contemporary with Jeremiah and Deutero-Isaiah, but his views differed from theirs considerably. Ezekiel seems to have retreated from the universal scene so as to focus on the contamination of the Jerusalem temple itself, from the introduction of idolatrous representations into its very buildings (Ezek 8), and to decry the extent of idolatry among the Judeans (Ezek 6). He saw idolatry both as a direct cause of the destruction, and the abolition of idolatry as a prerequisite for the national restoration that he predicted (11:17–21). In the spirit of the priestly school, for which Ezekiel spoke, the practice of idolatry was a contaminating force, degrading the people and rendering the land itself impure.

The postexilic prophets have little more to say specifically about idolatry. Second Zechariah (13:2) predicts that Yahweh in anger will eliminate all idols from the land so that they will be forgotten, and along with them the false prophets who spoke in their name.

Idolatry as a Phenomenon

The Meaning of Idolatry

The Hebrew Bible's derisive characterizations of idolatry as the worship of manufactured objects, which are lifeless and powerless, leads directly to a discussion of the fuller meaning of idolatry for the peoples of the ancient Near East. The Israelite prophets, and others who speak in the Bible, were hardly insulated from contemporary forms of religious practice. They surely realized that idolatry rose far above fetishism, but they chose to voice the strongest argument against its credibility, declaring that cult images are products of human manufacture. As such, the veneration of idols can be taken to mean that humans are worshipping the works of their own hands, objects that can neither see nor speak. Such veneration is not only absurd, but also demeaning. Thus we read in Jer 16:20: "Can a person make gods for himself, who are [after all] no gods at all?"

The nations of the world were every bit as aware of this logic as were the ancient Israelites. We are fortunate in having elaborate texts, from ancient Egypt and from Syria-Mesopotamia, which describe in great detail the fashioning and ceremonial induction of cult images. Perhaps the best known are those reporting on the *mīs pî*, "mouth-washing" rituals of ancient Mesopotamia. From such texts we learn that the first principle applicable to cult images is that they realized a dual process. The image was "born in heaven, made on earth," to cite a recent book title. The governing concept of image phenomenology is autogenesis, the notion that the image created itself in heaven. A variant of autogenesis is the belief that gods create divine images, a case of gods creating other gods. The ritual induction of the manufactured idol on earth was a reenactment, or dramatization, of what had already happened in heaven, where the cult image had been conceived. We thus observe the dynamic relationship between myth and ritual, whereby ritual confirms myth. It has been suggested that, by its very ambiguity, the narrative of the golden bull-calf (Exod 32) reflects an awareness of the autogenesis of cult images, or of something close to it. Although we read that Aaron fashioned a molten image out of gold, he later asserts, in reporting to Moses: "I threw it [the gold] into the fire, and out came this bull-calf" (32:24), suggesting that the bull-calf was created magically and not by human manufacture.

The rituals of "constitution," as they have been called, completed the process. Consecration effectively animated the cult image, once fashioned and installed, so that it actually manifested the divine presence and became numinous. The cult image was believed to be empowered so that it could speak, see, and do precisely what the biblical polemicists had denied it could do. It is reasonable to conclude that biblical spokesmen purposely omitted the mythological background of the cult image in their polemical parodies, alluding only cursorily, if at all, to its consecration, while emphasizing the implications of human manufacture.

Although idolatry was ridiculed in polemic, biblical authors seem to have recognized that humans feel a deep need for a visible manifestation of the divine presence. Worshipping the numinous cult image, or emblem, offered a ready approach to the deity and nurtured the hope for a divine response. In the earlier discussion of the view of the Deuteronomist (Deut 4:15–20), mention was made of the normal expectation that a deity would manifest his or her presence in visible form. In this respect, the aniconic cult of Aten in Egypt held an advantage over the similarly aniconic cult of Yahweh. The sun, personified as the god Raʿ, was visible to everyone; the power of the sun could hardly be doubted. The Israelite cult of Yahweh was making a more severe demand on its adherents: The people must worship Yahweh notwithstanding his invisibility, while at the same time resisting idolatry, notwithstanding the visible presence of the divine that it afforded the worshipper.

What we observe is that biblical religion accommodated human needs in ways just short of idolatry. The epic traditions speak of a cloud envelope that obscures the deity in heaven (1 Kgs 8:12), whereas the cloud tradition of the tabernacle narratives, for example, produces the same concealment of the deity on earth (Exod 13:32). Related to the cloud traditions is the *kābôd* (glory) theology, which speaks of Yahweh's glorious presence that was visible to the people in special moments and within sacred space (Exod 16:10). There were also angels who appeared as humans, and other materializations such as fire, and visible signs. Biblical anthropomorphisms suggested to worshippers that Yahweh was human in form. We read of certain exceptional individuals who experienced visions and dreams in which Yahweh appeared to them. According to one tradition, even Moses was permitted to behold only Yahweh's backside as he passed by, but not his countenance (Exod

33:12–23), while another tradition has it that only Moses among mortals could see Yahweh's likeness while speaking to him (Num 12:6–8). Exodus 24:9–11 has Moses and the elders of Israel catching a glimpse of the Deity, and Ezek 1:26–27 envisions an enthroned Yahweh bearing a human appearance. In the later apocalypse of Daniel (7:9–10, 13, 22) the "ancient of days" is envisioned seated on a fiery throne, surrounded by myriads of ministering angels. Quite clearly, biblical authors went as far as they could to meet the need for divine presence without compromising the aniconic principle. At the same time, they progressively clamped down even on emblems such as the cultic stelae and the Asherah tree (Deut 16:21–22), which had been legitimate at an earlier time.

Perhaps the most interesting variation on the phenomenon of idolatry is to be found in the priestly account of the creation of the first humans (Gen 1:26–27):

> Then God said: "Let us make a human being in our image, after our likeness. They shall rule over the fish of the sea, the birds of the sky, and over the cattle and over the entire earth, and over all the creeping creatures that creep on the earth." Then God created the human being in his image, in the image of God he created him; male and female he created them.

One senses instinctively that, in its wording, this statement recalls the fashioning of a cult image. It employs a biblical term for prohibited idols, namely, *ṣelem*, "statue," and also the intrinsically morphic term *dĕmût*, "likeness." In the account of Gen 2 (v. 7), which is a text of earlier authorship, we read that Yahweh formed the first human, a male, from earth, and that he animated him by breathing the breath of life into his nostrils, so that he became a living creature. It may not be "reaching" to see in this brief description a reflex of the ceremonial induction of a cult image, discussed above, whereby images were animated and empowered ritually. The creation narratives can be read to mean that Yahweh/Elohim, a deity who desired to remain hidden from human view and had no wish to be represented pictorially, fashioned the human being so as to represent his form as well as his spirit. In this way, all who beheld the human being would be reminded of the Creator and would acknowledge his ubiquitous presence. The human being is perceived as an avatar of a unique sort, assigned stewardship over the created world, a veritable agent of God.

The Terminology of Iconography

What kinds of cult objects are targeted in the Hebrew Bible? Answering this question requires us to define the iconographic terms employed in the Hebrew Bible for what they can tell us about methods of manufacture and materials used, as well as the forms of cult objects. In some instances biblical terms reflect negative attitudes toward the relevant objects. We will classify the biblical terminology according to orientational categories:

Attitudinal terms. Certain terms tell us only that a cult object is detested, or abominable, and reveal nothing specific about its form or manufacture. In such instances, whatever else we know is learned from immediate context and usage. An example is the term *šiqqûṣ*, with its plural, *šiqqûṣîm*, "abominable object(s)." Most biblical scholars parse the term as a *šapʿel* form of the verb *q-w-ṣ*, "to loathe, feel disgust or disaffection" (Lev 20:23; Num 21:5), hence, "that which produces loathing." There is also the segollate form (with vowel *e*, called *sĕgōl*), *šeqeṣ*, a term often applied to forbidden water creatures, insects, and fowl (Lev 11:9–25). Conceivably, the form of such creatures was regarded as loathsome to start with, but it would be unwarranted to conclude that cult images identified in this way necessarily bore the appearance of such living forms. A rare exception is to be found in Ezek 8:10, where we are told that the prophet saw on inner walls of the Jerusalem temple incised pictorial descriptions "of every design of creeping creature and cattle, *šeqeṣ*, and all the idols of the house of Israel." Often, the term *šiqqûṣ* is attached to national gods such as Milkom (Milcom) of the Ammonites and Kemosh (Chemosh) of the Moabites (1 Kgs 11:5), as well as Ashtoreth of the Sidonians (2 Kgs 23:13). Reference is undoubtedly to anthropomorphic statues of these deities that were installed at a *bāmâ*, or in a temple.

Another attitudinal term is *tôʿēbâ*, "abomination," which is of uncertain etymology. In addition to its more abstract meanings, this term designates, in context, idolatrous objects that are abominable (Deut 7:26; 27:15; Isa 44:19; Ezek 18:12, 24). This term is highly charged; it often characterizes the most heinous sins and breaches of morality. The term *ʾelîl*, most often in the plural, *ʾelîlîm*, "idols," may possibly represent a pejorative of *ʾēl*, "deity," but it more likely derives from Hebrew *ʾal* "the negative; nothingness" (Job 24:25). As such, it is attitudinal and genuinely derisive, denying any power or significance to idols. Once again, the term *ʾelîl* itself tells us nothing about form. It is of broad, general usage, occurring in both early and late biblical texts.

Terms of manufacture. Terms for idols may relate to the methods and materials of their manufacture. A classic example is *pesel*, "a sculpted object" (only the singular of the segollate form is attested). There is also the variant plural *pesîlîm* (Aramaistic passive). These nouns are derived from the verb *p-s-l*, "to sculpt." The term *pesel* occurs in texts that describe manufacture in detail, listing the tools and materials used. The most informative are the prophetic parodies cited above, such as Deutero-Isaiah 40:18–20; 44:9–19; Jer 10:1–5. Materials include wood; metals such as iron, gold, and silver; and stone; there are references to craftsmen working in wood and metal smiths. Idols were often carved out of wood, then to be overlaid with silver and gold. Many craftsmen's tools are mentioned in detail. These terms are not form-specific, although it is likely that at least some were anthropomorphic. This is explicit in Isa 44:13, which is exceptional in referring to the manufacture of a *pesel* in human form.

The term *massēkâ* means "cast, molten image," cult images cast in wood molds, a task usually performed by a metal smith (Judg 17:4). Paired with *pesel*, it represents one of the two principal types of manufactured cult images (Deut 27:15; Judg

17:3-4; 18:14; Nah 1:14): carved or sculpted images, and cast images. Another blatant example of a term of manufacture is the plural ʿăṣabbîm, "crafted objects," deriving from a rare verb ʿ-ṣ-b, "to form, shape" (Job 10:8). All that this term tells us is that the object was shaped or formed, but we are not told how this was done. Its distribution ranges from Hosea to Chronicles and late Psalms. This term is implicitly pejorative; it emphasizes manufacture.

Morphic terms. These are terms that relate to the form assumed by the cult object. We begin with the frequent term ṣelem, "statue, image " (cf. Akkadian ṣalmu). Most often it designates a standing object bearing the form of whatever it represents: a divine being, king, or even hemorrhoids fashioned for magical use (Num 33:52; 1 Sam 6:5)! The term is applicable to any number of forms, including anthropomorphic representations. It is not specific as regards the method of its manufacture. It seems that ṣelem can also designate reliefs incised on walls (Ezek 23:14). A second morphic term is the plural *gillûlîm*, "idols," assuming that a derivation from the geminate verb g-l-l, "to pile up, roll" is correct. That verb is used to describe large stones piled up so as to produce a rotund, or conic, form. This term is attested in various biblical sources, but it is most evident in Ezekiel (8:10; 16:6), where it occurs more than thirty times. It is pejorative, suggesting that a cult image so designated was in truth nothing more than a heap of stones!

Perhaps the most thoroughly morphic term is děmût, "likeness" (Gen 1:26; 5:1), because it literally designates an artifact that looks like what it represents, deriving from the verb d-m-h, "to be like, comparable"—in form, dimensions, and even actions. A similarly morphic term is těmûnâ, "pictorial depiction" (Exod 20:4) that which is aligned, or measured in space. Still another is tabnît, "plan, design," a term elsewhere used in connection with construction (Exod 25:9, 40). Then there is the rare term (ʾeben) maśkît, "a decorated stone," perhaps a mosaic floor; or one decorated attractively (Lev 26:1; Num 33:52).

Borderline cases. Several terms are difficult to classify. The first is sēmel, a Hebrew form of Greek *symbolon*, "symbol." This term also occurs in Phoenician-Punic, where it designates an anthropomorphic statue, not necessarily cultic. Usage in the Hebrew Bible is severely limited and unclear. The term first appears in Deut 4:16, part of a major Deuteronomist statement cited above, where it is synonymous with *pesel*, "sculpted object." In Ezek 8:3, 5 it refers to a forbidden cult image located in the Jerusalem temple, whose form is not specified. Its characterization is decidedly attitudinal; it is said to be an infuriating cult object. In 2 Chr 33:7, 15 we read that Manasseh first installed and then, as an act of repentance, removed hassemel from the Jerusalem temple. This is a late term, and may have been interpolated in Deut 4:16, for all we know. In context, it would seem to be morphic, probably anthropomorphic, based on usage in Phoenician-Punic. However, we normally differentiate between the figurative and the symbolic, with the latter being less representational.

Hebrew ʾăšērâ presents a problem of a different sort. It is the well-attested name of a West Semitic goddess (cf. the Ugaritic Athirat) and in several biblical passages occurs as a divine name, as distinct from designating an artifact. Thus 1 Kgs 18:19 mentions "the prophets of Asherah" who were confronted by Elijah, and elsewhere we read of altars and other objects being dedicated to this goddess (Judg 3:7; 1 Kgs 15:13; 2 Kgs 23:4, 7). Conceivably, there was a time when Asherah was venerated as Yahweh's consort, just as we know that this goddess was at times identified as Baal's consort. Such a relationship may be suggested by the early inscriptions from Kuntillet ʿAjrud, which refer to Yahweh and Asherah in some relationship to each other.

In many cases, however, this term refers to a fashioned cult object, prohibited in Deut 16:21: "Do not plant for yourself an Asherah, any arboreal object, adjacent to the altar of Yahweh, your God, which you may construct for yourself." This statement, although not entirely clear, suggests that, as a goddess, Asherah was symbolized as a tree, which connoted fertility. Others conclude that the Asherah image was simply a post, or pole, something like a cultic stela. Biblical statements seem to corroborate its form as that of a tree, because we find references to "cutting down" such objects, expressed by the verb *k-r-t*, which is used in connection with felling trees (Judg 6:25–30; 2 Kgs 18:4). The masculine plural *ʾăšērîm* is, in contrast, consistently artifactual. Without engaging the larger subject of cults of Asherah, we can say that biblical usage reflects metonymy, using the same term for deity and cult object.

The meaning of the Hebrew *maṣṣēbâ*, "stela," is not at all obscure. It represents a widely attested artifact that commemorates the presence of a deity (or hero!) or a momentous visitation at a sacred site. The many excavated examples reveal it to be conic in form and uninscribed. However, since stelae were often coated with plaster (Deut 27:2–3), it is quite possible that they had originally been inscribed, but that the plaster surface had corroded. The prohibition of the cultic stelae immediately follows that of the Asherah in Deut 16:22: "Do not erect for yourself a stela, which Yahweh, your God, detests." We may conclude that both the Asherah and the cultic stela had once been permitted but were henceforth forbidden. In the case of the stela, this progression from permitted to prohibited may be inferred from Hos 3:4–6, part of an early prophecy:

> For the Israelites will go many years without a king and without officials; without sacrifices [or "an altar"], and without the cultic stela, and without ephod and teraphim.

A functioning society would possess all of the above, whereas northern Israel will experience societal breakdown for many years.

This brings us to *tĕrāpîm* (always plural), most likely a term of Hittite derivation, whose usage indicates that objects so called were employed in necromancy or magic of other sorts (Ezek 21:26; Zech 10:2). From the patriarchal narrative of Gen 31, and the tale about Michal, Saul's daughter, in 1 Sam 19, we learn that teraphim were household objects, small enough to be hidden under the covers, and that they belonged to the family. They have been compared to the Lares and Penates of Roman times. Whereas the above narratives imply that there was nothing at all objectionable about retaining teraphim in the home, at least in northern Israel, other biblical statements clearly classify them as prohibited idols. This emerges from Judg 17–18, discussed earlier, and from statements in 1 Sam 15:23 and 2 Kgs 23:24. Once again, we observe the effects of growing cultic stringency during the protracted conflict with polytheism. Mention should also be made of the many so-called "Astarte figurines" found by archaeologists on the soil of ancient Israel. None of these objects is inscribed, but their form, often depicting a pregnant female, suggests fertility as their function.

Degrees of pictorial representation. We can differentiate among three basic types of idolatrous cult objects referred to in the Hebrew Bible: (1) Images fashioned in the form or appearance of a deity, as that deity was conceptualized. This is the highest degree of graphic representation. In many cultures, it translated into anthropomorphic images, because deities were so often conceptualized or visualized as having human form. This was true in ancient Israel as well, but given the fact that the cult of Yahweh was aniconic, this conceptualization was not actualized in image form, but reserved for exceptional visions of the divine and dramatic theophanies. The only "icon" of Yahweh is the human being, fashioned in the form of God. There is only one, explicit reference to an anthropomorphic image of an unnamed, foreign deity in the Hebrew Bible, and that is in Deutero-Isaiah (44:13), already mentioned, within the famous parody of manufacturing idols, probably written in Babylonia during the exile. (2) Images suggestive of qualities associated with a particular deity, such as great strength. An example of this type would be the image of the bull, utilized in the cult of El, which was discussed in detail above. Such images were progressively discredited in the Hebrew Bible. Nevertheless, biblical epic poetry, in expressing awe of El's great strength, compares it to that of the wild ox (Num 23:22; Deut 33:17). In a sense, this category would also include the copper serpent, originally fashioned by Moses at Yahweh's instruction (Num 21:8–9), but piously removed at a later time by Hezekiah from the temple court after the people were given to venerating it (2 Kgs 18:4). In that case, the principle at work was sympathetic magic: the power of the numinous, hypostasized snake overcame the ill effects of the poisonous snakes. (3) Less representational and more stylized symbols or emblems identified with certain deities, more by custom than necessarily by form. Examples from ancient Israel would be the Asherah tree and the cultic stela. (The form of the teraphim is unknown.) To this category we may also assign the Saturn emblems, *Sikkût* and *Kiyyûn* in Amos 5:26. The Israelites will carry these failed divine symbols with them into exile. Finally, it could be argued that the ark of the covenant, carried into battle (Num 10:35–36; 1 Sam 4:3–6), functioned as a divine emblem.

Recent studies of Mesopotamian iconography, in particular, have recognized progressive movement away from anthropomorphic divine images in the direction of less-representational symbols and emblems over a period of millennia. Certain variables are evident in ongoing decisions affecting the form of cult images, most notably the venue in which they were to be displayed. Anthropomorphic cult images seem to be concentrated in temples (see Isa 44:13), whereas more often, nonanthropomorphic cult objects, and especially emblems, were displayed outside temples, or were carried about in military campaigns, for example. Some scholars have maintained that this long-term trend accounts, at least in part, for the biblical ban on cult images. However, this hypothesis is reductionist: it projects a progressive reduction of anthropomorphic imagery to "zero," or total aniconism.

It must be conceded that we do not fully comprehend the phenomenology of aniconism. Logically, it could have emerged from cosmic astral cults, or pantheistic nature cults, where the concern was to retain direct contact with the sun or moon, or with mountains and the vast sea, avoiding the utilization of intermediary objects of worship. As already reported, the great temple to Aten was open to the sky and devoid of cult images, most likely for this reason. For the purposes of the present discussion of idolatry, suffice it to say that the Hebrew Bible, although it is a rich source for the study of religion, is not a systematic presentation of the history of Israelite religion. It does not explain itself. The most that we can do is to trace the ascendancy of the Yahwist movement in broad outline, from henotheism to universal monotheism, as the Israelites broke free of the overarching, West Semitic pantheon and committed to the worship of Yahweh alone. As part of this protracted process, opposition to cult images of all sorts became more severe as the scope of the ban extended to idolatry, so characteristic of world empires.

2

Rabbinic Reading

Idolatry and Paganism

Jacob Neusner

In its land, Israel is to wipe out idolatry, even as a memory. Yet the land encompasses not only Israelites but also diverse, undifferentiated Gentiles. Gentiles by definition are idolaters, and Israelites by definition are those who worship the one, true God who has made himself known in the Torah. In the rabbinic system of Judaism, that is the difference—the only consequential distinction—between Israel and the Gentiles. What is at stake is that Israel stands for life; the Gentiles, like their idols, stand for death. That view is expressed in the law, which compares an object of idolatrous worship with a corpse: both convey uncleanness to what passes beneath them. That is, an Asherah tree that is worshipped conveys uncleanness to those who pass underneath it, just as at Num 19 the corpse conveys uncleanness to whatever is in the shadow of the same roof as the corpse itself. Mishnah *Abodah Zarah* 3:8 treats an idol as comparable to a corpse in its capacity to convey uncleanness: "And he should not pass underneath its shade [that of a tree worshipped as an idol], but if he passed underneath it, he is unclean."

While Scripture concerns itself with the disposition of idolatry—destroying idols and tearing down altars and the like—and the eradication of idolatry from the Holy Land, rabbinic Judaism in its Halakhic statement takes as its problem the relationship of the Israelite to the Gentile, who by definition is assumed to practice idolatry. At issue is how the Israelite can interact with the idol-worshipping Gentile without being uncorrupted by his idolatry.

The Halakhah of idolatry is set forth in the rabbinic category "idolatry," called in Hebrew "alien worship," *Abodah Zarah*, in the tractate by that name found in the Mishnah, Tosefta, Yerushalmi, and Bavli. The laws of rabbinic Judaism rest squarely on the foundations of Scripture, supplying rules and regulations that carry out the fundamental Scriptural commandments about destroying idols and everything that has to do with idolatry. But the Halakhah so formulates matters as to transform the entire topic of idolatry into an essay on Israel's relationships not with idolatry in particular, but with the Gentiles in general, all of them idolaters by definition

Scripture does not contemplate Israel's coexisting in the land with Gentiles and their idolatry. But the Halakhah of the rabbinic heirs of Scripture does. For it speaks to a world that is not so simple. In theological theory the Holy Land may belong to Israel to the exclusion of idolaters, but in political fact Gentiles live there too—and from 70 CE have run things. The Halakhah further takes for granted that Gentiles live side by side with Israelites. Its Israelites therefore have to sort out the complex problems of coexistence with idolatry. Thus rabbinic Judaism in its Halakhic statement uses the occasion of idolatry to contemplate a condition entirely beyond the imagination of Scripture, which is the hegemony of idolatrous nations and the subjugation of holy Israel. In the Talmuds the rabbis take the discussion of idolatry as the occasion for considering Israel's place among the nations of the world and Israel's relationships with Gentiles.

As to its topical program, the Halakhah deals first with commercial relationships, such as at fairs, which invariably are devoted to pagan gods, second with matters pertaining to idols, and finally with the particular prohibition of wine, part of which has served as a libation to an idol. There are relationships with Gentiles that are absolutely prohibited, particularly occasions of idol worship; the Halakhah recognizes that these are major commercial events. When it comes to commerce with idolaters, Israelites may not sell or in any way benefit from certain objects, may sell but may not utilize certain other things, and may sell and utilize yet other items. There are these unstated premises within the Halakhah: (1) What serves idolatry is prohibited for use and for benefit. (2) What may serve not as part of an idol but as an appurtenance thereto is prohibited for Israelite use but permitted for Israelite commerce. (3) What a Gentile is not likely to use for the worship of an idol is not prohibited. The laws on idolatry and idols are represented by the following passages of the Mishnah:

M. *Abodah Zarah* 3:1: Images are prohibited that have in its hand a staff, bird, or sphere.

M. *Abodah Zarah* 3:2: He who finds the shards of images—lo, these are permitted. [If] one found [a fragment] shaped like a hand or a foot, lo, these are prohibited, because objects similar to them are worshipped.

M. *Abodah Zarah* 3:3: He who finds utensils upon which is the figure of the sun, moon, or dragon, should bring them to the Salt Sea. . . . One breaks them into pieces and throws the powder to the wind or drops them into the sea. . . . [Also] they may be made into manure, as it is said, "And there will cleave nothing of a devoted thing to your hand" [Deut 13:18].

M. *Abodah Zarah* 3:5: Gentiles who worship hills and valleys—these [hills or valleys] are permitted, but what is on them is forbidden [for Israelite use], as it is said, "You shall not covet the silver or gold that is upon them nor take it" [Deut 7:25]. . . . On what account is an *Asherah* prohibited? Because it has been subject to manual labor, and whatever has been subject to manual labor is prohibited.

Of particular interest to the rabbis was the prohibition of wine that has been touched by Gentiles. The rabbis assumed that a Gentile would make a libation of a drop of wine from any bottle of wine that they possessed, and that libation rendered the remainder of the wine forbidden as having served idolatry. It goes without saying that meat of animals sacrificed to idols could not be consumed by Israelites for the same reason. Here is how the Halakhah of the Mishnah sorted out the issues involving libation-wine:

> Mishnah *Abodah Zarah* 4:8: They purchase from Gentiles [the contents of] a winepress that has already been trodden out, even though [the Gentile] takes [the grapes] in hand and puts them on the heap [apple], for it is not made into wine used for libations until it drips down into the vat. [And if wine has] dripped into the vat, what is in the cistern is prohibited, while the rest is permitted.
>
> M. *Abodah Zarah* 4:9: [Israelites] tread a winepress with a Gentile [in the Gentile's vat]. But they do not gather grapes with him. An Israelite who prepares [his wine] in a state of uncleanness—they do not trample or cut grapes with him. But they do take jars with him to the winepress, and they bring them with him from the winepress.

The sages differentiate between actual commercial relationships on the occasion of festivals and fairs, on the one side, and transactions of a normal, humane character, on the other. They do not require Israelites to act out Scripture's commandments utterly to destroy idolatry; they permit them to maintain normal social amenities with their neighbors, within some broad limits. First, while the general prohibition covers all Gentiles on the occasion of fairs and festivals, it pertains to individuals' celebrations in a limited way. All Gentiles are not subjected to a prohibition for all purposes and at all times, and that is the main principle that the extension and the amplification of the law instantiates in many concrete cases. The effect is to reshape Scripture's implacable and extreme rulings into a construction more fitting for an Israel that cannot complete the task of destroying idolatry but is not free to desist from trying.

The basic theory of Gentiles, all of them assumed to be idolaters, is the following: First, Gentiles always and everywhere and under any circumstance are going to perform an act of worship for one or another of their gods. Second, Gentiles are represented as thoroughly depraved (not being regenerated by the Torah), so they will murder, fornicate, or steal any chance they get; they routinely commit bestiality, incest, and various other forbidden acts of sexual congress. The rabbis then consider how Israel is to protect itself in a world populated by utterly immoral persons, wholly outside of the framework of the Torah and its government. Basically, the Halakhah embodies the same principle of compromise where possible, but at whatever cost maintains rigid conformity to the principles of the Torah under all circumstances involving commercial transactions. Just as Israel must give up all possibility of normal trading relationships with Gentiles, depriving itself of the most lucrative transactions, those involving fairs, so Israel must avoid more than routine courtesies and necessary exchanges with idolaters.

That involves the principle that one must avoid entering into situations of danger, such as allowing opportunities for Gentiles to carry out their natural instincts of murder, bestiality, and the like. Cattle are not to be left in their inns, a woman may not be left alone with Gentiles, nor a man: the woman because of a Gentile's probable fornication with her, and the man because a Gentile might murder him. Their physicians are not to be trusted, though when it comes to using them to treat beasts, that is all right. One also must avoid appearing to conduct oneself as if he were an idolater, even if he is not actually doing so; thus if someone is in front of an idol and feels a splinter in his foot, he should not bend over to remove it, because he would look as though he is bowing down to the idol. But if it does not look that way, he is permitted to do so. Yet there are objects that are assumed to be destined for idolatrous worship, and these under all circumstances are forbidden for Israelite trade. Israelites simply may not sell to Gentiles anything that Gentiles are likely to use, or that they explicitly say they are intending to use, for idolatry. That includes wine and the like. Whatever Gentiles have used for idolatry may not be utilized afterward by Israelites, and that extends to what is left over from an offering, such as meat or wine. Israelites also may not sell to Gentiles anything they are going to use in an immoral way, such as wild animals for the arena, materials for the construction of places in which Gentile immorality or injustice will occur, ornaments for an idol, and the like.

The Halakhah takes as its task the realization of the theological principle that those who hate Israel hate God, those who hate God hate Israel, and God will ultimately vanquish Israel's enemies as his own—just as God too was redeemed from Egypt. So the theory of idolatry, involving alienation from God, accounts for the wicked conduct imputed to idolaters, without regard to whether that is how idolaters actually conduct themselves. That matter of logic is stated in so many words:

Sipre on Numbers 84.4.1:
A. "And let them that hate you flee before you" [Num 10:35]:
B. And do those who hate [come before] him who spoke and brought the world into being?
C. The purpose of the verse at hand is to say that whoever hates Israel is as if he hates him who spoke and by his word brought the world into being.

The same proposition is reworked. God can have no adversaries, but Gentile enemies of Israel act as though they were God's enemies:

D. Along these same lines: "In the greatness of your majesty you overthrow your adversaries" [Exod 15:7].
E. And are there really adversaries before him who spoke and by his word brought the world into being? But Scripture thus indicates that whoever rose up against Israel is as if he rose up against the Omnipresent.
F. Along these same lines: "Do not forget the clamor of your foes, the uproar of your adversaries, which goes up continually" [Ps 74:23].

G. "For lo, your enemies, O LORD" [Ps 92:10 (9 Eng.)].
H. "For those who are far from you shall perish; you put an end to those who are false to you" [Ps 73:27].
I. "For lo, your enemies are in tumult, those who hate you have raised their heads" [Ps 83:2]. On what account? "They lay crafty plans against your people; they consult together against your protected ones" [Ps 83:3].

Israel hates God's enemies, and Israel is hated because of its loyalty to God (a matter to which we shall return presently):

J. "Do I not hate those who hate you, O LORD? And do I not loathe them that rise up against you? I hate them with perfect hatred; I count them my enemies" [Ps 139:21–22].
K. And so too Scripture says, "For whoever lays hands on you is as if he lays hands on the apple of his eye" [Zech 2:12 (8 Eng.)].
L. R. Judah says, "What is written is not, 'the apple of an eye' but 'the apple of *his* eye'; it is as if Scripture speaks of him above, but Scripture has used a euphemism."

Those who hate Israel hate God, those who are enemies of Israel are enemies of God, those who help Israel help God—and then all this is systematically instantiated by facts set forth in Scripture. The systematic proof extends beyond verses of Scripture, with a catalog of the archetypal enemies assembled: Pharaoh, Sisera, Sennacherib, Nebuchadnezzar, Haman. So the paradigm reinforces the initial allegation and repertoire of texts. The context of all thought on Israel and the Gentiles then finds definition in supernatural issues and the context in theology. In rabbinic Judaism in its Halakhic statement, sages at no point deem as merely secular the category the Gentiles.

Clearly, the moral ordering of the world encompasses all humanity. But God does not neglect the Gentiles or fail to exercise dominion over them. For even now, Gentiles are subject to a number of commandments or religious obligations. God cares for Gentiles as for Israel; he wants Gentiles as much as Israel to enter the kingdom of heaven, and he assigns to Gentiles opportunities to evince their acceptance of his rule. There are seven such religious obligations that apply to the children of Noah. It is not surprising—indeed, it is predictable—that the definition of the matter should find its place in the Halakhah of *Abodah Zarah*:

Tosefta *Abodah Zarah* 8:4:
A. Concerning seven religious requirements were the children of Noah admonished:
B. Setting up courts of justice, idolatry, blasphemy [cursing the Name of God], fornication, bloodshed, and thievery.

Where is the justice in all this, and why are the Gentiles punished for not obeying the Torah? When the Gentiles protest the injustice of the decision that takes

30   *Idolatry and Paganism*

> Bavli tractate *Abodah Zarah* 1:1 I.2/2a–b: A. R. Hanina bar Pappa, and some say, R. Simlai, gave the following exposition [of the verse, "They that fashion a graven image are all of them vanity, and their delectable things shall not profit, and their own witnesses see not nor know" (Isa 44:9)]: "In the age to come the Holy One, blessed be He, will bring a scroll of the Torah and hold it in his bosom and say, 'Let him who has kept himself busy with it come and take his reward.' Then all the Gentiles will crowd together: 'All of the nations are gathered together' [Isa 43:9]. The Holy One, blessed be He, will say to them, 'Do not crowd together before me in a mob. But let each nation enter together with [2b] its scribes, 'and let the peoples be gathered together' [Isa 43:9], and the word 'people' means 'kingdom': 'and one kingdom shall be stronger than the other' [Gen 25:23]."

effect just then, they are shown the workings of the moral order, as the following quite systematic account of the governing pattern explains:

We observe that the players are the principal participants in world history: the Romans first and foremost, then the Persians, the other world-rulers of the age:

> C. The kingdom of Rome comes in first.
> H. The Holy One, blessed be He, will say to them, "How have you defined your chief occupation?"
> I. They will say before him, "Lord of the world, a vast number of marketplaces have we set up, a vast number of bathhouses we have made, a vast amount of silver and gold have we accumulated. And all of these things we have done only in behalf of Israel, so that they may define as their chief occupation the study of the Torah."
> J. The Holy One, blessed be He, will say to them, "You complete idiots! Whatever you have done has been for your own convenience. You have set up a vast number of marketplaces, to be sure, but that was so as to set up whorehouses in them. The bathhouses were for your own pleasure. Silver and gold belong to me anyhow: 'Mine is the silver and mine is the gold, says the Lord of hosts' [Hag 2:8]. Are there any among you who have been telling of 'this,' and 'this' is only the Torah: 'And this is the Torah that Moses set before the children of Israel' [Deut 4:44]." So they will make their exit, humiliated.

The claim of Rome—to support Israel in Torah-study—is rejected on grounds that the Romans did not exhibit the right attitude, always a dynamic force in the theology. Then the other world rule enters in with its claim:

> K. When the kingdom of Rome has made its exit, the kingdom of Persia enters afterward.
> M. The Holy One, blessed be He, will say to them, "How have you defined your chief occupation?"

N. They will say before him, "Lord of the world, we have thrown up a vast number of bridges, we have conquered a vast number of towns, we have made a vast number of wars, and all of them we did only for Israel, so that they may define as their chief occupation the study of the Torah."

O. The Holy One, blessed be He, will say to them, "Whatever you have done has been for your own convenience. You have thrown up a vast number of bridges, to collect tolls; you have conquered a vast number of towns, to collect the corvée; and as to making a vast number of wars, I am the one who makes wars: 'The LORD is a man of war' [Exod 15:3]. Are there any among you who have been telling of 'this,' and 'this' is only the Torah: 'And this is the Torah that Moses set before the children of Israel' [Deut 4:44]." So they will make their exit, humiliated.

R. And so it will go with each and every nation.

As native categories, Rome and Persia are singled out, and "all the other nations" play no role, for reasons with which we are already familiar. Once more the theology reaches into its deepest thought on the power of intentionality, showing that what people want is what they get.

But matters cannot be limited to the two world empires of the present age, Rome and Iran, standing in judgment at the end of time. In a further formulation of the same view, the Gentiles are not just Rome and Persia but also others; and of special interest, the Torah is embodied in some of the Ten Commandments—not to murder, not to commit adultery, not to steal; then the Gentiles are rejected for not keeping the seven commandments assigned to the children of Noah.

Sipre on Deuteronomy 343.4.1:

A. Another teaching concerning the phrase, "He said, 'The LORD came from Sinai'" [Deut 33:2]:

B. When the Omnipresent appeared to give the Torah to Israel, it was not to Israel alone that he revealed himself but to every nation.

C. First of all he came to the children of Esau. He said to them, "Will you accept the Torah?"

D. They said to him, "What is written in it?"

E. He said to them, "'You shall not murder' [Exod 20:13]."

F. They said to him, "The very being of 'those men' [us] and of their father is to murder, for it is said, 'But the hands are the hands of Esau' [Gen 27:22]. 'By your sword you shall live' [Gen 27:40]."

At this point we cover new ground: other classes of Gentiles that reject the Torah. Now the Torah's own narrative takes over, replacing the known facts of world politics, such as the earlier account sets forth, and instead supplying evidence out of Scripture as to the character of the Gentile group under discussion:

G. So he went to the children of Ammon and Moab and said to them, "Will you accept the Torah?"

H. They said to him, "What is written in it?"
I. He said to them, "'You shall not commit adultery' [Exod 20:14]."
J. They said to him, "The very essence of fornication belongs to them [us], for it is said, 'Thus were both the daughters of Lot with child by their fathers' [Gen 19:36]."
K. So he went to the children of Ishmael and said to them, "Will you accept the Torah?"
L. They said to him, "What is written in it?"
M. He said to them, "'You shall not steal' [Exod 20:15]."
N. They said to him, "The very essence of their [our] father is thievery, as it is said, 'And he shall be a wild ass of a man' [Gen 16:12]."
O. And so it went. He went to every nation, asking them, "Will you accept the Torah?"
P. For so it is said, "All the kings of the earth shall give you thanks, O LORD, for they have heard the words of your mouth" [Ps 138:4].
Q. Might one suppose that they listened and accepted the Torah?
R. Scripture says, "And I will execute vengeance in anger and fury upon the nations, because they did not listen" [Mic 5:14].

At this point we turn back to the obligations that God has imposed upon the Gentiles. These obligations have no bearing upon the acceptance of the Torah; they form part of the ground of being, the condition of existence, of the Gentiles. Yet even here, the Gentiles do not accept God's authority in matters of natural law:

S. And it is not enough for them that they did not listen, but even the seven religious duties that the children of Noah indeed accepted upon themselves they could not uphold before breaking them.
T. When the Holy One, blessed be He, saw that that is how things were, he gave them to Israel.

What accounts for Gentile idolatry is the Gentiles' rejection of the Torah. The Torah deprived them of the very practices or traits that they deemed characteristic and essential to their own being. These are not matters of historical narrative but analyses of the very definition of *Gentiles*. The Gentiles' own character, the shape of their conscience, then, now, and always, accounts for their condition—which, by an act of will, they can change. The Torah is at the heart of matters. What they do not want, that of which they were by their own word unworthy, is denied them. And what they do want condemns them. So when each nation comes under judgment for rejecting the Torah, the indictment of each is spoken out of its own mouth: its own-self-indictment then forms the core of the matter. Given what we know about the definition of Israel as those destined to live and the Gentile as those not destined to live, we cannot find it surprising that the entire account is set in that age to come, to which the Gentiles by reason of their status are denied entry. That is why the advent of another scriptural community of monotheists, besides Israel, would complicate matters for the rabbis.

3

Early Christian Interpretation

The Case of Justin Martyr

Bruce D. Chilton

Justin Martyr, the second-century writer who brought Christian belief into the realm of philosophical discourse, followed the ruling of the Apostolic Council under James (Jesus' brother) in Jerusalem that food sacrificed in honor of idols (see Acts 15:29),[1] and idolatry itself, were incompatible with Christ.[2] Yet Justin also develops an understanding of how the Spirit of God, known principally through the prophets of Israel, spoke through ancient pagan culture.

Justin's account in his *Dialogue with Trypho* (3-8) of how he converted to Christianity sets out a model of conversion whose pivot is the Prophetic literature of Israel. What Justin goes on to say in the *Dialogue*, together with his earlier treatment of the Prophets in his *Apology*,[3] permits the reader to see how Justin understands this model to function. Our approach takes Justin's narrative in its context as exemplary, rather than raising historical issues in regard to the circumstances of Justin's personal conversion.

Considerable attention has been accorded the identity of the *palaios tis presbytēs* (3.1) who spoke with Justin during a conversation that occasioned his conversion. Typically, he is called "the Old Man" in English translation, although Justin's language at this point emphasizes the antiquity and the traditional wisdom of his interlocutor more than the English phrase does. Oskar Skarsaune has described him as a "Christian Socrates," a designation that will serve well, provided the limits of the statement are observed, as well as its positive comparison.

Skarsaune specifies the limits of comparison with Socrates:[4]

> On one point Justin the Platonist and the Old Man agree: true knowledge of God only comes through direct encounter with God. As we have seen already, Justin in the *Apologies* hints that Socrates himself had only a partial and incomplete knowledge of God or His Logos, and that he therefore was content with exhorting others to *seek* the Unknown God. At this point the Old Man, the Christian Socrates of the *Dialogue*, goes one significant

step further: The Old Testament prophets really had such a direct and complete knowledge of God that they could impart it to others without any inhibition.

The sage convinced Justin that the highest good that Platonism can attain, the human soul, should not be confused with God himself, since the soul depends upon God for life (chap. 6). Knowledge of God depends rather upon the revelation of God's Spirit (chap. 7). Here is a self-conscious Christianity, which proclaims itself the true and only adequate philosophy. Justin's account of the truth of the *Logos* depends upon two sources of revelation, resonant with one another: the Prophetic Scriptures that attest the Spirit and the wise reader who has been inspired by the Spirit.[5]

To this extent, it would complement Skarsaune's approach to balance the characterization of a Christian Socrates with that of a Platonic Moses or Isaiah. After all, what merits faith in the Prophets, according to Justin's interlocutor, is not only their words but also their "powers" (*dynameis*, as in *Dialogue* 7), a consequence of their direct apprehension of divine truth. In any case, the identity of the *presbytēs* within Justin's presentation appears less important than what the *presbytēs* points to: the Prophetic Scriptures of Israel that speak to all who believe in them "much knowledge of the beginning and end of things, and all else a philosopher ought to know."

Skarsaune has devoted a monograph to this issue, assessing the text type as well as the usage of Scripture in Justin.[6] Following Dominique Barthélemy,[7] he characterizes Justin's text as a rendering that corresponds to its Hebrew antecedent more formally than the Septuagint, in this regard appearing closer to the *Kaige* translation (named from the Greek terms *kai* + *ge*, representing the Hebrew conjunction *gam*) unearthed at Nachal Chever, Murabbaʿat, and Qumran Cave 4. This leads Skarsaune to suggest that Justin used a source of "testimonies," proof texts used for purposes of evangelism within a "Jewish Christian" environment, which exerted a powerful influence on "the mainstream-theology of the second century."[8] Skarsaune then goes on to suggest that Justin's account of the origin of his translation in his *Apology* is the introduction of this testimony source.[9]

Justin's description of this translation departs from the account of the Septuagint's origins in the *Letter of Aristeas*, insisting that precise copies of the Hebrew Bible, going back to originals five thousand years earlier in some cases, were sent to Alexandria, and translated under the aegis of Herod (*1 Apol.* 31.1–8). This account corresponds to a degree with Barthélemy's suggestion, but two cautions are in order, both of which are consonant with Skarsaune's contribution. First, establishing text types of the Septuagint has proved parlous. In the case of Justin, he agrees sometimes with the *Kaige* recension, sometimes with the Septuagint (in its wide diversity of witnesses), sometimes with the way Paul cites the Scriptures of Israel in Greek, and actually varies from one citation to the next. These observations militate against the finding of a single text type, as Judith Lieu has commented.[10]

Similar considerations suggest that the model of a fixed source of "testimonies" for apologetic purposes can become too restrictive. Influenced by the identification of catena fragments, especially from the Byzantine period, Rendell Harris tried to explain the origins of the Gospels in those terms,[11] but subsequent discussion has not confirmed the existence of a first-century source of testimonies, as he suggested. The second century has proved no more productive for the hypothesis. It appears, rather, that Justin spoke within the terms of reference of a *tradition*, a way of conceiving of the significance of the prophets of Israel in respect of a stable of favorite passages as expressed in preferred recensions, rather than a fixed set of Scriptural proof texts. On the basis of this tradition, Justin insists that (1) the prophets, beginning with Moses and including David, attested Christ; (2) inspired the best of Greek philosophy; (3) forecast the transfer of the prophetic Spirit from Israel to Christians; and (4) agreed that the divine *Logos* lies at the heart of human cognition of God.

Each of these four assertions might be instanced in many citations from the *Apology* and the *Dialogue*. In aggregate, they have been well established in previous studies, to which references will be made as we proceed. The purpose here is less to argue that these themes are Justin's—which has already been demonstrated—than to assess them and then to observe that, at each of these points, Justin puts himself into a philosophical argument with the Judaism *of his time*, as reflected in the Mishnah and some Targumim rather than later rabbinic literature, on the basis of patterns of thought for the most part already traditional within Christianity.

The Prophets, Beginning with Moses and Including David, Attested Christ

Justin sets his *Dialogue with Trypho*, a Jew, in the period after the revolt under Simon called Bar Kokhba (*Dial.* 1.3), 132–135 CE. Thematically, Justin disputes Trypho's conception of the permanent obligation of the law (chaps. 1–47) and sees the purpose of Scriptures in their witness to Christ's divinity (chaps. 48–108), which justifies and indeed requires the extension of the divine covenant to Gentiles (chaps. 109–136). Trypho is portrayed as arguing in agreement with the axiom of the Mishnah that the systemic meaning of the Scriptures is the law, while Justin argues that their systemic meaning is Christ.

Justin spells out the structure of the prophetic tradition beginning with Moses more precisely in his *Apology* (32.1), insisting that "all we affirm to have learned from Christ and the prophets who preceded him is only truth" (23.1). He invokes Moses as the "first prophet," citing Gen 49:10–11, Jacob's prophecy that the scepter would not depart from Judah (32.1). By treating Moses in this way, as the author of Jacob's blessing and the agent of the prophetic Spirit (cf. chap. 44), Justin can proceed through the Prophets (Isaiah, above all) to speak of their reference to Christ, and then conclude in David's testimony—as both prophet and king—within the Psalms (40.1).

These extensive citations over a long run of chapters systematize the claim of the risen Jesus among the disciples in Luke 24:44 (cf. v. 27) that "it was necessary for all the Scriptures to be fulfilled in the law of Moses and the Prophets and the

Psalms concerning me." A setting of communal instruction and worship—akin to the meetings of Christian worship as Justin briefly describes them (*1 Apol.* 67.3), at which the apostles' memoirs or the writings of the Prophets were read and studied—is the likely point of origin of Justin's christological tradition of reading the Scriptures.

In concluding her penetrating reading of the *Dialogue*, Tessa Rajak suggests:[12] "It is perhaps not wholly far-fetched to suggest that the *Dialogue with Trypho*, though presented as an apologetic dialogue, is less a discussion than a Christian *pesher* on Isaiah and the other prophets." Rajak is appropriately tentative in making this suggestion, because the *Dialogue* does not comport with the genre of *pesher* (interpretation) in providing a *continuous* commentary on Isaiah or any other prophet. But a similar technique is instanced in episodic exegeses of Scripture also discovered at Qumran.

A recent study of the usage of Scripture attributed to James in Acts 15, citing Amos 9:11, has pointed out that an analogy to the episodic usage of that passage by James is offered by the texts of Qumran designated florilegia by the editors. In one citation (in 4Q174 3.10–13), the image of the restoration of the encampment of David is associated with the promise to David in 2 Sam 7:13–14 and with the Davidic "branch" (cf. Isa 11:1–10), all taken in a messianic sense.

Given the expectation of a son of David as messianic king within early Judaism (see *Pss. Sol.* 17:21–43), the messianic application of the passage in Amos, whether in 4Q174 3.10–13 or by James in Acts 15, is hardly strange. On the other hand, it is striking that the passage in Amos—particularly "the fallen hut of David"—is applied in the *Damascus Document* (CD 7.15–17), not to a messianic figure but to the law, which is restored. Clearly, neither Trypho nor the rabbis innovated the insistence that the Prophets attested the Mosaic law.

Indeed, the book of Amos itself makes Judah's contempt for the Torah a pivotal issue (2:4) and calls for a program of seeking the Lord and his ways (5:6–15); so it is perhaps not surprising that "the seeker of the law" is predicted to restore it in the *Damascus Document*. Still, CD 7.15–20 directly refers to the "books of the Torah" as "the huts of the king," interpreted by means of the "fallen hut of David." Evidently there is a precise correspondence between the strength of the messiah and the establishment of the Torah, as is further suggested by the association with the seeker of the law *not only* in the *Damascus Document*, but also in the florilegium (4Q174 3.10–13). This kind of interpretation—although pursued to different ends, by means of briefer citations, and without a framing argument such as Justin's— offers a useful analogy to the treatment of Scripture in the *Dialogue* as well as in the *Apology*.

The Essene interpretation and Justin evidently go their separate ways when it concerns the Torah. By insisting upon Moses' role as a *prophet*, indeed the first prophet, Justin contends with the portrait of Moses that animated rabbinic literature from the second century onward, where Moses appears preeminently as the giver of the Torah, both in writing and in the oral tradition of the sages. Justin does not engage rabbinic literature in any detail (even as interpreted in the *Mekilta*, the only second-century midrash) and sometimes makes apparent errors in what he takes to be the practice of Judaism in his time. Yet he does know that he is confronting a Jewish *paradosis* unlike his own, and he warns Trypho away from it (*Dial.* 38.2; 120.5) while maintaining his own ground within a setting of traditional learning (2 *Apol.* 10.1-2).[13] The particular passage that Justin uses to make his case is quite striking, because rabbinic interpretation in its most popular form during the second century—as represented in the Targumim, designed for usage within synagogues—also understood Gen 49:10-11 as a messianic prophecy.[14]

The Prophets Inspired the Best of Greek Philosophy

In taking Moses as a prophetic figure, Justin certainly aligns himself with the portrait of Philo, and appreciating that alignment bears fruit. Like Philo (*De aeternitate mundi* 17-19), Justin believes that Plato imitated Genesis in the *Timaeus* (1 *Apol.* 59-60).[15] His statement of the analysis is actually more aggressive than Philo's (1 *Apol.* 44.9): "Whatever both the philosophers and poets said concerning the immortality of the soul or punishments after death or about perception of things heavenly or similar doctrines, they were able to understand and explain because they borrowed the essential features from the Prophets." This perspective is by no means limited to cosmological issues, but specifically includes ethics (44:8): "So when Plato said, 'The responsibility of choice is for him who makes it, God is not responsible,' he took it from the prophet Moses."

The paucity of explicit reference to Philo in Justin has troubled some commentators,[16] but it should be kept in mind that Justin is sometimes least explicit when he is most influenced by other literary sources. He paraphrases the satire against those who make idols (1 *Apol.* 9), for example, without citing its source in Isa 44 or its repetition in Acts 17. Justin explicitly writes as a philosopher,[17] and for that reason he absorbs literary influences more than he cites them. Citation is not routine; Scripture as specified occurs when there is a matter of doubt or Justin believes the scriptural meaning is deeper than a literary motif.

Justin famously portrays Socrates as executed for his opposition to idols (1 *Apol.* 5.3-4), so close is the fit between the Prophets and Greek sages. To Justin's mind, a rejection of *eidōlothyta* (meats offered to idols) remains a constitutive feature of faith in Jesus (*Dial.* 35), as was the case in James's teaching, according to Acts 15:19-21. That agreement with the Apostolic Decree is striking, because Justin goes very much his own way as compared to James when it comes to circumcision.

The comparison between Philo and Justin shows the extent to which Judaism in the first century and Christianity in the second century relied upon the revival of Platonism to provide them with a way of expressing how their respective religions were philosophically the most appropriate. The Platonic picture of perfect intellectual models was their common axiom, invoked in Philo's rhythmic, elegant Greek, and in Justin's controversial, rhetorical Greek. One can easily imagine a debate between Philo and Justin. Had it occurred, that would have been an encounter between Judaism and Christianity in antiquity on philosophical terrain that they both claimed and with which both were comfortable. Had they met and disputed,

Judaism and Christianity would have been represented as approximate equals and on a level playing field.

But that meeting never happened. By the second century, what divided the two different religions[18] was not only one hundred years, but also watershed events. The temple in Jerusalem had been burned under Titus in 70 CE, and taken apart by Hadrian's order in 135. Judaism was still tolerated in a way Christianity was not, but it was now under suspicion, the remnant of a destroyed nation that had rebelled, and it needed to reconstitute itself as a postnational and postcultic religion in the wake of the failed revolts against Rome that resulted in the double destruction of the temple. The rabbis who invented a new form of Judaism during the second century did so, not on the basis of Platonism, but on grounds of a fresh intellectual contention. They held that the categories of purity established in their oral teaching, as well as in Scripture, were the very structures according to which God created and conducted the world. Mishnah, the principal work of the rabbis, is less a book of law (which it is commonly mistaken for) than a science of the purity[19] that God's humanity—Israel—is to observe.

So complete was the rabbinic commitment to systematic purity at the expense of Platonism that Philo's own work was not preserved within Judaism, but only became known as a result of the work of Christian copyists. And the very philosophical idiom that the rabbis turned from as a matter of survival, apologetic argument, was what Justin turned to, also as a matter of survival.

The Prophets Forecast the Transfer of the Prophetic Spirit from Israel to Christians

In his recent study of the *Akedat Yitschak* (Binding of Isaac), that is, interpretations of Genesis 22, Edward Kessler has characterized Justin as illustrating "a pervasive patristic supersessionist teaching, which is known as the doctrine of replacement theology."[20] The basis of this teaching, however, as Kessler clearly indicates, is not a claim about the standing of one community in relation to another, but an analysis of prophecy. Thus Justin says:

> For these words have neither been prepared by me, nor ornamented by human art; but David sang them, Isaiah evangelized them, Zechariah proclaimed them, and Moses wrote them. Are you acquainted with them, Trypho? They are contained in your Scriptures, or rather not yours, but ours. For we are persuaded by them; but you, though you read them, do not recognize the mind that is in them. (*Dial.* 29.2; see also 32.2)

At its theological foundation, Justin's "supersessionism" is no greater than Paul's, who offered an analysis of the obscured reading of Scripture among Jews (2 Cor 3:12–18)[21] that has clearly influenced Justin here as much as Paul's teaching of the "mind" of Christ (1 Cor 2:16).

In his *Dialogue*, Justin portrays Trypho as being limited to the immediate reference of Scripture, enslaved by its specification of laws. Justin is committed to a typological reading of Scripture, the Christian norm during the second century. The prophets were understood to represent "types" of Christ, impressions on their minds of the heavenly reality, God's own Son. Trypho, by contrast, is portrayed as becoming lost in the immediate minutiae of the prophetic text. So prevalent was this understanding of Judaism by the end of the century that Christians such as Clement of Alexandria and Tertullian called any limitation to the immediate reference of Scripture (its "literal meaning") the "Jewish sense."

Justin presents the shift in the possession of the Spirit that animates the Scripture, moreover, in a way that Paul does not. While Paul famously still hopes that "all Israel will be saved" (Rom 11:26), Justin is categorical—by means of Isa 51:4 and Jer 31:31—that "there is to be an ultimate Law and Covenant superior to all, which now must be kept by all people who claim God's inheritance" (*Dial.* 11.2–3). This eternal covenant (Isa 55:3-4) establishes who is a true, spiritual Israelite *and* Judahite, and who is not (*Dial.* 11.5), taking the place of all other aspirants to those names. Thus Philippe Bobichon has said, "Nous ne sommes plus dans une logique d'accomplissement (comme dans le Nouveau Testament), mais de substitution."[22] Bobichon makes plain that supersession and replacement are not one and the same. The way in which Justin makes the transition from one to the other is instructive and prepares the way for yet another move.

The periodization of prophecy is the key to Justin's position in this regard. In taking this position, I adopt a different view from those who try to explain Justin on the basis of a periodization of Scripture. Philippe Bobichon attempts such a reading, arguing that "Pour l'Apologiste, preceptes 'éternels' (destinés à toute l'humanité) et preceptes de la Loi (réservés à Israël) entretiennent un rapport d'inclusion: ils eminent du même Dieu et s'inscrivent dans une même économie salvatrice."[23] That "inclusive" reading is accurate, it seems to me, but in Justin its generative term of reference is "the prophetic Spirit," rather than being determined by the nature of particular texts or a specific view of salvation history.

Bobichon's reading represents a simplification of the argument of Theodore Stylianopoulos, who argues that Justin divides Scripture into "(1) ethics, (2) prophecy, and (3) historical dispensation."[24] Treating Scripture as conditional indeed permits Justin to get out of the force of Trypho's observation that Jesus kept the law (*Dial.* 67.5–6), but that is because the whole of Scripture is prophetic; any part of it might prove to be binding or to be conditional in the light of what attests to Christ. For that reason, a "ritual" requirement, such as avoiding *eidōlothyta*, might remain crucial, while an "ethical" requirement, such as leaving part of field unharvested for the benefit of the poor (treated in an entire tractate of the Mishnah, *Peʾah*), might receive no emphasis.

Basic to Justin's view of prophecy is the Gospels' portrayal of John the Baptist as the successor of the prophets, and Justin's claim that prophecy came to an end after Jesus' death (*Dial.* 51.1–52.4). The former theme is taken directly from the Gospels (Luke 16:16; Matt 11:13), but the latter idea is also attested, and in surprising sources. From the time of 1 Maccabees (4:46), Jewish teachers had held that the era of prophecy had come to an end, so that the time had come to await a prophet, and this notion is specifically endorsed by rabbinic literature during the second century and later as part of the explanation for the destruction of the temple.[25] Although no connection is made to Jesus, the Talmud also dates portents of the temple's demise to the period "forty years before the destruction of the temple" (b. Yoma 39b, cf. y. Soṭah 6:13). As in the case of his messianic exegesis and his recourse to arguments reminiscent of Philo's, Justin appears to adapt motifs of Judaism available to him.

His purpose, however, goes beyond the supersession or even the replacement of Judaism. Justin appears clearly to believe that, with the defeat of Bar Kokhba, Judaism is coming to an end. Referring again to Gen 49 (this time v. 8), Justin declares there will be two comings of Christ, "that in the first he would be suffering, and that after his coming there would be neither prophet nor king in your race, and—I added—that the Gentiles who believe in the suffering Christ will expect his coming again" (Dial. 52.1). Once these sufferings of Christ had been accomplished,[26] Israel no longer had a place, which is why Isaiah predicts the devastation of Judea (1 Apol. 47) as well as the conversion of the Gentiles (1 Apol. 49), and why, finally, even the seal of the covenant in Gen 17 itself is, as Rodney Werline has explained, completely reinterpreted (citing Dial. 16): "For Justin, then, circumcision is the sign for the recent historical national disaster for the Jews."[27] To this extent, Justin stands not simply for supersession or replacement, but also for the elimination of Israel as commonly understood on the basis of the prophetic Spirit. Now "those who justify themselves and say they are children of Abraham will desire to inherit along with us even a little place, as the Holy Spirit cries aloud by Isaiah [a citation of Isa 63:15 follows]" (Dial. 25.1; cf. 55.3).

The "Spirit of prophecy" is precisely what *Targum Jonathan to the Prophets*, largely extant during the second century, said would return to Israel in the mouths of the prophets at the end of time.[28] Justin's reply, echoing targumic language, is that "the prophetic Spirit" has already made its move. He produces a hermeneutic of Christian experience out of Jesus' prophecy in Matthew, that "the kingdom of God shall be taken from you and given to a nation producing its fruit" (Matt 21:43), as well as the declaration of Paul and Barnabas that, having tried to speak to the Jews in Pisidian Antioch, "we turn to the Gentiles" (Acts 13:46). The speech of Paul in Pisidian Antioch bears comparison with Justin's approach to Scripture and the range of texts cited. At the same time, when Paul and Barnabas make their claim, they do so as envoys of the Holy Spirit (13:2).

Prophecy as a contemporary phenomenon is an emphatic theme of Luke-Acts, and it is a major aspect of Justin's argument (Dial. 88). Indeed, Justin becomes so enthusiastic in his argument that he makes false prophecy among Christians into an argument that the Spirit is among them (Dial. 82). Christian failings, on this reading, become stronger than Jewish virtues. In an attempt to save Justin from his own trenchancy, Sylvain Sanchez has argued that there were, after all, other forms of Judaism in the second century that Justin does not mention.[29] Given what he says about any form of Judaism he can think of, that was their good fortune.

The Prophets Agreed That the Divine Logos Lies at the Core of Human Cognition of God

Justin believes that the apostles preach the *Logos* of God (*Dial.* 109), and that is also what Paul and Barnabas say they articulate (Acts 13:46) after the synagogue leaders invite them to speak a *logos paraklēseōs* (13:15). God's *Logos* is so closely tied to prophecy for Justin that he attributes Balaam's oracle—the Scriptural justification for the Bar Kokhba revolt—to Moses (*Dial.* 106.4; 126.1). Eric Osborn has observed the role of the Logos in prophecy of all types in Justin:[30] "Prophecy is the word of the logos and not merely a part of the logos." The fit is so tight, Osborn claims, that Justin sometimes does not distinguish the *Logos* from the prophetic Spirit. In discussing the appearance at Mamre, Justin invokes what the "Word" says, or the "holy prophetic Spirit" (*Dial.* 56). The connection of the *Logos* with inspiration becomes explicit when Justin says (*1 Apol.* 36:1): "When you hear the utterances [*lexeis*] of the prophets spoken as by a player, don't think that they were spoken by those inspired, but think rather by the divine *Logos* who moved them." His picture of the *Logos* is indeed dynamic, and the distinction between the Logos and the Spirit needs sorting out. Appreciating Justin's context, both Judaic and Hellenistic, permits a resolution of the question.

Philo's *Logos*, together with its Stoic and Platonic resonances and its relationship to Justin, has long been a part of discussion, and generally this ground has been better covered than most aspects of the study of Justin.[31] The closer the association with Socrates (*1 Apol.* 46.3), and the more universal the claim of the reach of the *Logos* "in which the whole human race partakes" (46.2), the more natural this seems. Philo's case, argued in his brilliant continuous commentary on the Pentateuch in Greek, identifies the creative *Logos* behind our world and in our minds as the Torah that God revealed perfectly to Moses. Justin, in a less voluminous way, more the essayist than the systematician, insists that our knowledge of the *Logos* implies that it is eternally human (cf. *Dial.* 62). More specifically, he calibrates his case to address the reason (*Logos*) that should animate imperial policy (*1 Apol.* 2.1):[32] "Reason (*Logos*) enjoins those who are truly reverent and philosophers to honor and desire only the true." Yet it is striking when Justin says that *both Jews and Christians* agree that "those who prophesy are God-born by nothing other than divine *Logos*" (*1 Apol.* 33.9). He even has Trypho say that the *Logos* speaks in Scripture (*Dial.* 68.5). Something of the qualities of Justin's conception should, therefore, be discernible in Judaic sources apart from Philo.

Skarsaune has suggested that biblical works such as Proverbs (to which Justin refers in *Dial.* 61) and pseudepigraphic references such as *4 Macc* 5:22–25 should be taken into account.[33] If we pursue this line of inquiry, the fit between prophecy and "word" in the Judaism of Justin's period, we are brought to *Targum Jonathan to the Prophets* and its usage of the term *Memra* (creative word of God). In the past this term has been explored in relation to John's Gospel,[34] but it may even more fruitfully be investigated in relation to second-century literature. The *Memra* is portrayed in the *Targumim* as active at the beginning of creation, as being directed in the mouths of the prophets by the Holy Sprit, and as being subject to rejection as well

42   *Idolatry and Paganism*

as acceptance by the people of God, among other usages. As a result, like the *Logos* in *Dialogue* 141, the *Memra* may also speak of punishment as well as blessing.

This range of usage is only to be expected, because the noun *memra* is closely related to *ʾamār*, the verb of speaking; only an emphasis distinguishes the noun *memra* from the infinitive *mēmar*. So, in the Targumim as in Justin, the *Memra/Logos* is the act of speaking, while Spirit of Prophecy/prophetic Spirit is the power of speech. Justin can be bold in his application of the possibilities that these usages offer precisely because they are so widely agreed as to be axiomatic. Even the *presbytēs*, like the Prophets, speaks the "divine word" (*theion logon*; *Dial.* 23.3).[35]

Conclusion

After the *presbytēs* left Justin, a fire suddenly kindled in his soul, and he found the one sure and useful philosophy (*Dial.* 8.1). Bobichon observes the Platonic connection with fire,[36] but that is another case of a widely appearing image, specifically connected in Luke 24:32 to the moment when the risen Jesus "opened" the Scriptures to two of his disciples. Justin also compares fire to how, when we say something, "we engender a word," but without any diminution or loss to ourselves (*Dial.* 61.2).

With knowing innovation, Justin appropriates the prophetic Spirit and *Logos* to Christianity. And he uses this appropriation to articulate a consistent eucharistic theology (*1 Apol.* 66.2).

> Because we do not take as ordinary bread or ordinary drink, but in the same way as through God's *Logos* Jesus Christ our incarnate savior had flesh and blood for our salvation, so also the food given thanks for through an oath of a *Logos* from him, from which our blood and flesh are nourished by assimilation, is—we have learned—the flesh and blood of that incarnate Jesus.

In this case Justin builds upon the Johannine understanding of Eucharist as consumption of Jesus, which can only have offended Jewish readers and hearers.[37] To a dramatic extent, Justin locates himself with this conscious separation from Judaism; at the same time he perfects his synthetic understanding of the *Logos*.

PART TWO

The Nazirite

4

Scripture's Account

The Nazirite

Baruch A. Levine

Biblical references to the Nazirite (the Hebrew term is *nāzîr*) serve as a window into the practice of private religion in ancient Israel, and these texts reveal one of the ways that women participated in religious life. The underlying concept of Nazirite devotion, in all of its forms, is that of surrender and renunciation, perceived as ways of drawing nearer to God so as to partake of his power; or to put it differently, so as to become an instrument of divine power. The goal of the Nazirite could be defined as the attainment of holiness. The detailed Torah legislation preserved in Num 6 (vv. 1–21) represents a relatively late, priestly codification of a very ancient but sparsely documented form of dedication. Although its provisions only partially cover all aspects of Nazirite devotion, as we know the phenomenon, these provisions address selective aspects in great detail. Most notably, Num 6 identifies the Nazirite's act of devotion as a form of the private vow (Heb. *neder*), a human-divine contract that also has a long history. In effect, it formalizes an already-existing connection between the two. Earlier poetic and narrative sources speak primarily of persons who are dedicated for life, whereas Num 6 institutionalizes a limited, time-constrained form of devotion.

Viewing Num 6 in this way, as the end of a process, recommends tracing the requirements of Nazirite devotion prescribed therein to their roots in the culture of biblical Israel. The earlier texts reveal the heroic and even military provenance of the Nazirite, pointing to an elite status, and illustrating the role of divine designation alongside human initiative in the assignment of this status. Against this background, Num 6 is to be seen as an expression of the more focused priestly agenda. Prominent in that agenda is the unprecedented notion that the time-constrained Nazirite must preserve cultic purity by avoiding contact with a human corpse, much in the manner of a priest (Heb. *kōhēn*), as prescribed in Lev 21.

The Meaning of the Term *Nāzîr*

An examination of all biblical texts referring to the Nazirite, and of usage of the verb *nāzar*, reveals ambiguities and calls for an analysis of forms before treating the subject of Nazirite devotion, in substance. The Hebrew verb *nāzar*, from which we derive the term *nāzîr*, is probably a phonetic variant of the verb *nādar*, yielding the noun *neder* "vow," except that each has taken on specialized connotations. The core concept of both realizations is "separation." Hebrew *nādar* is a transitive verb whose base meaning in the simple stem is "to set aside, devote." The connotation of Hebrew *nāzar* is restrictive, or prohibitive, and expresses avoidance, whereas the form *nādar* is constitutive and describes a positive act. Because Biblical Hebrew does not attest verbal examples of the simple stem of the root *nāzar*, its precise force remains less certain. Usage of the derived stems suggests that it is a verb of motion, a stative verb meaning "to be separate, to stay apart." In the *nipʿal* it exhibits a reflexive meaning, "to keep one's self apart from . . ." (Lev 22:2; Ezek 14:7), or "to turn aside to . . ." (Hos 9:10). In Zech 7:3 the *nipʿal* bears a functional meaning: "Shall I weep in the fifth month, practice abstinence [*hinnāzēr*] as I have been doing for some years?" To express the transitive sense requires recourse to the *hipʿil*, which means "to set aside, reserve, devote."

The biblical lexicons usually associate the noun *nēzer*, "crown" (Exod 29:6; Prov 27:24; Zech 9:16; etc.) with the verb *nāzar*, but it is probable that there is no etymological connection between the two; they are homonyms. And yet, the inflected homophonous form *nēzer*, as in Hebrew *nizrô*, "his Nazirite (status)," derives from the root under discussion (Num 6:4–5, et passim).

The specific term *nāzîr* realizes the *qāṭîl* form, which in Hebrew represents more than one phenomenon and is undifferentiated phonologically. It may represent (1) an active participle, characterizing the actor; and (2) a passive participle, characterizing one who is acted upon. This distinction has been masked by the Masoretic vocalization systems but is evident in other Semitic languages. In many cases, however, the force of the *qāṭîl* form in Hebrew could be either active or passive. Thus, for example, a word for "harvest," *ʾāsîp*, means either "what is gathered in" (passive) or the act of "ingathering," and the same is true of *qāṣîr*, which can be translated "what is reaped, the harvest," or the act of "cutting, reaping."

Since usage of the verb *nāzar* indicates that it is not a transitive verb, it is less likely that it represents a passive form meaning "one who has been separated." Those who favor this interpretation point to the case of Samson, who was divinely designated as a Nazirite, as we shall observe, so that it would make sense to say of him that he had been "separated." And yet, the force of *nāzîr* appears to be different from that of *nātîn*, for instance, which clearly means "one who had been handed over, dedicated," or from that of *nāśîʾ*, which means "chieftain, one who has been raised" to a leadership position.

Although scholarly opinions vary, it is more likely that *nāzîr* means "one who keeps/stays apart," in the same way that Hebrew *ḥāsîd* means "one who acts with trust, who shows kindness" (and not "one who has received God's kindness"). If the above analysis is correct, the Nazirite is so-called because of how he (or she) behaves over time, in terms of what one avoids or renounces. The Nazirite is the actor, the avoider. It must be noted that the *qāṭîl* form, whether it expresses an active participle, or a passive participle, is durative; and functions as a title, signifying a customary, or regular status.

The Priestly Nazirite Rule of Numbers 6:1–21

Yahweh spoke to Moses as follows: Speak to the Israelite people and say to them: When anyone, man or woman, sets himself apart by pronouncing a vow as a Nazirite, to place restrictions upon himself for Yahweh, he must restrict [himself] from wine or any other intoxicant, not drinking the vinegar of wine, or any other intoxicant; nor may he imbibe any liquid in which grapes have been steeped. He may not eat either moist or dried grapes. For the entire term of his restriction, he may not ingest any product of the grapevine, neither seeds nor skins.

For the entire term of his restriction, a razor may not pass over his head. Until the completion of the days during which he placed restrictions on himself for Yahweh, he is to remain sacred, allowing the hair of his head to grow loose.

For the entire term during which he placed restrictions on himself for Yahweh, he may not come near the body of a dead person. Even on the account of his father and his mother, or for his brother and his sister—even on account of them he may not render himself impure at their death. For hair reserved for his God covers his head. For the entire term of his restriction, he remains sacred to Yahweh. Should any person related to him pass away suddenly, so that he has defiled his dedicated hair, he must shave his head on the day of his purification. On the seventh day he must shave it. On the eighth day he must deliver to the priest two turtledoves or two young pigeons, at the entrance to the Tent of Meeting. The priest shall assign one as a sin offering and the other as a burnt offering, and perform expiation on his behalf for the guilt he has incurred concerning a corpse. He must reconsecrate his "head" on that day. He must recommit the days of his restriction for Yahweh and deliver a yearling lamb as a guilt offering. The prior days shall fall away because his state of restriction has been impaired by an impurity.

This is the prescribed instruction for the Nazirite: On the day that his term of dedication is complete, he is to be brought to the entrance of the Tent of Meeting. He is to present, as his offering to Yahweh, a yearling lamb without blemish for a burnt offering, and one ewe a year old without blemish for a sin offering, and one ram without blemish for sacred gifts of greeting; a basket of unleavened bread made of semolina flour, prepared as loaves with oil mixed into them, as prepared as thin cakes of unleavened bread smeared with oil, along with their grain offerings and libations.

The priest shall draw near to the presence of Yahweh and perform his sin offering and his burnt offering. He shall sacrifice the ram as an offering of sacred gifts of greeting in the presence of Yahweh, together with the basket of unleavened bread. The priest shall likewise perform his grain offering and his libation.

The Nazirite shall then shave his restricted "head" at the entrance of the Tent of Meeting. He shall take the hair of his restricted "head" and place it on the fire that is under the sacred gifts of greeting. The priest shall take the boiled shoulder of the ram and one loaf of unleavened bread from the basket, along with one thin, unleavened cake, and place them on the palms of the Nazirite, after he has shaved off his restricted [hair]. The priest shall raise them as a presentation in the presence of Yahweh. This shall be a sacred offering for Yahweh, in addition to the breast of the presentation offering and the shoulder of the levied donation. Only afterward may the Nazirite drink wine.

This is the prescribed instruction for the Nazirite. But one who pledges his offering in excess of the instruction, in accordance with what his means allow, must fulfill the vow he has pledged in excess of the instruction prescribed for his restriction.

The Background of Numbers 6:1–21

Numbers 6:1–21 stipulates three basic, behavioral restrictions assumed by the Nazirite for the duration of the vow: (1) The prohibition against shaving the hair of one's head, and the corollary duty of offering a shock of hair to the Deity at the appointed time. (2) Abstinence from wine and other products of the grapevine. (3) Avoidance of contact with the dead, an unprecedented prohibition for the Nazirite. The first two prohibitions, against shaving the hair of the head and against drinking wine, are the most frequent features of Nazirite devotion and are given a particular turn in the cycle of Samson narratives (Judg 13–16). Samson is designated a Nazirite in the annunciation to his unnamed mother, the wife of Manoah:

> Then the angel of Yahweh appeared to the woman, and said to her: "Behold, you have been barren and have not borne children, but you shall conceive and bear a son. Now, then, be careful not to drink wine or other intoxicants, or to eat impure food. For behold, you are going to conceive and bear a son; let no razor be applied to his head, for the boy is designated a Nazirite to God, from the womb until the day of his death. (Judg 13:3–5)

This theme is repeated in the woman's report to her husband (Judg 13:7). The prohibition against drinking wine is imposed on the mother, not on the Nazirite himself, as is the ban on eating impure food, an item significantly absent in Num 6. Upon reflection, it would strain credulity if Samson, depicted in the cycle of narratives as a carousing hero, were to be required to abstain from drinking wine!

Most probably, this well-documented prohibition was translocated, in the present instance, from Samson to his mother. The ban on shaving the head certainly does apply to Samson himself. Anthropologists have long recognized that one's hair, as a self-replenishing part of the physical person, represents that person's vitality.

This theme is clearly expressed in Judg 16:17:

> Then he [Samson] confided to her [Delilah] all that was in his heart, saying to her: "No razor has ever been applied to my head, for I have been a Nazirite for God since I was in my mother's womb. If I were to be shaved, my strength would leave me, and I would become as weak as all other humans."

If Samson were to shave off his hair, that would amount to violating his divinely designated status, and in punishment his God-given Herculean strength would leave him. So much for the devotional dimension of the narrative; in terms of the heroic role, Samson was sent by God to rescue Israel from its Philistine oppressors. As unbridled as he was, Samson exercised his prowess in the service of his God, like the other so-called "judges." What happened is that his heroic foible did him in, so that the shaving of his hair was accomplished by a woman in the employ of Israel's enemies. Though mutilated and in chains, Samson's hair grew back, and he entreated Yahweh to restore his strength so that he could avenge himself against the Philistines. His petition was granted, indicating that his lapse had been pardoned.

In the heroic tradition generally, hair symbolized strength. Esau, notwithstanding the enmity between him and his brother, Jacob, was a heroic figure, a hirsute hunter, whereas the pacific herdsman, his brother, was smooth (Gen 25:23–27). Absalom, David's son, rebellious but nonetheless heroic, had a heavy head of hair (2 Sam 14:26). There are indications that those who answered the call to fight in the wars of Yahweh customarily let their hair grow long. It is not clear whether such fighters took lifelong vows, or only treated their hair in this way when they went into battle. Thus runs the opening verse of the Song of Deborah, an heroic ballad of victory in battle: "When locks go untrimmed in Israel, / When fighting men dedicate themselves, / Give blessing to Yahweh" (Judg 5:2). Admittedly, the meaning of this verse from early Hebrew poetry remains unclear. The translation given here is suggested, among other things, by the fact that Num 6:5 requires the Nazirite "to let his hair grow loose" (Heb. *peraʿ*, "untrimmed, loose hair"), just as Judg 5:2 speaks of a time when hair grew loose and untrimmed (Heb. *bipĕrōʿa pĕrāʿôt*). The same diction is encountered in another cryptic verse, Deut 32:42: "From the blood of the slain and the captive, / From the long-haired [*parĕʿôt*] enemy chiefs." The wide application of the theme of untrimmed hair is evident from the fact that Lev 25:11 refers to grapevines that were not pruned as "your 'Nazirite' grapes." The Hebrew Bible attests to further rituals involving the shaving of one's hair. According to Lev 14:8–9, the impure person afflicted with a pernicious skin ailment was required to shave his hair prior to reentry into the religious community. A captive woman taken as wife by an Israelite must shave her head and pare her nails while mourning for her slain husband (Deut 21:10–14). In Jer 7:29 the form *nēzer* means untrimmed hair: "Shave off your 'Nazirite' hair, and cast it away."

The requirement in Num 6:18–20 that the Nazirite offer his shorn hair to God by casting it into sacrificial flames at the termination of the votive period has no explicit parallel in biblical literature, undoubtedly because it reflects a specifically priestly practice. The closest we come is in Ezek 5:1–4:

> And you, O mortal, take a sharp knife: use it as a barber's razor [*ta'ar haggallābîm*], and pass it over your head and beard. Then take scales and divide the hair. When the days of siege are over, destroy a third part in fire within the city. Take a third and strike it with the sword all around the city, and scatter a third to the wind, unsheathing a sword after them Take also a few [hairs] from there and tie them up in your skirts. Then take some more of them and cast them into the fire, and burn them in the fire. From this a fire shall go out upon the whole house of Israel.

The hair of the prophet is systematically destroyed or scattered, and finally burned in fire. In this prophecy, hair represents life, the lives of the inhabitants of the city, and of all Israel. The Nazirite's hair, burned in the altar fire, represents his special power, which had now to be returned to God, who had conferred it on him. There is some significance in the fact that the Nazirite places some of his shorn hair under the *šĕlāmîm*-offering, into the altar fire (Num 6:18). This may be simply because it was the final altar offering in the composite ritual, but it is also relevant that the disposition of the sacred meal involved boiling the parts of the offering that were spared from the altar fire. These were placed on the palms of the Nazirite, after which the officiating priest raised them in a rite known as *tĕnûpâ*, "presentation offering" (6:19). This act asserted the innocence of the Nazirite; he is adjudged *nĕqî kappayim*, "one whose palms are innocent, clean" (Ps 24:4), and his offering qualifies as *maśĕʾat kappay*, "the tribute of my palms" (141:2). In the same manner, Num 5:18 prescribes that the requisite grain offering was to be placed on the palms of a wife suspected of adultery during her ordeal.

We now have a Phoenician inscription from Kition, on Cyprus, dated before 800 BCE and first published in 1970 by the French scholar Dupont-Sommer. It was inscribed on a bowl found in a temple, and although it is only partially preserved, we can decipher a statement to the effect that the hair of a devotee of the goddess Ashtart (Astarte = Heb. Ashtoreth) was shaved as part of a ritual.

> śʿr z glb.wypg[ʿ (brbt) ʿš[trt] wʿ[štrt
> ... the hair which he shaved. He prayed to (Rabbat) Ashtart, and Ashtart...

The man in question had prayed to the Phoenician goddess Ashtart. The Phoenician verb for praying is *pgʿ* (cf. Heb. *pāgaʿ* in Jer 7:16; Ruth 1:16). Presumably the goddess heard his petition. He had shaved his hair and offered it to her. The verb for shaving is Phoenician *glb*, whose Hebrew cognate, *gālab*, occurs only once in the Hebrew Bible, precisely in Ezek 5:1–4, the passage just cited above! Further on in the unfortunately fragmentary inscription we can read the verb *wytkrb*, "and it was sacrificed," although it remains unclear whether reference is to the hair itself or to the sacrificial animals enumerated in the inscription. In another broken line, we can also restore the words *ś[ʿr]*, "hair" and *bnd[r]*, "by means of a vow." So it is that notwithstanding the poor condition of the Phoenician inscription, it attests to the votive practice of devoting hair to deities, and this in a neighboring culture that shared some of the votive practices of the Israelites.

Returning to avoidance of wine by Nazirites, we find this prohibition reflected in Amos 2:11–12. Chastising the Israelites, the prophet proclaims in the name of Yahweh:

> Furthermore, I raised up prophets from among your sons,
> And Nazirites from among your select young men.
> Is that not so, O people of Israel? . . .
> But you made the Nazirites drink wine,
> And you commanded the prophets, saying:
> "Do not prophesy!"

With characteristic ingratitude, the people were preventing both prophets and Nazirites from performing their proper functions, since Nazirites who imbibed wine were no longer acceptable. The prohibition against wine should be understood as part of the nomadic mind-set, which was resistant to urban life. Thus the Rechabites of Jeremiah's time dwelled in tents and avoided the products of the vine. They had come to live in Jerusalem only for protection in the face of the Babylonian invasion (Jer 35). The cultivation of vines symbolizes settled life, so that the divine promise of restoration to the land is expressed both as the building of homes and the planting of vineyards (Jer 31:4–5; Ezek 28:26).

The prophecy of Amos (2:11–12) also implies that the Nazirite held a preeminent status in ancient Israel, comparable with that of prophets. High status is likewise reflected in the blessing of Joseph, the eponym of the northern Israelite tribes of Ephraim and Manasseh, in Gen 49:26, paralleled in Deut 33:16: "May these [blessings] rest on the head of Joseph, / On the pate of the 'Nazirite' among his brothers." Lamentations 4:7, in bemoaning the Babylonian destruction of Jerusalem, speaks of Nazirites who were "purer than snow, whiter than milk." By referring to *han-nezîrîm*, "*the* Nazirities, "in parallelism with *hannebîʾîm*, "*the* prophets," the Amos (2:11–12) prophecy suggests that just as there were associations or guilds of prophets, usually called *bĕnê hannĕbîʾîm* (e.g., 1 Kgs 20:35; 2 Kgs 2:3), so there may also have been operative bands of Nazirites, so that one could refer to them collectively. Ironically, the same gap in our knowledge of ancient Israelite society that prevents us from knowing much about how one became a "professional" prophet likewise keeps us in the dark as to how one might become a lifelong Nazirite. The case of Samson illustrates divine designation, an annunciation to the mother of an as-yet unborn child, much in the mode of the divine designation of Jeremiah while in his mother's womb (Jer 1:5).

Although the cult prophet Samuel is never explicitly referred to as a Nazirite, his cultic dedication by his mother bears many similarities to the status of the Nazirite and is uniquely informative in its own right (1 Sam 1–2). Whereas Manoah's wife, Samson's mother, was commanded by the Deity to surrender her son as a Nazirite, Hannah on her own initiative vows to dedicate her son to Yahweh for all of his life:

> She pronounced a vow, saying: "O Yahweh of Hosts! If you will, indeed, regard the suffering of your maidservant, and remember me and not forget your maidservant, and *give* your maidservant a male child, I will (in return) *give* him to Yahweh for all of the days of his life; no razor shall ever be applied to his head." (1:11, emphasis added)

We observe that the child would, just like the Nazirite, never shave his head. Beyond that, the formulation of the vow plays on the nuances of the Hebrew verb *nātan*, "to give, grant, pay, dedicate." Its usage conveys precisely what the vow represents; it is a human-divine negotiation, a principle expressed in Latin as *Do ut des*, "I give so that you may give." The vow represents a conditional pledge to the Deity, made in advance. The votary is obligated to fulfill the pledge/contract only after the Deity of the regional temple in Shiloh has fulfilled the request. The report of that dedication provides considerable detail on the cultic acts celebrating the fulfillment of the vow. On that occasion, Hannah offered sacrifices of animals, grain, and wine, a triad basic to the biblical system (1:24–28). First Samuel 1 also establishes the cultic venue of the private vow, so that one pronounces the vow in a sanctuary or similar installation, and to fulfill it customarily repairs to a sacred site, often the same site where the vow was first pronounced. Hannah then gave her son to Yahweh.

What Hannah had asked of God, once granted, was now being given back to God, namely, her own son.

Numbers 6:1–21: The Focus of the Priestly Agenda

Three elements in the priestly legislation of Num 6 are innovative, in full or in part. (1) A time-constrained form of Nazirite devotion, activated through human initiative and configured as a restrictive vow. (2) The prohibition of contact with a dead body by the Nazirite for the term of the vow. (3) Specific, sacrificial rites of purification at various points during the term of Nazirite restriction and at its conclusion, performed at the Tent of Meeting.

It is conceivable that professional warriors resembled temporary Nazirites and let their hair grow long only when in battle, but it is equally possible that untrimmed hair was a permanent feature of their status. Be that as it may, the priestly writers who gave us Num 6, in a customary manner, prescribed time-constrained Naziritism in unambiguous detail. In three similar statements, Num 6 speaks of the "the entire term" of the restrictions imposed by the Nazirite's vow.

As observed (above), a connection between Nazirite devotion and the private vow is reflected in narratives such as 1 Sam 1, but this connection was not made explicit. Numbers 6 utilizes one aspect of the vow in setting forth the proper procedure for becoming a Nazirite: the pronounced vow as solemn pledge. The standard vow of biblical times, also known in Ugaritic literature and among the Phoenicians, consisted of a prior conditional pledge made to a deity, so that when the deity subsequently granted the petitioner's request, the petitioner would dutifully fulfill it. This negotiation determines the formulation of the vow. In Num 6, however, there is no indication of such conditionality; no "if" (Heb. *ʾim*), as in Hannah's vow (1 Sam 1:11), or as in the pronouncements of Jacob and Jephthah (Gen 28:20; Judg 11:30). The person assuming the status of a Nazirite was doing so unconditionally, promising to adhere to certain restrictions without asking for something specific in return. This is not to say that the Nazirite would not be rewarded or be strengthened by self-denial, only that no prior negotiation was involved. It was believed that self-denial in the service of God would bring its own rewards. It is as if a person swore to fulfill the specified requirements. The nexus of vow and oath is exemplified in the priestly code of practice set forth in Num 30. One either "pronounces a vow" or "takes an oath," with no difference implied. For itself, Num 30 proceeds to limit the liability of a father or husband, as the case may be, for the obligations pledged by vow or oath by an as-yet unmarried daughter or by one's wife.

The prohibition of contact with a dead body, imposed on the Nazirite, requires explanation. It is not because we lack corollary evidence, but rather because, in this mode, the Nazirite restriction connects with a whole range of mourning practices and burial customs; it reflects an aversion to the cult of the dead, the worship of dead ancestors. The most immediate source for discussion of this feature of Nazirite devotion is Lev 21:1–8, 11, a series of laws forbidding a priest from attending to the burial of any of his kin, with the exception of consanguineous relatives. These are specified as his mother and father, his son and daughter, his brother and as-yet unmarried, virginal sister. Even the wife of a priest was excluded from the permitted category. The "Great Priest" is absolutely prohibited from any contact with the dead, with no exceptions. The wording of these prohibitions is significant: The priest "may not render himself impure" (Heb. *lōʾ yiṭṭammāʾ*, 21:11; cf. Ezek 44:25–27).

According to Num 6:6–12, the temporary Nazirite was restricted as severely as was the Great Priest of Lev 21! In fact, contingencies are dealt with in case a sudden death occurs during the period of the vow. In that event, the Nazirite must start counting the days all over again. The head must be shaved and a waiting period of seven days initiated, so that the original vow was effectively undone. Even though the Nazirite was not at fault, a sin offering and burnt offering were required, because the purity of the Nazirite had actually been breached.

To understand the procedure of purification after contact with a dead body, we turn to Num 19, which specifies not only the spatial and tactile conditions that produce corpse contamination, but also the exceptional procedures for purification, including use of the ashes of the red heifer. The Nazirite becomes impure in the same manner as any other Israelite, except that the Nazirite has initially been admonished to avoid being so affected. Perhaps in an effort to induce a person seeking holiness to start over again, Num 6:6–12 does not require the full purification dictated in Num 19. This is also the case with respect to warriors who fought in the Midianite war, and who were presumably in contact with the slain while battle raged on (Num 31:19).

The question that begs discussion is why contact with a corpse produced such severe impurity, to start with. Was this always so in ancient Israel? There is evidence, first of all, of a deep-rooted and long-held aversion to the cult of ancestor worship in biblical Israel. This is not to say that no such activity occurred, although scholarly opinion is divided as to its extent. Deuteronomy 26:14 requires one remitting his tithes to the sanctuary to declare: "I have not partaken of it while in mourning." Jeremiah assures Zedekiah, king of Judah, that he will not die in battle, but rather peacefully. "And like the fire offerings of your ancestors, the earlier kings who preceded you, so will they burn offerings for you, and 'Ah, lord!' will they lament over you" (Jer 34:5). The psalmist (106:28) knows about "sacred meals honoring the dead" (Heb. *zibhê mētîm*). To believe that the dead held some power over the living, and that on this basis they should be propitiated, was seen to conflict with the belief that all power over the living and the dead was held by God.

In the priestly tradition, the adverse attitude toward the cult of the dead took a particular turn, evident in the specific distancing of funerary activity from sacred sites and in prohibiting priestly participation, as is set forth in Lev 21. Attending to the dead was henceforth to be regarded as a duty relegated to the family, requiring no cultic sanctification. Outside of the Torah, the first specific indication that the corpse contaminated everything and everyone that came in contact with it or was in proximity to it is reflected in the activities of Josiah, king of Judah, near the end of the seventh century BCE. In his effort to reform the cult of Yahweh, he intentionally defiled the necropolis of Bethel in a distinctive way:

> Then Josiah turned and saw the graves that were there on the hill, and he had the bones exhumed from the graves, and burned them on the altar, thereby defiling it. (2 Kgs 23:16)
>
> And as well, Josiah abolished all of the enclosed cult platforms that were in the towns of Samaria, which the kings of Israel had provocatively built, and he dealt with them in the same manner as he had acted in Bethel. He slaughtered all of the *bāmâ*-priests who were there atop the altars, and he burned human bones upon them. (2 Kgs 23:19–20)

Logically, Josiah's method of defilement presumes a belief that the bones of the dead contaminated all that came into contact with them, otherwise it would be ineffective. Therefore, in order to deter Israelites from worshipping at the illicit *bāmôt* (platforms/high places) and to defile them permanently, bones of the dead were burned on the relevant altars. This notion, that the bones of the dead contaminate, accounts for the prophetic condemnation of royal burials in the palace, which was divided from the first temple by only one wall and stood under the same roof as the temple (Ezek 43:7–9). A sequence of ritual changes thus emerges: In the near-exilic period, Josiah takes strong measures to render the cult platforms, some of which stood at major grave sites, inactive by defiling them with bones of the dead, and subsequently we find in Ezek 43 a prophetic ruling prohibiting the age-old practice of royal burials in the Jerusalem temple. These developments in religious ritual underlie the priestly legislation of Leviticus and Num 19, and also the Nazirite laws of Num 6. This is why the prohibition against contact with the dead is not attested in any of the earlier sources that refer to the Nazirite. In effect, the Nazirite resembled the priest, and his purity, though usually time-constrained, consisted in part of avoidance of contact with the dead. Like the priest, the Nazirite is *qādōš*, "consecrated, holy," if only temporarily (Num 6:3, 5). For the rest, Num 6 prescribes many specific sacrifices and rites associated with the ritual status and behavioral obligations of the Nazirite, most of which fit into the overall pattern of priestly practices. Although purity is consistently associated with Nazirite devotion, it is nowhere else spelled out as it is in Num 6.

Conclusion

What remains obscure about the practice of Nazirite devotion in biblical Israel far exceeds what is known about this elusive status. More can be said about the history of the Israelite priesthood(s), or even about the Levites and prophets, notwithstanding serious gaps in available knowledge of these roles. One has the sense that the cumulative evidence regarding Nazirite devotion only touches the surface of what may well have been a deeply rooted, functional aspect of Israelite religion, one having cultic as well as ecstatic features and intersecting with differing institutional affiliations. Most of all, we are unable to identify organized groups of Nazirites, as is possible to a degree with respect to priests and prophets, and even Levites. Was Nazirite devotion a practice "on its way out"? If so, we would regard the priestly legislation of Num 6 as an attempt to retain at least some of what had been a more life-changing status by subsuming Nazirite devotion under the category of vows.

5

Rabbinic Reading

The Nazirite

Jacob Neusner

The Halakhah of *Nazir* on the special vow of the Nazirite and of Nedarim on generic vows investigates the power of a person through invoking the name of Heaven to affect the classification in which he or she is situated and so to define one's concrete and material relationships with other people. This is done in the generic vow by stating, "May what I eat of your food be prohibited to me as is a sacrifice prohibited to me," all conveyed in the word "Qorban [or Korban]." Having said that, the person who uttered the statement may not eat the food of the other, to whom the statement was addressed. The reason is that the other person's food has been declared by the individual who took the vow to be in the status of a sacrifice.

That does not mean the food is intrinsically holy, as if on the altar. What makes an ordinary beast into a holy beast, subject to the laws of sacrilege and set aside for the altar, is a verbal designation as a sacrifice. Here in the case of vows and the special vow of the Nazirite, by contrast, it is a subjective transaction, affecting only the one who uses the affective language. What makes ordinary food into food in the status of holy things, so far as the given individual is concerned, is the verbal designation of that ordinary food as holy things. The difference is that designating an animal as a beast for sacrifice is a public act, affecting society at large. No one can then make use of said animal. Declaring that a dish of oatmeal is in the status of a Qorban, by contrast, has no affect upon the cereal, except for the person who made that declaration. Now let us examine the Nazirite vow in particular.

The Nazirite is comparable to a *kōhēn*, or priest, who is subject to certain prohibitions and is assigned a particular position in the conduct of the temple cult. The priest cannot serve if he is drunk or contaminated by a corpse or bald (a bald-headed man is invalid to serve as a priest; so *m. Bekorot* 7:2A). From the perspective of Scripture, once the Nazirite vow takes effect, prohibitions are invoked against wine, haircutting, and corpse-uncleanness. The other point of interest is the offerings that are required if the Nazirite is made unclean with corpse-uncleanness and that are in any case imperative when the Nazirite completes the vow in a state of cleanness. All this the rabbinic Halakhah both takes for granted and in the main simply ignores. What Scripture holds does not require detailed analysis; by contrast, more attention is given to the process by which the woman or man becomes a Nazirite: the vow itself. To that problem fully half of the Halakhah, as defined by the Mishnah with the Tosefta, is devoted. So while the triple taboo is merely restated by the Halakhah, it is the exposition of the vow that defines the tough problems, generates interesting conundrums, and entails the rich exposition that the Tosefta and two Talmuds would ultimately provide.

The Halakhah focuses not on the black-and-white language that invokes the vow, but on euphemisms that may or may not pertain, just as we shall see with Mishnah *Nedarim*.

> M. *Nazir* 1:1: All euphemisms for [the form of words for] a Nazirite vow are equivalent to a Nazirite vow [and binding]. He who says, "I will be [such]"—lo, this one is a Nazir. Or: "I shall be comely"—he is a Nazir. [If he says,] "Naziq" or "Naziah" or "Paziah"—lo, this one is a Nazir. [If he says,] "Lo, I shall be like this one," "Lo, I shall curl [my hair]," "Lo, I shall tend [my hair]," "Lo, it is incumbent on me to grow [my hair] long"—lo, this one is a Nazir. [If he says,] "Lo, I pledge myself [to offer] birds"—he is not a Nazir.
>
> M. *Nazir* 1:2: [He who says,] "Lo, I shall be an abstainer [Nazir] from grape pits" or "from grape skins" or "from haircuts" or "from uncleanness [of corpses]"—lo, this one is a Nazir [in all regards]. And all the details of a Nazirite vow pertain to him. [He who says,] "Lo, I shall be like Samson" or "like the son of Manoah" or "like the husband of Delilah" or "like the one who tore down the gates of Gaza" or "like the one whose eyes the Philistines plucked out"—lo, this one is a Nazir in the status of Samson. What is the difference between a lifelong Nazirite and a Nazirite in the status of Samson [also a Nazirite for life]? A lifelong Nazirite: [If] his hair gets too heavy, he lightens it with a razor and brings three [offerings of] cattle [Num 6:14]. And if he is made unclean, he brings an offering on account of uncleanness. A Nazirite in the status of Samson: [If] his hair gets too heavy, he does not lighten it. And if he is made unclean, he does not bring an offering on account of uncleanness.
>
> M. *Nazir* 1:3: A Nazirite vow that is unspecified [as to length] is for a period of thirty days. [If] he said, "Lo, I shall be a Nazir for one long spell," "Lo, I shall be a Nazir for one short spell," [or] even, "From now until [for as long as it takes to go] the end of the world"—he is a Nazir for thirty days. [If he said,] "Lo, I shall be a Nazir and for one day [more]," "Lo, I shall be a Nazir and for one hour [more]," "Lo, I shall be a Nazir for one spell and a half"—lo, he is a Nazir for two spells [of thirty days]. [If he said,] "Lo, I shall be a Nazir for thirty days and for one hour," he is a Nazir for thirty days and for one day, for Nazirite vows are not taken by the measure of hours.

Language that is similar in sound or in sense takes effect. What about stipulations that might affect the vow, conditions under which the vow is or is not invoked, the taking of sequences of Nazirite vows at a single moment? That is the next problem. The duration of the vow, undefined in Scripture, occupies attention. Then comes the husband's intervention into the applicability of the vow his wife has taken.

Individual conditions are null, as shown here:

> If one said, "Lo, I am a Nazir on condition that I shall drink wine and become unclean with corpse uncleanness," lo, this one is a Nazir. But he is prohibited to do all of these things that he has specified as conditional upon his vow. If he said, "I recognize that there is such a thing as Naziriteship, but I do not recognize that a Nazir is prohibited from drinking wine," lo, this one is bound by the Nazirite oath. (*m. Nazir* 2.4)

But legitimate stipulations bear consequences, such as conditions that do not violate the law of the Torah: "If my wife bears a son" or "a daughter" (2:7–10).

Because the husband has the power to nullify the vows of the wife (or the father, those of the daughter), the Halakhah attends to the case of nullification. While the husband may nullify the wife's vow, he may not nullify his own. If his vow is contingent upon her vow, by contrast, neither is subject to the Nazirite rule. Limits are set upon intentionality; if one intended to violate the vow but in fact was not subject to the vow, there is no penalty. If her husband annulled the vow for her, but she did not know that her husband had annulled it for her and nonetheless continued to go around drinking wine and contracting corpse uncleanness, she does not receive forty stripes. So, too, someone who violated the vow but had a sage annul it is not penalized; the vow never took effect. Here intention to violate the vow is insufficient to precipitate sanctions; the actualities intervene. Or to put it otherwise, improper intention not confirmed by improper deed is null. Mere intention on its own is null: language and action decide everything, and when it comes to the vow, the language constitutes the act.

When it comes to the restrictions upon the Nazirite, which Scripture has defined, the Halakhah is devoted to the familiar problem of differentiating among a sequence of actions of a single type, that is, the general theme of the many and the one, the one and the many, that preoccupies the Halakhah in one topic after another. This routine problem comes to expression in the language: "A Nazir who was drinking wine all day long is liable only on one count. If they said to him, 'Don't drink it! Don't drink it!' and he continues drinking, he is liable on each and every count [of drinking]" (6:4). The problem is particular, the resolution and consequent rule are general. So too the conundrum about the high priest and the Nazirite, both of them subject to the same restriction against corpse-uncleanness; if they share the obligation to bury a neglected corpse, it requires us to hierarchize the sanctity of each in relationship to that of the other. This too represents a particular form of a general problem of the Halakhah in its work of hierarchical classification, here of competing sanctities: who is holier than whom, and so what? For the same reason, we need not be detained by the Halakhah covering cases of doubt. They merely illustrate prevailing principles on how cases of doubt are to be resolved.

The upshot is, people bear direct, personal responsibility for what they say, and while statements made in error are null, those made in jest bear real consequences. That is why euphemisms form so central a concern. There is no fooling around with God, no language exempt from God's hearing. Accordingly, the Halakhah of vows and the Nazirite vow finds an appropriate situation here because it is coherent in its generative problematics with the Halakhah of the household in general. For what makes the Nazirite vow effective is language that an individual has used, and it is the power of language to bring about profound change in the status of a person that forms the one of the two centers of the Halakhah's interest in life within the walls of the Israelite household: the focus of sanctification.

Within the framework of the Halakhah, vows—including the special vow of the Nazirite—present the message that people had best use the power of language in a wise and astute manner. That is not only because sages want to tell people to watch their words and not pretend to joke when it comes to matters where intentionality makes a difference as to personal status. It is also because sages take a negative view of vowing. While they approve of oaths taken in court with full deliberation, invoking the name of God, they despise vows. They are explicit on that matter: people who take vows show their weakness, not their strength. Vows represent the power of the weak and put-upon, the easy way to defend oneself against the importunities of the overbearing host, the grasping salesman, the tormenting husband or wife. But sages do not honor those who take the easy way, asking God to intervene in matters to which we ought to be able to attend on our own.

Sages do not treat respectfully the person who takes vows, including those of the Nazirite, as we shall see in a moment. Vow-takers yield to the undisciplined will, to emotion unguided by rational considerations. But intentionality must (ideally) take form out of both emotion and reflection. Vows explode, the fuel of emotion ignited by the heat of the occasion. "Qonam [= Qorban; cf. *m. Nedarim* 1:2] be any benefit I get from you" (2:5) hardly forms a rational judgment of a stable relationship; it bespeaks a loss of temper, a response to provocation with provocation. Right at the outset the Halakhah gives a powerful signal of its opinion of the whole: suitable folk do not take vows, only wicked people do. That explains in so many words why, if one says something is subject to "the vows of suitable folk," he has said nothing. Suitable people, *kesheyrim* (kĕšêrîm), make no vows at all, ever. Here is the counterpart for vows using euphemistic language, as we observed earlier in the Nazirite vow:

> Mishnah *Nedarim* 1:1: All euphemisms [substitutes for language used to express] (1) vows are equivalent to vows, and [all euphemisms] for (2) bans [ḥerem] are equivalent to bans, and [all euphemisms] for (3) oaths are equivalent to oaths, and [all euphemisms] for (4) Nazirite vows are equivalent to Nazirite vows. He who says to his fellow [euphemisms such as], (1) "I am forbidden by vow from you," (2) "I am separated from you," (3) "I am distanced from you," "if I eat your [food]," [or] "if I taste your [food],"

is bound [by such a vow]. [He who says], "As the vows of the evil folk ... ," has made a binding vow in the case of a Nazir, or in the case of [bringing] an offering, or in the case of an oath. [He who says,] "As the vows of the suitable folk," has said nothing whatsoever. "As their [suitable folks'] freewill-offerings ... ," he has made a binding vow in the case of a Nazir or in the case of [bringing] an offering.

A distaste for vowing and a disdain for people who make vows then characterize the law. People who take vows are deemed irresponsible; they are adults who have classified themselves as children. They possess the power of intentionality but not the responsibility for its wise use. That is why they are given openings toward the unbinding of their vows; at the same time, they are forced to take seriously what they have said. Vows are treated as a testing of Heaven, a trial of heavenly patience and grace. Sanctification can affect a person or a mess of porridge, and there is a difference. Expletives, with which we deal here, make that difference; these are not admired.

But because the Halakhah begins and ends with the conviction that language is power, the Halakhah also takes account of the sanctifying effect of even language stupidly used. That is the message of the Halakhah, and it is only through the Halakhah at hand that sages could set forth the message they had in mind concerning the exploitation and abuse of the power of language. It is a disreputable use of the holy. And language is holy because language gives form and effect to intentionality—the very issue of the Halakhah at hand! That is why we do admit intentionality—not foresight but intentionality as to honor—into the repertoire of reasons for nullifying vows, as we see in the Halakhah of *Nedarim*:

> Mishnah *Nedarim* 9:1: In a matter which is between him and his mother or father, they unloose his vow by [reference to] the honor of his father or mother.
>
> *Nedarim* 9:9: They unloose a vow for a man by reference to his own honor and by reference to the honor of his children. They say to him, "Had you known that the next day they would say about you, 'That's the way of So-and-so, going around divorcing his wives,' "and that about your daughters they'd be saying, 'They're daughters of a divorcée! What did their mother do to get herself divorced' [would you have taken a vow]?" And [if] he then said, "Had I known that things would be that way, I should never have taken such a vow," lo, this [vow] is not binding.

The normative law rejects unforeseen events as a routine excuse for nullifying a vow; foresight on its own ("Had you known . . . , would you have vowed?") plays a dubious role. But when it comes to the intentionality involving honor of parents or children, that forms a consideration of such overriding power as to nullify the vow.

So the sages' statement through the Halakhah of the two tractates on vows, *Nedarim* and *Nazir*, is clear. Vows are a means used on earth by a weak or subordinated person to coerce the more-powerful person by invoking the power of Heaven. They form an intangible but solid defense against overbearing hosts, for example. They are taken under emotional duress and express impatience and frustration. They are not to be predicted. They do not follow a period of sober reflection. They take on importance principally in two relationships, (1) between friends (e.g., host and guest), and (2) between husband and wife. They come into play at crucial, dangerous points, because they disrupt the crucial relationships that define life, particularly within the household: marriage on the one side, and friendly hospitality on the other. They jar and explode. By admitting into human relationships the power of intentionality, they render the predictable—what is governed by regularities—into a source of uncertainty, for who in the end will penetrate what lies deep in the heart, as Jeremiah reflected, which is beyond fathoming? But language brings to the surface, in a statement of will best left unsaid, what lurks in the depths; the result, Heaven's immediate engagement, is not to be gainsaid. That is why vows form a source of danger. What should be stable if life is to go on is made capricious. So far as marriage is concerned, vows rip open the fabric of sacred relationships.

Language represents power, then, and it is a power not to be exercised lightly. The weaker side to the party is represented as taking a vow, whether the milquetoast husband or the abused wife. It is the wife against the husband, the harried guest against the insistent host, the seller against the buyer, the boastful storyteller against the dubious listener, the passive against the active party, that the vow is taken. The strong incites, the weak reacts; and the language of reaction, the vow, contains such power as is not to be lightly unleashed even against the one who gives and therefore dominates, whether in sex or food or entertainment. Vows then are the response: the mode of aggression exercised by the less-powerful party to the relationship. The weak invoke Heaven, the strong do not have to. A vow will be spit out by a guest who has been importuned to take a fourth portion in a meal he does not want to eat. A wife will exclaim that she will derive no benefit whatsoever from her husband. A whole series of cases emerges from a vow taken by a person not to derive benefit from his friend, with the consequence that the friend, who wants to provide some sort of support for the dependent person, does so through a third party. The dependence then is less obtrusive. So once more: who gives, dominates, and the vow is the instrument to escape earthly domination in the name of Heaven.

The same negative view pertains to the Nazirite vow. It is a mark of arrogance. The special vow of the Nazirite arrogates to the person who takes it the special status of a holy man or woman, even though Heaven has not endowed him or her with that status by nature, by birth. The priest by birth cannot function drunk or subject to corpse-uncleanness. The Nazirite takes on himself the same prescriptions and beautifies himself with abundant hair, held by sages as a mark of pride.

> Tosefta *Nazir* 4:7:
> A. Said Simeon the Righteous, "In my entire life I ate a guilt-offering of a Nazirite only one time.
> B. The Story Concerns the Following: "A man came to me from the south,

and I saw that he had beautiful eyes, a handsome face, and curly locks. I said to him, 'My son, on what account did you destroy this lovely hair?'

C. "He said to me, 'I was a shepherd in my village, and I came to draw water from the river, and I looked at my reflection, and my bad impulse took hold of me and sought to drive me from the world.

D. "'I said to him, "Evil one! You should not have taken pride in something which does not belong to you, in something which is going to turn into dust, worms, and corruption. Lo, I take upon myself to shave you off for the sake of Heaven."'

E. "I patted his head and kissed him and said to him, 'My son, may people like you become many, people who do the will of the Omnipresent in Israel. Through you is fulfilled this Scripture, as it is said, "A man or a woman, when he will express a vow to be a Nazir, to abstain for the sake of the LORD."'" [Num 6:2]

But the Nazirite is one who lets his hair grow long, cutting it only at the end of the process, when the vow has been fulfilled. So the Nazirite has undertaken important restrictions incumbent on the priesthood and beautified himself with long hair. Only at the end does the Nazirite make himself praiseworthy, in line with Simeon's judgment, by cutting off all the hair. Thus the sages treat the Nazirite vow as they treat vows in general, as a mark of inferior character or conscience, and here, of pride.

What is at stake, then, in the Halakhah of tractates *Nedarim* and *Nazir*? It is the sages' interest in defining the source of the power of language. This they find in Heaven's confirmation of man's or woman's affirmation. By using formulary language, the man or woman invokes the response of Heaven more really by throwing up words toward Heaven and so provoking Heaven. That is how patterns of behavior and relationship—such as are defined by the vow, the Nazirite vow, the act of sanctification of a woman to a particular man, or a marriage contract—are subjected to Heaven's concerned response. Relationships and deeds are subjected to Heaven's engagement by the statement of the right words. So the Halakhah explores the effects of words, and it is in the Halakhah of rabbinic Judaism—and not that of Scripture, with its powerful bias toward priestly concerns—that that exploration takes place.

6

The New Testament's Interpretation

The Nazirite Vow and the Brother of Jesus

Bruce D. Chilton

In the New Testament the vow is associated specifically with James, the brother of Jesus, who is identified as a principal authority within the primitive church. That association provided a precedent for much of the *ritual* character of early Christianity.

Acts attributes to James (and to James alone) the power to decide whether non-Jewish male converts in Antioch needed to be circumcised. He determines that they do *not* need circumcision.[1] Under the influence of the thesis of F. C. Bauer, it is sometimes assumed that James required circumcision of all such converts,[2] but that requirement is attributed to Christian Pharisees in Acts (15:5), not to James. Nonetheless, James does proceed to command non-Jewish Christians to observe certain requirements of purity (so Acts 15:1-35). That explains why emissaries from James make their appearance as villains in Paul's description of a major controversy at Antioch.[3] They insisted on separate fellowship meals for Jews and non-Jews, while Paul with more than equal insistence (but with little or no success) argued for the unity of Jewish and non-Jewish fellowship within the church (Gal 1:18-2:21). How precisely James came to such a position of prominence is not explained in Acts; his apostolic status was no doubt assured by the risen Jesus' appearance to him (see 1 Cor 15:7).

Like Josephus (*Antiquities* 20.9.1 §§197-203), Hegesippus (in concert with Clement, Eusebius reports; see his *Ecclesiastical History* 2.23.1-18) portrays James as killed by Ananus at the temple. In addition, Hegesippus describes James in terms that emphasize his purity in such a way that, as in Acts, his association with the Nazirite vow is evident (cf. Acts 21:17-36). James's capacity to win the reverence of many Jews in Jerusalem (not only his brother's followers) derives from this practice and his encouragement of others in the practice. The fact is frequently overlooked, but needs to be emphasized, that the Mishnah envisages the Nazirite practice of slaves, as well as of Israelites, both male and female (see *Nazir* 9:1).[4] James's focus was purity in the temple under the aegis of his risen brother, the Son of Man, but

64   *The Nazirite*

there is no trace of his requiring circumcision of Gentiles. It needs to be kept in mind that Jesus himself had expelled traders from the temple, not as some indiscriminate protest about commercialism, but as part of Zechariah's prophecy (see Zech 14) of a day when all the peoples of the earth would be able to offer sacrifice "to the LORD" without the intervention of middlemen.[5] James's Nazirite practice helped to realize that prophecy in his brother's name.

Josephus indicates that James was killed in the temple in 62 CE at the instigation of the high priest Ananus during the interregnum of the Roman governors Festus and Albinus (*Ant.* 20.9.1 §§197–203). Hegesippus gives a more circumstantial, less politically informed, account of the martyrdom. James is set up on a parapet of the temple, being known and addressed by his opponents by the titles "Righteous and *Oblias*," Hegesippus reports. The second title has caused understandable puzzlement (especially when Hegesippus's rendering of the term as "bulwark" is accepted),[6] but it is easily related to the Aramaic term *ʾābal*, which means "to mourn." Recent finds in the vicinity of the Dead Sea (not only near Qumran) have greatly enhanced our understanding of Aramaic as spoken in the time of Jesus and his followers. The use of the term is attested there.[7] James was probably known as "mourner."

A minor tractate of the Talmud lays down the rule that a mourner (*ʾābal*) "is under the prohibition to bathe, anoint [the body], put on sandals and cohabit" (*Semaḥot* 4:1). This largely corresponds to the requirements of a Nazirite vow and to Hegesippus's description of James's practice; for Jesus himself to have called his brother "mourner" would fit in with his giving his followers nicknames. A tight association with the temple on James's part is attested throughout and from an early period, but not a universal requirement of circumcision.

Hegesippus's account of James's prominence is confirmed by Clement, who portrays James as the first elected bishop in Jerusalem (also cited by Eusebius, *Eccl. Hist.* 2.1.1–6), and by the pseudo-Clementine *Recognitions*, which makes James into an almost papal figure, who provides the correct paradigm for preaching to Gentiles. Paul is so much the butt of this presentation that the *Recognitions* (1.43–71) even relates that, before his conversion to Christianity, Saul physically assaulted James in the temple. Martin Hengel refers to this presentation as an apostolic novel (*Apostelroman*), deeply influenced by the perspective of the Ebionites, and probably to be dated within the third and fourth centuries.[8]

Yet even in Acts 15, the use of Scripture attributed to James, like the argument itself, is quite unlike Paul's. James claims that Peter's baptism of non-Jews is to be accepted because "the words of the prophets agree, just as it is written" (15:15), and he goes on to cite from the book of Amos. The passage cited will concern us in a moment; the form of James's interpretation is an immediate indication of a substantial difference from Paul. As James has it, there is actual agreement between Symeon (Simon Peter) and the words of the prophets, as two people might agree: the use of the verb *symphōneō* is nowhere else in the New Testament used in respect of Scripture. The continuity of Christian experience with Scripture is marked as a greater concern than within Paul's interpretation, and James expects that continuity to be verbal, a matter of agreement with the prophets' words, not merely with possible ways of looking at what they mean.

The citation from Amos (9:11–12, from the Septuagint, the Bible of Luke-Acts) comports well with James's concern that the position of the church should agree with the principal vocabulary of the prophets (Acts 15:16–17):

> After this I will come back and restore the tent of David, which has fallen, and rebuild its ruins and set it up anew, that the rest of men may seek the Lord, and all the Gentiles upon whom my name is called.

In the argument of James as represented here, what the belief of Gentiles achieves is not the redefinition of Israel (as in Paul's thought), but the restoration of the house of David, with Gentile recognition of the Torah as it impinges upon them.[9] The argument is possible because a Davidic genealogy of Jesus—and, therefore, of his brother James—is assumed.[10]

James's devotion to the temple and to his brother as the Danielic Son of Man after the resurrection made him the most prominent Christian leader in Jerusalem. The practice of the Nazirite vow was his distinguishing feature, and his belief in his brother as the gate of heaven, the heavenly portal above the temple, made him a figure to be revered and reviled in Judaism, depending upon one's evaluation of Jesus. Among Christians, he promulgated his understanding of the establishment of the house of David by means of an interpretation reminiscent of the Essenes, although he insisted that baptized, uncircumcised non-Jews had an ancillary role. As the bishop or overseer (*mebaqqer*, as in the Dead Sea Scrolls) of his community, he exercised a function that entered the Greek language as *episkopos*, and the influence of his circle is attested in the New Testament and later literature (including the *Gospel according to Thomas*, the *Apocryphon of James*, the *Protoevangelium of James*, the *First* and *Second Apocalypse of James*, the *Gospel of Peter*, the *Apocalypse of Peter*, the *Kerygma Petrou*, the *Kerygmata Petrou*, the *Acts of Peter*, the *Letter of Peter to Philip*, and the *Acts of Peter*).

Within the terms of reference of early Judaism and primitive Christianity, no single issue can compare in importance to that of the temple. The Nazirite practice attributed to James and those in contact with him provides a highly focused degree of devotion to the temple. As usually practiced, the social history of primitive Christianity and early Christianity has been Hellenistic in orientation. That is perfectly natural, given the actual provenance and language of the New Testament and the bulk of the corpus of Christianity in late antiquity. Still, social histories such as those of Wayne Meeks,[11] Abraham Malherbe,[12] and Dennis Smith and Hal Taussig[13] have tended not to engage the sources of Judaism, and especially the Judaism of Aramaic and Hebrew sources, with the same vigor that has been applied to the Hellenistic dimension of analysis. That is perfectly understandable, given the particular documents they have dealt with, and the specific questions that they applied to those documents. But a figure such as James will simply remain a cipher, and in all probability a cipher for some form of Paulinism or its negation, as long as he is not located within the milieu that not only produced him, but also was embraced as a consciously chosen locus of devotion and activity. Many teachers associated with the movement of Jesus managed at least partially to avoid the temple altogether; James is found virtually only there after the resurrection.

The specificity of that location raises the issue of James's relation to other forms of Christianity, to other forms of Judaism, and especially to those responsible for the operation of the temple. Here the analysis of James in socially historical terms comes closest to classic history in its specificity.

Whether in the key of an emphasis on the "social" or the "historical" within socially historical analysis, what emerges from our consideration is a distinctive, cultic focus upon the validation of the covenant with Israel, which blesses all nations on the authority of Jesus, understood in his resurrection to be identifiable with the "one like a son of man" of Dan 7.

The Interplay of Sources and the Assessment of James and His Vow

Within the portrayal of the status of being a Nazirite within the New Testament, there is a strong difference between a direct and stringently practical depiction, and an evidently metaphorical characterization.

The Practical Nazirite

Acts 18:18 says that Paul shaved his head in Cenchreae (the eastern port of Corinth) because he had a vow.[14] The reference to the cutting of hair naturally associates Paul's practice with the Nazirite vow, because a Nazirite was held to have completed his vow at the time he shaved his hair and offered it at the altar (see Num 6:18). As set out in Num 6, a Nazirite was to let his hair and (if at issue) beard grow for the time of his vow, abstain completely from grapes, and avoid approaching any dead body. At the close of the period of the vow, he was to shave his head and offer his hair in proximity to the altar (so Num 6:18). The end of this time of being holy, of being the LORD's property, is marked by enabling the Nazirite to drink wine again (6:20).

Although the identification of the vow may seem straightforward, such a simple reading is immediately complicated by any attempt to read Acts 18 within the terms of reference of Num 6. After all, Num 6:18 is quite specific that the Nazirite is to shave his head at the opening of the tent of appointment and put the shorn hair on the fire under the sacrifice of sharings. The reading seems to suggest that the vow could only be fulfilled by shaving one's head at the threshold of the sanctuary and by placing one's hair on the fire in the sanctuary. That has caused commentators to be cautious about equating Paul's vow and Nazirite practice.

The text of Numbers itself, however, invites further consideration. Numbers 6:2 opens with the explicit statement that the vow might be undertaken by a man or a woman. Evidently, therefore, the Nazirite practice would not always have included their admission into the sanctuary, where the presence of women was regularly prohibited and the presence of men was not infrequently prohibited, so that the presentation of the hair in that place must have been by means of a surrogate.

Indeed, the Mishnah conceives of Nazirite vows as being undertaken by slaves as well as Israelites, so that a strict association with the sanctuary would have been untenable (*Nazir* 9:1). The Mishnah holds such vows even in regard to hair alone as equating to a Nazirite vow (*Nazir* 1:1); the opening of the tractate is also emphatic that a precise pronunciation of the term *Nazir* was not necessary to engage the full requirements of the vow. So whatever Paul or Acts thought of his vow from his own perspective, many would have seen him as falling in with the program of what is referred to in the Mishnah, and some would have seen him as obligated by the prevailing custom.

In his careful evaluation of Paul's practice, Maas Boertien has crafted a skillful association between Acts 18:18 and Acts 21:23–26, where Paul is convinced to undertake the expenses of four Nazirites.[15] The reference to their shaving their heads makes the association with Num 6 evident, especially since the context within the temple makes the identification with a Nazirite vow straightforward. Boertien's overall argument is that Paul had his hair shorn in Cenchreae to fulfill the temporal requirements of his vow, and then took part in an offering in the temple to fulfill the sacrificial requirements of his vow. To make out that case, Boertien must show that the moment of cutting of the hair and the moment of sacrifice could in fact be dissociated from one another.

Particularly with regard to hair, he must answer a question: If Paul's vow is as a Nazirite, what would he have done with the hair he had cut? After all, one was holy to the LORD, all the days that one vowed (Num 6:5, 13), by virtue of that uncut hair. Two institutions enable Boertien to reply to that question.

First, within the terms of reference of Num 6 itself, the problem of what we might call the missing hair is addressed in the Mishnah. When a Nazirite's head is rendered impure by the sudden death of one near to him, he shaves on the seventh day, the day of purification (6:9), and then on the eighth day he brings offerings to the opening of the tent of appointment (6:10). The priest takes these offerings as a sacrifice for sin and a whole sacrifice, and he makes appeasement; the Nazirite's head is consecrated again (6:11), and the vow starts all over again (6:12). Numbers accounts for everything but the hair that has been cut in view of impurity. Mishnah *Temurah* 7:4 provides the answer: such hair is buried, in an evident analogy to the blood of a slaughtered animal, which is poured into the ground when it is not poured out in sacrifice.

But cutting hair in view of purity is obviously different from cutting one's hair to fulfill the vow, which is what Paul is portrayed as doing in Acts 18:18. That is why the second institution is crucial to Boertien's analysis. *Nazir* 3:6 attributes to Beth Shammai the regulation of those who undertake Nazirite vows outside of Israel: when they fulfill the requirement of time abroad, they are to serve out an additional thirty days in the land of Israel. Implicitly, the hair is cut outside Israel, and the offering is accomplished in the temple.[16] The only question left open by the Mishnah is whether an additional thirty days is really necessary. The fact of the temporal fulfillment of Nazirite vows abroad is taken for granted.

The case of hair shorn abroad in fulfillment of the vow is analogous to hair shorn in view of contamination. In both cases, shearing is performed under conditions of impurity. *Nazir* 6:8 stipulates that the sacrificial offering of the hair by the Nazirite is to be carried out, even when he has been shorn outside of Jerusalem, but that the "shearing of impurity" is not to be offered.[17] But that still leaves the Nazirite from abroad with the problem of missing hair: what is he to offer? Beth Shammai solves the problem by providing for an additional month to grow some more. But what of those who proceed directly to the sacrificial moment specified by Num 6?

Boertien addresses that question by referring to the practice of association within a Nazirite offering. *Nazir* 2:5 sets out an at-first-sight complicated arrangement, which addresses what to do when a Nazirite pledges himself to bring both his own hair offering and the hair offering of another Nazirite. Under those circumstances, the recommendation is to make this offering with a fellow, to economize on the costs involved. Since each Nazirite was to offer three animals and grain with oil and the accompanying wine (so Num 6:14–15), the expense involved was considerable. So one could make a commitment that doubled the value of these sacrifices. In this way, even a person of relatively modest means, by taking on the expenses of Nazirites, could imitate the prosperous piety of Agrippa I (Josephus, *Ant.* 19.293–294).

Boertien brings all of these elements together in order to account for Paul's practice as narrated in Acts. Paul first completed his Nazirite vow outside Israel (Acts 18:18) and then, after his arrival in Jerusalem, offered the sacrifices of dedication in association with other Nazirites (21:23–26).[18] In this regard, Boertien calls particular attention to Acts 21:26, where Paul observes a period of seven days of purification before he completes the offering. That corresponds to the seven days stipulated in Numbers (6:9–10) for cases in which a Nazirite has encountered impurity. In effect, residence outside of Israel was itself treated as an instance of impurity.[19]

The question of Paul's vow in Acts 18:18 has been dogged by the problem that, although some relationship to Num 6 seemed to be implicit, Paul is not near enough to the temple to accord with the requirements of the Nazirite vow. Boertien resolved that problem by showing that the issue of Nazirites outside of Israel was addressed in the Mishnah. He was aware that the Mishnah cannot be assumed to be contemporaneous with the New Testament, and in fact attributed this section of the tractate *Nazir* to Yudah (Judah) ben Ilai, the Tannaite of the second century. Whether or not that association is fully tenable, the assumption within the tractate is that such vows can be effectuated, much as in the case of the vow of *Qorban*.[20]

Beyond that, however, Boertien seems to press Acts into the mold of the Mishnah. *Nazir* 2:5 assumes that, at the time one pledged, one might agree to take on the expenses of someone else. Acts clearly separates Paul's own vow (18:18) from the suggestion of James and the elders that Paul should, as a public display of piety, demonstrate his fidelity to the Torah (21:24). Paul and his companions arrive in Jerusalem and are confronted by James and the elders, who report to them that Paul's reputation in Jerusalem is that he is telling Jews in the Diaspora to forsake

Moses, and especially to stop circumcising their children (21:17–21). Paul is then told to take on the expense of four men who had taken a vow, entering the temple with them to offer sacrifice (21:22–26). The indications of time in Acts simply do not allow for Paul to accord with the halakhah of Beth Shammai; he delays one week, not one month.

Further, James's attempt to have Paul correspond to the halakhah on a more-liberal understanding is a failure, according to the narrative in Acts: once in Jerusalem, Acts portrays Paul as being received joyfully (21:17), and then as proceeding to follow the advice given him the following day (21:26). That advice had disastrous consequences. Paul's entry into the temple caused a riot, because it was supposed that he was bringing Greeks in. As a result, he was arrested by a Roman officer, and so began the long, legal contention that resulted ultimately in his death (21:27–28:21). Even Acts has to admit that there was some substance in the accusation of the "Jews from Asia": they had seen Paul in the city, not with a quartet of Nazirites, but with a Greek from Ephesus (21:27–29). And when Paul defends himself before Felix, his own protestation of innocence is not framed in terms of his own or others' Nazirite vow, but in terms of his bringing alms and offerings, the occasion of his having purified himself (24:17–19).

Acts, in other words, agrees substantially with Paul's own statement of his program in regard to the temple: the priestly service of preaching the gospel is to lead to the presentation of the offering of the Gentiles (Rom 15:16). The tangible generosity of congregations in Greece is a matter of pride for Paul, and he boasts that, "having sealed this fruit," he will return "with the fullness of Christ's blessing" (15:25–29). Openly boastful though he is at this stage (so 15:17), Paul is also cautious: he urges his Roman supporters to pray that he might escape the unpersuaded in Judah, and that his service for the saints in Jerusalem might be an acceptable offering (15:30–33).

And then, having mentioned both his sacrificial offering in Jerusalem and his fear of some in Judah, Paul goes on in the present text of Romans to recommend Phoebe to the Romans, the servant of the congregation among the Cenchreaens, whom Paul describes as an aid of many, including himself (16:1–2). The Romans are asked to accept her and to aid her "in whatever matter in which she has need of you." Chapter 16 of Romans opens with a famously long list of Paul's associates and helpers, but Phoebe is the only person who is commended in this way. She is called a servant (*diakonos*, the same term used of Christ in 15:8) just after Paul has referred to his own collection as service (*diakonia*, in 15:31) and to his own activity as serving (15:25).

The importance of these links is attenuated if one follows the argument that chapter 16 is an addition to the original letter, perhaps initially destined for Ephesus. Pierre Benoit has nonetheless come to the conclusion that Phoebe is the bearer of the letter, and that the salutations are designed to underscore Paul's familiarity with those known to the congregation(s) in Rome.[21] If the reference to Phoebe and the congregation in Cenchreae is Pauline, then we can correlate the itinerary of Acts with Paul's implicit itinerary. If, on the other hand, the chapter is an appendix, then it reflects a later correlation of the two itineraries. Either way, Cenchreae turns up as a linking moment between Paul's activity among the Gentiles and what is about to happen in Jerusalem.

The Cenchreaen moment is a time when Paul is well aware of enmity in Judah, and when he is disquieted by it. His response is to align himself as best he can with the most powerful Christian group in Jerusalem, the one associated with James. That, indeed, is the best explanation for Paul's willingness to take on a Nazirite vow and to bear the expenses of other Nazirites. As cited by Eusebius (see *Eccl. Hist.* 2.23.1–18),[22] Hegesippus characterizes James, Jesus' brother, as the person who exercised immediate control of the church in Jerusalem. Although Peter had initially gathered a group of Jesus' followers in Jerusalem, his interests and activities further afield left the way open for James to become the natural head of the community there. That change, and political changes in Jerusalem itself, made the temple the effective center of the local community of Jesus' followers. James practiced a careful and idiosyncratic purity in the interests of worship in the temple. He abstained from wine and animal flesh, did not cut his hair or beard, and forsook oil and frequent bathing. According to Hegesippus, those special practices gave him access even to the sanctuary. These practices of holiness are for the most part consistent with the requirements made of those undertaking a Nazirite vow. The additional notice that James avoided oil is consistent with the especial concern for purity among Nazirites. They were to avoid any contact with death (Num 6:6–12), and the avoidance of all uncleanness, which is incompatible with sanctity, follows naturally. Josephus also attributes the avoidance of oil to the Essenes (*Jewish War* 2.8.3 §123), and the reason seems plain: oil, as a fluid pressed from fruit, was considered to absorb impurity to such an extent that extreme care in its preparation was vital.[23] Absent complete assurance, abstinence was a wise policy. James's vegetarianism also comports with a concern to avoid contact with any kind of corpse. Finally, although Hegesippus's assertion that James could actually enter the sanctuary of the temple seems exaggerated, his acceptance of a Nazirite regime, such as Acts 21 explicitly associates him with, would account for such a remembrance of him, in that Nazirites were to be presented in the vicinity of the sanctuary where sacrifice was offered.

The Metaphorical Nazirite

Alongside the stringent reflection of Nazirite practice, another source within the New Testament is willing to call Jesus a Nazirite, although he is not reported to engage in any such vow and regularly engages in practices contrary to the requirements of Num 6. The existence of this source evidently complicates the analysis of James and his influence.

The first exorcism story in Mark's Gospel represents this alternative source. The demon "speaks," but the people in the synagogue hear only inarticulate shrieks. Jesus alone understands the meaning of the sounds. The demon identifies itself with all unclean demons of the spirit world in a fascinating switch of pronouns in the text (here italicized; Mark 1:24): "*We* have nothing for you, Nazarene Jesus! Have you come to destroy *us*? *I* know who you are—the Holy One of God!"

The slip back and forth between plural and singular surprises any reader of Mark's text.[24] Multiple demons—like Mary Magdalene's seven (Luke 8:2) and the demon that found seven colleagues to repossess a person in Jesus' saying (Luke 11:24–26; Matt 12:43–45)—signaled the resistance of the demonic world as a whole. Like a military commander who claims that acts by insurgents only prove that they are desperate, Jesus viewed the violence of demons as part of the impending defeat of their regime. In addition to the demon's identification with unclean spirits as a whole, the demon in the synagogue also specifies the purpose of Jesus' exorcisms: not simple banishment, but their definitive removal from power. That is what the demon fears on behalf of the whole realm of unclean spirits: regime change instigated by Jesus as the agent of God's kingdom, the kind of demonic retreat Mary Magdalene had experienced. She was the source of the most detailed stories of exorcism in the Gospels.

Fearing destruction, the unclean spirits act before Jesus speaks, initiating a preemptive strike by naming him. The situation is the same in Mark 5:7, where the verb *horkizō* appears with the meanings "to bind with an oath" (which is the point of an exorcism). The oath was a formula that exorcists usually employed to invoke divine power and force demons to obey their commands. Such spells were more effective when they identified a demon by name. In this case (cf. Mark 1:24 and 5:7), however, the demon jumps in with a spell and a naming of its own. In effect, it is exorcising the exorcist, a notable departure from the well-documented form of exorcism stories in the ancient world.

Mary's source, within Mark, describes these as noisy events. The demon "cried out" (Mark 1:23; cf. 5:7). Jesus shouted back in the rough language of the street, "Shut up, and get out from him!" (v. 25, cf. 5:8). The demon's obedience comes under protest; it "convulsed" its nameless victim and departed with a scream (v. 26; cf. 5:13).

These acute observations all point toward a storyteller with keen knowledge of the deep combat with evil that Jesus' exorcisms involved, their raucous quality, and the danger that the exorcist would be defeated. Moreover, the storyteller knows how Jesus interpreted the demons' wordless shout (1:34). Whoever conveyed this story had to know both what went on and what Jesus thought about it. Mary Magdalene best fits the description of that storyteller.

Hand in hand with that identification, calling Jesus "Nazarene" finds its purpose. Jesus "the Nazarene" (*Nazarēnos* in Greek) is the grammatical equivalent of "Magdalene" (*Magdalēnē*), allowing for a change of gender. (In Aramaic, which both Jesus and Mary spoke, the antecedents would have been the equally resonant terms.) English pronunciation conceals a rhyme that would have caught the ear of any Greek or Aramaic speaker who heard these names spoken aloud: the texts reverberate with an implicit connection between Jesus and Mary.

To call Jesus "the Nazarene" naturally evokes Nazareth as his native village,[25] just as "Magdalene" evokes Magdala, on the Sea of Galilee. The verbal echo between the names reflects the geographical proximity between the two villages and their contacts with one another. Mark's Gospel, the earliest of the Gospels and the closest to the Aramaic idioms of Jesus' movement, preserves the resonance between Rabbi Jesus' nickname and Mary's.

The form "Nazarene" also resonates with the traditional word "Nazirite" (*nāzîr* in Hebrew), which means "consecrated." The name "Nazarene," paired with the designation "the Holy One of God," evokes Jesus' consecration and reinforces his spiritual threat to the world of the demons in the dramatic opening exorcism in Mark's Gospel (1:23-27). Just as Jesus' contemporaries are "astounded" when the demons in Capernaum shudder in the presence of his purity, the Magdalene and her companions are "completely astounded" by a vision of a young man who tells them Jesus "the Nazarene" has risen from the dead (16:1-8). Here too, revelation troubles those it comes to, and that disturbance echoes through the names "Nazarene" and "Magdalene."

To Jesus' mind, Mary was "the Magdalene," the woman who had embodied the impurity to which Herod had subjected Magdala. To Mary, Jesus was "the Nazarene," the force of Galilean rural purity that could vanquish her demons. "Nazarene" and "Magdalene" together invoke the way Jesus and Mary became joined, the enduring link between them, and the disturbing thought that the force of the holy cannot be contained by the ordinary conventions of this world.

This comes to expression also in the story of the man with the legion of demons, set in Decapolis, just on the other side of the Sea of Galilee from Magdala. There Jesus confronts a horde of demons that have taken up residence in a man who inhabits a cemetery (Mark 5:1-17; Luke 8:26-37; Matt 8:28-34). When Jesus demands to know the demons' names (a standard feature in exorcisms of the time), they say they are "legion," the designation for a six-thousand-man Roman military unit. The story is related in the same simple, vigorous, abrupt voice of the Capernaum exorcism (Mark 5:1-13; cf. 1:21-28).

By several stark images (the victim's habitation in a cemetery, his habit of wounding himself, his residence in Gentile territory), this exorcism targets uncleanness as the evil Jesus addressed in all his exorcisms. The possessed man embodies impurity and is named "legion," just in case a hearer or reader might miss the point of where the contagion came from. When Rabbi Jesus drove demons out of people, he acted on behalf of those possessed, but we can clearly see that he was also acting against the source of impurity: Rome and Rome's collaborator, Herod Antipas. Mary Magdalene, whose town lay adjacent to Antipas's new capital (Tiberias), knew the reality of this uncleanness and was the initial source of this story. With equal clarity, the narrative drives home the theme of the struggle involved in this exorcism. The demons were numerous, talked back to Jesus, and did not obey a direct command.

It was unusual in the ancient world to insist that the demons formed a violent, coordinated front of impurity, and bizarre to depict them as dictating how an exorcist should handle them. The legion story deliberately engages in exaggeration, to the point that no commentator[26] has been able to draw the line between the story's symbolic meaning and the literal event it depicts. Still, the symbolic meaning remains clear no matter how literally we take the details: as the divine kingdom takes root, Rome will be dislodged. Roman demons were no more threatening than panicked pigs; they will neutralize themselves in God's encompassing purity, which is as deep as the sea.

It is startling, however, that in this case, Jesus is not called "Nazarene" at all, as he is in the first exorcism story in Mark (which comes from the Magdalene source).[27] Just as the impurity in the Mark 5 story has been exaggerated, so any association with Nazirite practice is avoided. This attests the influence of James, for whom the practical meaning of the Nazirite vow superseded the metaphorical vision of Nazarite practice championed by Mary Magdalene, for whom the expulsion of Roman impurity was paramount.

Conclusion

The association of the Nazirite vow with James is well established and has long been acknowledged. But alongside that practical institution, language and imagery derived from Num 6 is also applied to Jesus in the New Testament in a metaphorical way, most notably in the Magdalene source. James's position should not be confused with the stance of Jesus, as if Jesus himself were a conscious Nazirite,[28] or as if James's stance can be applied to all the circles of belief and practice that contributed to the New Testament. Rather, the Nazirite vow could be understood both practically and metaphorically on the basis of the New Testament, so that ritual practices—including fasting, abstinence, and avoidance of oil and/or bathing—continued to be pursued in Christianity after the destruction of the temple and with varying degrees of literal conformity to the requirements of a Nazirite.

PART THREE

The Sabbath

7

Scripture's Account

The Sabbath

Baruch A. Levine

The Sabbath (Heb. *šabbāt*) as a day of rest is an Israelite-Jewish contribution to world civilization. Scholarly attempts to find precursors to the biblical Sabbath in other ancient Near Eastern cultures have yielded only speculative conclusions. Aside from the fact that the Sabbath is configured as a function of the mythic-magical number "seven," a perception shared by many ancient cultures, and that its interval is practical, there is nothing to which it can be authentically compared in the ancient Near East. It is, first of all, unique as a day of obligatory rest, and what is equally significant, its scheduling is not subject to, or affected by, any operative calendar, lunar or otherwise. Therefore, the suggestion that the biblical *šabbāt* is somehow related to Mesopotamian *šapattu*, a term designating the fifteenth day of the month, has no validity. Despite the similarity in sound, there is no etymological, or computational, connection between the two terms.

The institutionalizing of the Sabbath produced the week, as we know it; a seven-day unit of measured time, which continues uninterruptedly through time. The new moon and annual festivals and the Sabbath actually represent two, contrasting patterns of measuring time in biblical antiquity. The former was determined by the phases (or circuits) of the moon, whereas the latter was calculated by consecutive units of seven days, whose counting had begun at a particular moment in the past. In the priestly tradition, exemplified by the Exodus version of the Decalogue (Exod 20), that moment occurred at the completion of the creation of heaven and earth, which took six days (cf. Gen 2:1–3). There was a first Sabbath.

The Hebrew term *šabbāt* derives from the verb *šābat*, "to cease, desist" (e.g., Gen 8:22; Isa 14:4), and its *qaṭṭāl* noun form (in the *piʿel* stem) bears the durative sense of "a fixed (time of) cessation." As such, the Sabbath dramatizes the principle that humans (even draft animals!) need, and are entitled, to a time-out from their assigned tasks at regular intervals. The Sabbath was a central component of Israelite-Jewish religion and culture, and yet there is comparatively little information provided in biblical literature about its history and institutional development. It is necessary, therefore, to ferret out such knowledge from sparse literary references to the Sabbath, whose precise historical sequence is difficult to ascertain. For its part, Torah literature provides ample legal and ritual texts on the prescribed celebration and observance of the Sabbath, but these too range from early to late.

Normally the Hebrew Bible uses *yôm* to mean a day, beginning at dawn and ending at sunset. That is the working day, the daylight period. On this basis, *yôm haššabbāt*, "the Sabbath day" (e.g., Exod 20:8), and *yôm haššĕbî'î*, "the seventh day" (20:10), would also demarcate a daylight period of observance, rather than a twenty-four-hour "day" beginning the previous evening. This would be so notwithstanding the refrain of Gen 1: *wayĕhî-'ereb wayĕhî-bōqer yôm X* (e.g., v. 5). "Evening arrived, then morning arrived, day X." The sole exception in the priestly tradition is the Day of Atonement (*yôm hakkippūrîm*, as in Lev 23:27–28), which is merely likened to the Sabbath. It was scheduled annually on the tenth day of the seventh month. In Lev 23:32 it is specified that this sacred occasion was to last "from evening to evening." The exception proves the rule. For most of the biblical period, the Sabbath and festivals began in the morning, a reality noted by the medieval commentator, Rashbam. The earliest indication that the biblical Sabbath began on the previous evening is to be found in Neh 13:19, which dates from the postexilic period:

> It happened that when the gates of Jerusalem turned shadowy before the Sabbath [*lipnê haššabbāt*], I commanded that the portals be bolted, and I (further) commanded that they not be opened until after the Sabbath.

Literary References to the Sabbath

The Sabbath emerged at an early stage of Israelite history. Three prophetic sources bear special scrutiny in this regard.

1. Hosea 2:13 (11 Eng.) is part of a condemnation of northern Israelite society, which may go back to the ninth century BCE. There we read:

> I shall bring to an end [*wĕhišbattî*] all of her rejoicing:
> Her pilgrimage festivals, her new moons, and her Sabbaths.

The play on the verb *šābat*, expressed by the *hip'il*-causative, *wĕhišbattî*, has poignancy: God will cause the day of "cessation" itself to cease! In the Hebrew, the terms for the three occasions appear in the singular, with collective meaning: *ḥag*, *ḥodĕš* and *šabbāt*, respectively. These are all characterized as times of rejoicing, and as divine blessings, the rewards of fidelity to the God of Israel. Hence the prophet warns that all such rejoicing will be denied to an unfaithful Israel as punishment for its infidelity.

2. The prophet Amos (8:4–5) of the last half of the eighth century BCE refers to the Sabbath in his critique of the cult:

> Hear this, those who trample on the poor,
> To ruin [*lašbît*] the unfortunate of the land, saying:
> "When will the New Moon pass so we can acquire provisions,

And the Sabbath, so that we can unpack grain,
To charge more shekels for less weight, and to alter false scales?"

Once again, we observe a play on the verb *šābat*, "to desist," employing the *hipʿil*-causative, infinitive *lašbît*. The day of cessation had become a time for conspiring to deprive the poor of whatever little they possess. The wording of this reproach is significant because, in effect, the prophet represents Sabbaths and new moons as occasions when normal commerce was suspended.

3. First Isaiah, in his dramatic denunciation of the cult of Yahweh as conducted in the temple of Jerusalem (end of eighth century BCE), has this to say (Isa 1:12–14):

When you arrive to appear in my presence,
Who sought to receive this from your hand,
While (you) trample my courtyards?
Do not bring more useless grain offerings;
Incense is an abomination to me!
New moon and Sabbath,
Convoking sacred gatherings [*qĕrōʾ miqrāʾ*]—
I cannot bear iniquitous assemblies!
Your new moons and fixed festivals, my feelings detest;
They have become burdensome to me;
I am weary of enduring them!

The Isaiah passage attests several terms of reference, which confirm the status of the Sabbath in Jerusalem of the period. We find mention of the temple courts and of "appearing" before Yahweh, both descriptive of celebrating sacrifices in the temple and of pilgrimages. We read of *ʿăṣārâ*, "assembly," and *môʿēd*, "fixed festival," both collectives. The reference to *qĕrōʾ miqrāʾ*, "convoking a sacred gathering," resonates with the more-standard term *miqrāʾ qōdeš*, "sanctuary convocation," which in priestly texts characterizes the Sabbath and other occasions (see below).

The above citations illustrate that, aside from an oblique reference to the cessation of daily pursuits in Amos 8:4–5, the Sabbath is characterized positively rather than in terms of prohibited activity, which was to become the dominant theme in legal-ritual texts. In early prophecy the Sabbath is a time of rejoicing and cultic celebration at sacred sites, attended by large gatherings of Israelite worshippers. In practical terms, such celebrations undoubtedly brought daily pursuits to a halt in places where they were held, but nothing is said directly to forbid daily activities as such. It may also be relevant to call attention, at this point, to a tale about a Shunammite woman whose son was resuscitated by the prophet Elisha (2 Kgs 4). When she had informed her husband that she was going to consult a man of God on Mt. Carmel, he asked her: "Why are you going to him today? It is neither new moon nor Sabbath!" (2 Kgs 4:23). It was, after all, on Sabbaths and new moons that holy men were available to serve the worshippers in attendance.

Scanning the historical books of the Hebrew Bible further, we encounter a cluster of references to the Sabbath in 2 Kgs 11 and 16, the former set in Jerusalem at the beginning of the reign of Joash (836–798 BCE), and the latter during the reign of Ahaz (743–727 BCE), respectively, both kings of Judah. Second Kings 11 relates how the young prince, Joash, was secretly protected in the temple until he could be installed as king of Judah. At one point, the priest Jehoiada deployed the palace and temple guards for this purpose. He refers, en passant, to "those who go on duty each Sabbath" and "those who go off duty each Sabbath" (2 Kgs 11:5, 7, 9), indicating that the watches of temple and palace guards were scheduled on a weekly basis. In 2 Kgs 16 we read of certain renovations in the cultic trappings of the Jerusalem temple ordered by Ahaz, especially with respect to the main altar. Second Kings 16:18 mentions "the Sabbath drape," a screen that afforded the king privacy when he entered the temple on Sabbaths by way of a special passage known as "the king's entrance."

Exactly how much may be learned from these references is questionable, nor do we know when the narratives themselves were composed. One of them has the Judean king, Ahaz, and his court entering the temple on the Sabbath, presumably to worship, which would be significant information on the sacral role of Judean kings if its historicity could be confirmed. It is not until the latter chapters of Ezekiel, chapter 46, to be exact, that we have indications of the cultic role of the projected leader of the people, the *nāśîʾ* "chief, prince," who was to enter the rebuilt temple of Jerusalem by the eastern gate on Sabbaths.

We next encounter a cluster of references to the Sabbath in Jer 17:19–27, and only there, in all of Jeremiah. Modern scholarship has rightly questioned the authenticity of this prophecy, which resembles what we read in postexilic Nehemiah (e.g., Neh 10:32; 13:15–22) regarding measures taken to prevent commerce on the Sabbath day in Jerusalem. The speaker of Jer 17 was positioned at the main gate of Jerusalem, through which the kings of Judah pass in and out. He admonishes the people not to bring in their wares (literally, "loads") or take them out on the Sabbath day, or to perform other assigned tasks (Heb. *mĕlāʾkâ*). They are to sanctify (*qiddēš*) the Sabbath as they had been commanded. However we date the Sabbath prophecy of Jer 17, it marks a turning point in tracing the history of the Sabbath, because it clearly resonates with the language of the Decalogue and with other Torah statements regarding the Sabbath.

The book of Lamentations bears many affinities to Jeremiah, and some even attribute it to Jeremiah, or to his immediate circle. In Lam 2:6 we read the following description of the destruction of Jerusalem:

> He [Yahweh] trampled his covered abode like a garden plot,
> He destroyed his meeting place.
> Yahweh caused festivals and Sabbaths
> To be forgotten in Zion,
> And he rejected in his wrath
> Both king and priest.

Reference is to the Jerusalem temple, God's abode on earth, which was destroyed. The collapse of religious life, expressed as the discontinuation of the festivals and the Sabbath, brought an end to both the priesthood and the monarchy.

From this point on, every statement that we encounter regarding the Sabbath—

in Ezek 20; 40–48; in Trito-Isaiah (Isa 56; 58; 66); and in Nehemiah and Chronicles—is predicated on at least some of the Torah legislation affecting the Sabbath. For this reason, attention should now shift to Torah literature, returning to literary references at a later point.

The Sabbath in Torah Sources

Before examining pentateuchal sources on the Sabbath, it is necessary to recognize the literary composition of the Torah books, and to engage problems that persist regarding their sequence and dating. Torah literature is composed of three principal strata, each with its own internal divisions: (1) The Yahwist (J for Jahwist), a Judean source; the Elohist (E), a northern Israelite source; and their combination in JE, with appropriated early poetry and law. These sources have been identified according to which divine name is predominantly favored in each of them. (2) Deuteronomy and its interpretation by the Deuteronomist (D); (3) Priestly writings (P = *Priesterschriften*). The approach adopted here, one disputed by some scholars, is that the priesthood produced the final version of the Torah. In the priestly writings of the Torah we encounter responses to the Deuteronomic doctrine that all sacrificial activity is restricted to one, central temple, historically identified as the temple of Jerusalem. This so-called "reformation" was decreed by Josiah, king of Judah around 622 BCE. In historical terms this means that the priestly stratum in Torah literature is principally a product of the early postexilic period, and it therefore is descriptive of the cult of the second (postexilic) temple of Jerusalem, not of the first. In surveying Torah sources for information on the Sabbath, we will begin, therefore, with what is considered to be older material, and then proceed to analyze the priestly enhancement of Sabbath observance in law and ritual.

The antiquity of the Sabbath is documented in an early cultic calendar, preserved in Exod 23:10–19 as part of the so-called Book of the Covenant. This text is arguably older than either version of the Decalogue, in Exod 20 or in Deut 5. The second part of the calendar, Exod 23:14–19, pertains to annual festivals; the first part of the passage is of particular interest here (23:10–13):

> And for six years you shall sow your land and gather in its yield. But as for the seventh year, you must let it lie fallow and abandon it, so that the poor of your people may partake of it; and what is left by them, the beasts of the field may eat. Thus shall you do as well with respect to your vineyards and your olive groves. Six days shall you produce your products [*taʿăśeh maʿăśêkā*], but on the seventh day you shall desist [*tišbōt*], in order that your ox and mule may rest, and the son of your handmaiden and your resident alien may regain strength. You must exercise care regarding all that I have spoken to you. Do not pronounce the name of any other deity; let it not be heard from your month.

The Hebrew *taʿăśeh maʿăśêkā* is unique in statements on the Sabbath and is ambiguous, at that. It can either mean, "You shall do your deeds, perform your tasks," or it can mean, "You shall produce your products." In context, it seems more likely that reference is to the productive yield of an agrarian economy, which is where the Sabbath was born. The cessation occurring every seven days parallels the abandonment of the fields, vineyards, and olive groves every seven years. As has been stated, time units of seven, whether days or years, are very ancient configurations, and they also delimit two of the three annual festivals which are to last seven days. Though the verb *šābat* "to cease" is used in such regulations, the term *šabbāt*, itself, does not appear. The same omission is evident in a related statement in Exod 34:21, which is Deuteronomic in tone:

> For six days you shall work [Heb. *taʿăbōd*] [the land], but on the seventh day you must cease [*tišbōt*]; even in the season of plowing, and in the season of reaping shall you cease.

Enter the two versions of the Decalogue, to be examined for what they tell us about the Sabbath. From the outset of modern biblical scholarship, the intertextual relationship between the two versions, which differ in certain particulars, has been debated. For the purpose of the present discussion, the Deuteronomic version of the Sabbath commandment will serve as the base text. It contains the only direct reference to the Sabbath in all of Deuteronomy. In contrast to Exod 23, we find that Deut 15 addresses the theme of the seventh year yet never associates it with the weekly Sabbath. Thus:

> Take care to sanctify the Sabbath day as Yahweh, your God, has commanded you. For six days you shall work (the land) and accomplish all of your assigned tasks [*kol-mĕlaʾktĕkā*], but the seventh day is a Sabbath ordained by Yahweh, your God. You shall not perform any assigned tasks—neither you, your son or daughter, your male and female slaves; your oxen or mules, or any of your work animals; nor your resident alien who is within your gates, in order that your male and female servants may rest, as you do. Be mindful that you were slaves in the land of Egypt, and that Yahweh, your God, liberated you from there with a strong hand and an outstretched arm. For this reason Yahweh, your God, has commanded you to institute the Sabbath day. (Deut 5:12-15)

This version of the Sabbath commandment draws a direct contrast between the bondage of Egypt, on the one hand, and the Sabbath day as the exercise of human freedom, on the other. What sounds like a stern prohibition is actually a gift from God. The commandment to sanctify the Sabbath, expressed by the verb *qiddēš*, means that the Sabbath is a day set apart from other days. The version in Exod 20 rationalizes the Sabbath differently, making of it a commemoration of the six days of creation (Exod 20:11):

> Because for six days Yahweh made the heaven and the earth, the sea and all that is in it, and he rested on the seventh day. It is on this account that Yahweh blessed the Sabbath day and sanctified it.

In the priestly tradition, observing the Sabbath constitutes *imitatio Dei*; God rested on the seventh day, therefore Israel rests. This theme is elsewhere expressed in Gen 2:1–3, at the conclusion of the priestly account of the creation (Gen 1), and in other priestly statements.

Exodus (20:8) has *zākôr*, "mark, take note of," whereas Deuteronomy (5:12) has *šāmôr*, which connotes the performance of acts. Both versions highlight the pervasive category of *mĕlāʾkâ*, "assigned tasks." The precise meaning of this term has now been clarified by Ugaritic literature, which attests the fairly common verb *lak*, "to send." Previously, classical Hebrew had attested only the noun *malʾak*, "messenger, angel," literally, one who is sent. Understood in this way, the prohibition of *mĕlāʾkâ* on the Sabbath (and on some other sacred occasions) applies to tasks that one is mandated or assigned to perform in daily life. Every seven days an Israelite is free from performing such tasks himself, and if possessing the authority to assign tasks to others, is commanded by God to grant them similar respite on the Sabbath. The Moses saga may be alluding to the nexus of rest and freedom in describing Egyptian bondage. In response to Moses' request for respite, to allow the Israelites to worship God for three days in the wilderness, the Pharaoh had this to say: "The working population is now numerous, and yet you would be granting them leave [*wĕhišbattem ʾōtām*] from their corvée [forced labor]?" (Exod 5:5). The use of a form of the verb *šābat* is allusive: What Pharaoh's conscripts did not deserve, free Israelites did.

As observed above, the Exodus version of the Sabbath commandment is priestly in concept and language, and on this basis it may be later than the version preserved in Deuteronomy. Nevertheless, it can serve as a logical preamble to a discussion of the body of law and ritual found in the priestly writings of the Torah, elsewhere in Exodus, Leviticus, and Numbers. We begin with Lev 19, a major text within the so-called Holiness Code. This collection is generally considered to represent the primary stratum of priestly law, composed of core sections of Lev 17–27. Leviticus 19 resonates with the Decalogue, paraphrasing at least six of the Ten Commandments. Thus we read: "Each one of you is to revere his mother and father, and my Sabbaths you are to observe [*tišmōrû*]" (19:3). A Sabbath law also appears in Lev 23:3 as part of a cultic calendar of festivals:

> For six days you shall perform assigned tasks, and on the seventh day it is a Sabbath of complete cessation, a sanctuary convocation [*miqrāʾ-qōdeš*]. You may not perform any assigned tasks. It is a Sabbath day in all of your settlements.

This statement introduces the category known as *miqrāʾ-qōdeš*, here translated "sanctuary convocation," which is applied to the Sabbath and to some other sacred occasions. Both parts of the term are ambiguous. Hebrew *qōdeš* may represent an abstract noun "holiness," but it is also spatial, meaning "a holy place, sanctuary." Similarly, Hebrew *miqrāʾ* connotes the act of summoning, assembling, but it may also refer to the venue of assembly (thus Isa 4:5). The translation "sanctuary convocation" has the advantage of preserving the sense of sacred space, while also conveying the act of assembling the people to celebrate. There is a further implication to this statement on the Sabbath. It speaks of how Israelites are to conduct themselves *bekōl môšĕbōtêkem*, "in all of your settlements." This confirms that priestly law is, indeed, predicated on the Deuteronomic doctrine of cult centralization. Because sacrificial celebration had been restricted to the central temple, it became necessary to stipulate that Israelites, wherever they lived, were required to desist from their daily tasks in observance of the Sabbath, even though they could not celebrate it by offering sacrifices as they had once done. We begin, therefore, to observe two dimensions of communal religious observance: activity at the central temple's sacred space, for those in attendance; and nonsacral activity outside of it, for those at home.

The Holiness Code highlights the Sabbath in additional ways. It ordains the counting of forty-nine days, from the offering of the first barley sheaf during the *maṣṣôt* (Unleavened Bread) festival in the spring, until the presentation of the firstfruits of the new wheat harvest on the fiftieth day thereafter. What is significant is that the time span of seven weeks is stated as "seven complete Sabbaths." In effect, the fixed regularity of the Sabbath day has generated the week as a unit of measured time. The role of the Sabbath as a model of time measurement is further affirmed in Lev 25, which opens with a restatement of the law of Exod 23:10–13, cited above, that the land must lie fallow every seventh year. However, in Lev 25 Sabbatical terminology is employed throughout. The seventh year is *šěnat šabbātôn*, "a Sabbatical year" (cf. 25:4). What is more, Leviticus 25 calculates the Jubilee as a multiple of the Sabbatical year, seven times seven. We have come full circle: Exodus 23 had presented the seventh day as a reflex of the seventh year. The Holiness Code speaks of the period of counting in the spring of the year as a sequence of Sabbaths (Lev 23), and of the Sabbatical year as a reflex of the Sabbath day (Lev 25).

The festival calendar of Lev 23 is followed by a later cultic calendar in Num 28–29, also part of the priestly stratum. That group of texts focuses on the public, temple cult and has little to say about the meaning of sacred occasions. This is particularly true of the laconic Sabbath law (Num 28:9–10):

> And on the Sabbath day, two yearling lambs, without blemish, and two-tenths of an ephah of semolina flour as a grain offering, mixed with oil, together with its libation. This is to be the burnt offering on every successive Sabbath, in addition to the regular burnt offering [*ʿōlat hattāmîd*], and its libation.

This is how the public cult of ancient Israel came to be structured in the later biblical period: The regularity of the *tāmîd* (daily offering) was inviolable, overriding the Sabbath and festivals. On such occasions, additional sacrifices were added. Other priestly statements on the Sabbath, including brief narratives, provide further information pertaining to Sabbath observance.

1. Exodus 16 is a veritable medley of brief narratives about the manna supplied to the Israelites in the wilderness. It is likely that the primary version of the manna narrative was unrelated to the Sabbath, which is the case in Num 11, a similar, early narrative about manna. Priestly writers reconfigured the story to substantiate the

rule that food gathering is a task prohibited on the Sabbath. A double portion of manna was provided on the sixth day, thereby eliminating the need for gathering it on the Sabbath, for doing so would violate the day of rest. Exodus 16:23 implies that cooking and baking are also prohibited on the Sabbath:

> Tomorrow is a Sabbath of complete cessation [*šabbat šabbātôn*]. Whatever you intend to bake, bake, and whatever you intend to boil, boil, and whatever is left over—put aside for yourselves until morning.

2. Exodus 31:12–17 introduces into the tabernacle narrative a passage that resonates with both versions of the Decalogue and with other priestly statements, such as Gen 2:1–2. However, it adds a specific penalty for violation of the Sabbath: death. The passage concludes as follows:

> The Israelite people shall observe the Sabbath, to institute it for their generations as an eternal covenant. Between me and the Israelite people, it is a sign forever, that in six days Yahweh made the heavens and the earth, and on the seventh day he ceased, and regained strength. (31:16–17)

The symbolism of the Sabbath is enhanced; it is a sign and a covenant testifying to the unique relationship between God, the creator, and his people, Israel.

3. Exodus 35:3 restates the Sabbath law along the lines of Exod 31, including the death penalty, adding a specific prohibition, undoubtedly associated with cooking food: "You shall not kindle fire in any of your settlements on the Sabbath day."

4. Numbers 15:32–36 relates that in the wilderness an Israelite was caught gathering wood on the Sabbath. He was detained, because there had been no instruction on the penalty for such activity. Thereupon Yahweh instructed Moses to have that person put to death by stoning outside the encampment.

This concludes a survey of Torah references to the Sabbath. There is relatively little specificity as to what constituted *mĕlāʾkâ*, and yet there is the clear message that the Sabbath is a time-out from daily pursuits. In earlier periods it was celebrated in sacred sites all over the land. After the centralization of the cult, sacrificial celebration was restricted to the one, central temple in Jerusalem, while the Sabbath was observed locally through the cessation of all *mĕlāʾkâ*.

A reference to the Sabbath appears in a Hebrew ostracon inscription from Yavneh Yam (Mesad Hashavyahu), dated around 625 BCE, where we read in lines 5–6: *lpny šbt* [= *lipnê šabbāt*], "before the Sabbath" (cf. Neh 13:19). In the Aramaic papyri from the Jewish mercenary settlement of Elephantine in Egypt of the fifth century BCE, there are several references to the Sabbath. The name of the day is realized as *šbh*, apparently an absolute Aramaic form, whereas in a contemporary ostracon from Saqqara we find the forms *šbt* and *šbtʾ* (a determined Aramaic form). This information attests to some form of Sabbath observance by Jewish communities outside the land of Israel, specifically, in the Persian colonies of Egypt.

Exile and Return: The Sabbath in Late Biblical Times

It remains to examine later biblical sources on the Sabbath, some prophetic and other narratives, all of which postdate the destruction of the first temple of Jerusalem. It has already been suggested that Jer 17, and the passing references to the Sabbath in 2 Kgs 11 and 16 as well, may be late interpolations. The following are clearly late and shed light on further developments in the celebration of the Sabbath.

1. In Ezek 20, a series of prophecies cast in the Babylonian exile, the prophet explains to the elders of Israel that the destruction and exile were punishments for Israel's failure to obey God's statutes and judgments at successive periods of their history, most notably the Sabbath. Speaking in God's name, he repeatedly condemns Israel's desecration of "my Sabbaths" as a sin tantamount to idolatry, and the one which, more than any others, brought on God's punishment. The Sabbath is characterized as a gift granted to a chosen people by their divine liberator, so that its violation is a grievous act of disloyalty. There is clear intertextuality between Ezek 20 and certain passages in Leviticus, especially Lev 18 and 26, on the subject of Israel's sinfulness, exemplified by violation of the Sabbath. The same theme is briefly repeated in Ezek 22:8, and more elaborately expressed in 22:26:

> Her priests trampled on my teaching and desecrated my sacred offerings. They did not differentiate between the sacred and the profane, nor did they inform [the people] the difference between the impure and the pure. And they disregarded my Sabbaths, so that I became profaned in their midst.

Further references to the Sabbath occur in Ezek 40–48, whose status within the book of Ezekiel is a subject of debate. Whether or not original to the prophet, these compositions are exilic at the earliest, and more likely postexilic. Ezekiel 44:24 charges the Zadokite priests and Levites, among other things, to sanctify the Sabbath. Ezekiel 45:17, in a summary statement, stipulates that the *nāśîʾ* was responsible for providing all of the sacrifices in the rebuilt temple of Jerusalem "on pilgrimage festivals and on new moons, and on Sabbaths; on all fixed festivals of the house of Israel." What is more, he is assigned a sacral role in a series of sacrificial rites. By way of explanation, the title *nāśîʾ* represents the internal, Hebrew equivalent of *peḥâ*, "governor," in the Persian provincial administration. The author(s) of Ezekiel revived this early tribal title, which originally meant "chieftain," and applied it to the leader of the restored Judean community. Significantly, this leader was not entitled "king." Ezekiel 46 is remarkable in detailing how the *nāśîʾ* was to enter the temple on Sabbaths through the eastern gate, which was to remain closed during weekdays, and to perform specific sacrifices. He also officiated on new moons and festivals, and would offer his own voluntary sacrifices from time to time. There is little to inform us as to whether the sacral role here projected for this leader ever materialized in reality, but it is patterned after widespread ancient Near Eastern models of sacral kingship.

2. Chapters 56–66 of Isaiah are usually referred to as "Trito-Isaiah," meaning that they are of different authorship from Isa 40–55, usually known as Deutero-

Isaiah, and of later composition, bringing us into the period of the return from exile. The major theme of Trito-Isaiah is Israel's restoration and the ingathering of exiles. The prophet charges the Judean community with upholding God's commandment of justice, assuring the people of the reward for so doing (Isa 56:1–2):

> Thus spoke Yahweh: Preserve justice and do what is right, for my salvation is near at hand, and my vindication to be revealed. Fortunate is the person who acts in this way, and the human who fulfills it; who observes the Sabbath to avoid desecrating it [šōmēr šabbāt mēḥallĕlô], and who holds back his arm from doing evil.

In Isa 58:13–14 the prophet asserts God's promise:

> If you turn back from your pursuits on the Sabbath, (from) conducting your affairs on my sacred day, and proclaim the Sabbath as a joy, in honor of the Holy One of Israel; (if) you honor it by not attending to your pursuits, by not conducting your business or devising plans—then shall you rejoice over Yahweh, and I will transport you over the high places of the earth. I shall enable you to partake of the estate of Jacob, your forefather.

Finally, in Isa 66, the last chapter of Trito-Isaiah, the prophet envisions continuous celebrations in a rebuilt Jerusalem, when exiles from all lands will assemble on God's holy mountain:

> And it shall be on one New Moon after another, and on one Sabbath after another, that all flesh will come to bow down before me, said Yahweh. (66:23)

These passages from Trito-Isaiah, like Jer 17, expand on the activities prohibited on the Sabbath, although it is difficult to pinpoint the precise meaning of the unusual language used in Trito-Isaiah. In a broader sense, Trito-Isaiah links Sabbath observance to the future fortunes of the Judean community.

3. The book of Nehemiah contains important information on the status of the Sabbath in Jerusalem and Judea under Persian imperial rule. Nehemiah 9:14, within a confessional prayer, regards the Sabbath as foremost among the statutes and laws made known to the Israelites through Moses. In the famous ʾămānâ, "compact," of Nehemiah 10, one of the specific commitments undertaken by the people and its leaders assembled was to observe the Sabbath: One notes resonance with Deut 15:

> And as for the peoples of the land (or: "folks from the countryside") who bring items for sale and all sorts of provisions on the Sabbath day to sell—we will not purchase from them on the Sabbath, or a holy day. We will practice the abandonment of the seventh year, and (annul) all indebtedness. (Neh 10:32)

Nehemiah 13 is taken from "Nehemiah's memoirs" and contains a lengthy passage in which that leader asks God to remember his personal efforts in enforcing Sabbath observance in Jerusalem and Judea (13:14–22). He speaks contemptuously of those who bring loads of grape and fig wine on the Sabbath, some of which had been trampled in vats on the Sabbath. He is in conflict with the landowners of Judah, admonishing them not to act like their ancestors, who had desecrated the Sabbath and thereby brought destruction upon Jerusalem. Nehemiah makes mention of foreign merchants, if that is what is meant by "Tyrians" (13:16) and "peoples of the land" (10:32). He ordered the gates of Jerusalem to be closed at sunset before the Sabbath, and he stationed guards, including Levitical gatekeepers, to assure that the gates would not be reopened until after the Sabbath. His orders paraphrase Jer 17: "Let no 'load' enter on the Sabbath day" (Neh 13:19).

4. As for 1 and 2 Chronicles, there is little that is new on the subject of the Sabbath. We find the usual paraphrasing of earlier biblical pronouncements, as well as summary statements phrased in late biblical style (cf. 1 Chron. 23:31; 2 Chron 9:32). And then, there is the caption to Psalm 92: "A poetic song for the Sabbath day," which allows us to infer that the Sabbath was celebrated with singing, a finding that is amplified in 1 and 2 Chronicles.

Summary

In the last scene of the biblical drama, we find ourselves in Jerusalem, the restored capital of what came to be known as *yĕhūd mĕdîntāʾ*, "the province of Judea," under Persian imperial domination (cf. Ezra 5:8). We find Nehemiah, himself a provincial governor, endeavoring to uphold the observance of the Sabbath in Jerusalem, and elsewhere, in a mixed population of Jews and Gentiles. The main concerns relate to the urban life of Jerusalem as a capital and redistribution center, with produce and other wares being brought into the capital. We have moved from the Sabbath of an agrarian economy in northern Israel and Judah in early, pre-exilic times, when regional temples and smaller, local cult sites coexisted with the temple of Jerusalem. We pass through the loss of northern Israel to Assyria in the last quarter of the eighth century BCE, and cult centralization in Judah a century later. Israel survives the exile and reconstitutes itself as a vibrant though contracted postexilic Judean province in the Achaemenid period.

The information that the Hebrew Bible provides on the cultic celebration of the Sabbath becomes more specific in the priestly writings of the Torah, pursuant to the Decalogue. In contrast, it is surprising that there is relatively little to indicate which activities were specifically prohibited on the Sabbath, even in priestly writings or in the chapters of Ezekiel that elaborate on cultic celebration. Like most aspects of religious life in biblical Israel, the Sabbath was deeply affected by the Babylonian destruction of Jerusalem and Judea, and the resultant Diaspora. The Sabbath became a key index of Jewish identity in the now internationalized Jewish "settlements."

8

Rabbinic Reading

The Sabbath

Jacob Neusner

Scripture presents two accounts of the Sabbath day: (1) memorial to creation and (2) commemoration of the liberation of the Israelites from slavery in Egypt. Both theories of the holy day concur that servile labor is not to be done on the day of rest. But for the Halakhah of the Mishnah, Tosefta, Yerushalmi, and Bavli, in tractates *Shabbat* (the Sabbath) and *ʿErubin* (commingling of domains of space or of time for Sabbath purposes), the Sabbath celebrates only the perfection of creation at the end of the sixth day, when God completed creation and sanctified it. The Israelite household at rest recapitulates the celebration of God at the moment of the conclusion and perfection of creation. Then the Israelite household, like creation at sunset marking the end of the sixth day of creation, is sanctified: separated from the profane world and distinguished as God's domain. With all things in place and in order, at the sunset that marks the advent of the seventh day, the rest that signals the perfection of creation descends. The sanctification takes place through that very act of perfect repose that recapitulates the perfection celebrated at the climax of the creation. Like God at the celebration of creation, now humanity achieves perfect, appropriate rest. That takes place when time, circumstance, and also space come together. The advent of the Sabbath marks the time, the household, the space, and the conduct of home and family life on the seventh day, from sunset to sunset, the circumstance. The Sabbath marks the celebration of creation's perfection (Gen 2:1–3). Food for the day is to be prepared in advance (Exod 16:22–26, 29–30). Fire is not to be kindled on that day, and thus no cooking (35:2–3). Servile labor is not to be done on that day by the householder and his dependents, encompassing his chattel (20:5–11; 23:12; 31:12–17; 34:21). The *where* matters as much as the *when* and the *how*; people are supposed to stay in their place: "Let each person remain in place, let no one leave his place on the seventh day" (16:29–30), understanding by place the private domain of the household (subject to further clarification in due course).

The Halakhah stands back from the Sabbath and speaks of broad and general principles, expressed through concrete cases. Scripture forms a presence but rarely

90   The Sabbath

limits the inquiry. Indeed, the law expounded in the Mishnah-Tosefta-Yerushalmi-Bavli sometimes takes up in particular terms principles of a general character, such as intentionality and its effects in a variety of transactions, and sometimes it proves particular to a given topic, such as doing work on the Sabbath. Both perspectives pertain to the law of the Sabbath, the one transcending that law, the other limiting that law. Let us consider the recurrent Halakhic concerns that transcend the Sabbath altogether, starting with intentionality.

Taking Account of Intentionality

The classification of an action is governed by the intention by which it is carried out and also by the consequence:

1. One is not supposed to extinguish a flame, but if he does so for valid reasons, it is not a culpable action; if it is for selfish reasons, it is culpable. If one has deliberately violated the Sabbath, after the Sabbath one may not benefit from the action; if it was inadvertent, he may. We consider also the intentionality of Gentiles. One may not benefit indirectly from a source of heat. But what happens en passant and not by deliberation is not subject to prohibition. Thus if a Gentile lit a candle for his own purposes, the Israelite may benefit, but if he did so for an Israelite, the Israelite may not benefit.

2. If one did a variety of actions of a single classification in a single spell of inadvertence, he is liable on only one count.

3. In the case of anything that is not regarded as suitable for storage, the like of which in general people do not store away, but which a given individual has deemed fit for storage and has stored away, and which another party has come along and removed from storage and taken from one domain to another on the Sabbath—the party who moved the object across the line that separated the two domains has become liable by reason of the intentionality of the party who stored away this thing that is not ordinarily stored.

4. The act must be carried out in accord with the intent for culpability to be incurred. The wrong intention invalidates an act; the right intention validates the same act. Thus a person may break a jar to eat dried figs from it, on condition that he not intend [in opening the jar] to make it into a utensil.

The principle that we take account of what one plans, not only what one does, and that the intentionality of an actor governs—all this yields at least *four* quite distinct results, none of them interchangeable with the others, but all of them subject to articulation in other contexts altogether, besides *Shabbat*.

First, we deal with a familiar principle. Intentionality possesses taxonomic power. The status of an action—culpable or otherwise—is relative to the intent with which the action is carried out. That encompasses a Gentile's action; he may not act in response to the will of an Israelite (to break the Sabbath). But if he acts on his own account, then an Israelite en passant may benefit from what he has done. The law of *KiPayim*, *Shebiʿit*, and the shank of the *Baba*s goes over the same ground.

If the intention is improper, the action is culpable; if proper, it is not. But insofar as inadvertence is the opposite of intentionality, *second*, the result of the failure to will or plan is as consequential as the act of will. If one acts many times in a single spell of inadvertence, the acts are counted as one. This too is an entirely familiar notion.

The *third* entry is the most profound. To understand it, we have to know that the Halakhah in general takes account of what matters to people, and it treats as null what does not. Hence a sum of money or a volume of material deemed negligible is treated as though it did not exist. If one deliberately transports a volume of material of such insufficient consequence that no one would store that volume of that material, no violation of the law against transporting objects has taken place. Transporting objects from one domain to the other matters only when what is transported is valued. What, then, about a volume of material that people in general deem null, but that a given individual regards as worth something? For example, people in general do not save a useless shard or remnant of fabric. But in a given case, an individual has so acted as to indicate that he takes account of the shard. By his action he has imparted value to the shard, even though others would not concur. If then he has saved the negligible object, he has indicated that the shard matters. If someone else takes the shard out of storage and carries it from one domain to another, what is the result? Do we deem the one person's evaluation binding upon everyone else? Indeed we do, and the second party who does so is liable. The reason that ruling is not particular to the Sabbath becomes clear in the exegesis of the law, which carries us to a variety of other Halakhic topics altogether, such as what is susceptible to uncleanness must be deemed useful, and what is held of no account is insusceptible, and what a given person deems useful is taken into account, and the rest follows.

The *fourth* matter involving intentionality is a commonplace of the Halakhah and recapitulates the principle of the first. If someone acts in such a way as to violate the law but the act does not carry out his intent, he is not culpable; if he acts in accord with his intent and the intent is improper, he is culpable. So the match of intention and action serves to impose culpability.

The matter of causality produces a number of cases that make the same point: we take account of indirect consequences, not only direct causality. But the consequences that we impute to indirect causality remain to be specified.

Taking Account Not Only of Direct but Also of Indirect Consequences

Since one may not perform an act of healing on the Sabbath, one may not consume substances that serve solely as medicine. But one may consume those that are eaten as food but also heal. One may lift a child, even though the child is holding something that one is not permitted to handle or move about; one may handle food that one may not eat (e.g., unclean food) along with food that one may eat. One may not ask Gentiles to do what he himself may not do, but one may wait at the Sabbath limit at twilight to do what one may ask another person to do. Thus they do not go to the Sabbath limit to await nightfall to bring in a beast. But if the beast was standing outside the Sabbath limit, one calls it, and it comes on its own.

Once we distinguish indirect from direct causality, we want to know the degree to which, if at all, we hold a person responsible for what he has not directly caused; what level of culpability, if any, pertains? The point is that what comes about on its own, and not by the direct action of the Israelite adult, is deemed null. If one is permitted to eat certain foods, then those foods may be eaten on the Sabbath even though they possess, in addition to nourishment, healing powers. Indirect consequences of the action are null. One may carry a child, even though the child is holding something that one may not carry. We impose a limit on the effects of causation, taking account of direct, but not indirect, results of one's action. One may make the case that the present principle places limits upon the one that assigns intentionality taxonomic power; here, even though one may will the result, if one has not directly brought about the result, he is still exempt from liability. In no way is this law particular to the Sabbath.

So much for issues that transcend the specificities of the Sabbath. But what about the particularities? The principal conception is simply stated: the advent of the Sabbath transforms creation, specifically reorganizing space and time and reordering the range of permissible activity. First comes the transformation of space that takes effect at sundown at the end of the sixth day and that ends at sundown of the Sabbath day. At that time, for holy Israel, the entire world is divided into public domain and private domain, and what is located in the one may not be transported into the other. What is located in public domain may be transported only four cubits, that is, within the space occupied by a person's body. What is in private domain may be transported within the entire demarcated space of that domain. All public domain is deemed a single spatial entity, so too all private domain, so one may transport objects from one private domain to another. The net effect of the transformation of space is to move nearly all permitted activity to private domain and to close off public domain for all but the most severely limited activities. People may not transport objects from one domain to the other, but they may transport objects within private domain. So the closure of public domain from most activity, and from nearly all material or physical activity, comes in consequence of the division of space effected by sunset at the end of the sixth day of the week.

Taking Account of Space

On the Sabbath the household and village divide into private and public domain, and it is forbidden to transport objects from the one domain to the other:

1. Private domain is defined as at the very least an area ten handbreadths deep or high by four wide; public domain is defined as an unimpeded space open to the public. There one may carry an object for no more than four cubits, which the sages maintain is the dimension of man.

2. The sea, plain, *karmelit* (neutral domain), colonnade, and a threshold are neither private domain nor public domain. They do not carry or put (things) in such

places. But if one carried or put (something into such a place), he is exempt (from punishment).

3. If in public domain one is liable for carrying an object four cubits, in private domain, there is no limit other than the outer boundaries of the demarcated area of the private domain, as within the walls of the household.

4. What is worn for clothing or ornament does not violate the prohibition against carrying things from private to public domain. If one transports an object from private domain to private domain without bringing the object into public domain, such as by tossing it from private to private domain, he is not culpable.

The point of the division into private and public domain emerges in the exposition of the distinction; it concerns transporting objects. One may cross the line but not carry anything in so doing—hence the concern for what may or may not be worn as clothing. The same point emerges in the rule that one may move an object from one private domain to another, so long as public domain does not intervene. Carrying within public domain forms an equally important consideration; one may do so only within the space occupied by his very body, his person. But the four cubits a person occupies in public domain may be said to transform that particular segment of public domain into private domain, so the effect is the same. The delineation of areas not definitively public domain but also not private domain—the sea and the plain, which are not readily differentiated; the space within a colonnade; a threshold—simply refines and underscores the generative distinction of the two distinct domains.

So when it comes to space, the advent of the Sabbath divides into distinct domains for all practical purposes what in secular time is deemed divided only as to ownership, but united as to utilization. Sacred time then intensifies the arrangements of space as public and private, imparting enormous consequence to the status of what is private. On the Sabbath, there and only there is life to be lived. The Sabbath assigns to private domain the focus of life in holy time: the household is where things take place then. When, presently, we realize that the household (private domain) is deemed analogous to the temple or tabernacle (God's household), forming a mirror image to the tabernacle, we shall understand the full meaning of the generative principle before us concerning space on the Sabbath.

Second comes the matter of time and how the advent of sacred time registers. Since for the Sabbath the consequence of demarcating all space into private and public domain affects, in particular, transporting objects from one space to the other, how time is differentiated will present no surprise. The effects concern private domain, the household. Specifically, what turns out to frame the Halakhic issue is what objects may be handled or used, even in private domain, on the Sabbath. The advent of the Sabbath thus affects the organization of space and the utilization of tools and other objects, the furniture of the household within the designated territory of the household. The basic principle is simple. Objects may be handled only if they are designated in advance of the Sabbath for the purpose for which they will be utilized on the Sabbath. But if tools may be used for a purpose that is licit on the Sabbath, and if those tools are ordinarily used for that same purpose, they are deemed ready at hand and do not require reclassification; the accepted classification applies.

What requires designation for Sabbath use in particular is any tool that may serve more than a single purpose, or that does not ordinarily serve the purpose for which it is wanted on the Sabbath. Designation for use on the Sabbath thus regularizes the irregular, but it is not required for what is ordinarily used for the purpose for which it is wanted and is licitly utilized on the Sabbath.

Taking Account of Time

What is to be used on the Sabbath must be so designated in advance.

1. For example, on the Sabbath people do not put a utensil under a lamp to catch the oil. But if one puts it there while it is still day, it is permitted. But they do not use any of that oil on the Sabbath, since it is not something that was prepared (before the Sabbath) for use on the Sabbath.

2. What one uses on the Sabbath must be designated in advance for that purpose, either in a routine way (what is ordinarily used on the Sabbath, e.g., for food preparation, does not have to be designated especially for that purpose) or in an exceptional manner. But within that proviso, all utensils may be handled on the Sabbath, for a permitted purpose. If something is not ordinarily used as food but one designated it for that purpose, such as for cattle, it may be handled on the Sabbath.

The advent of sacred time calls into question the accessibility and use of the objects and tools of the world, but with a very particular purpose in mind. That purpose emerges when we observe that if an object is ordinarily used for a purpose that is licit on the Sabbath, such as for eating, it need not be designated for that purpose for use on the Sabbath. Since on the Sabbath the object is used for its ordinary and licit purpose, that suffices. So the advent of the Sabbath requires that things licit for use on the Sabbath be used in the manner that is standard. If one wishes to use those things for a given purpose that is licit on the Sabbath, but that those objects do not ordinarily serve, then in advance of the Sabbath one must designate those objects for that purpose, to regularize them. That rule covers whole, useful tools, but not broken ones or tools that will not serve their primary purpose.

The Sabbath then finds all useful tools and objects in their proper place. That may mean that they may not be handled at all, since their ordinary function cannot be performed on the Sabbath. Or it may mean that they may be handled on the Sabbath exactly as they are handled every other day, the function being licit on the Sabbath; or it may mean that they must be designated in advance of the Sabbath for licit utilization on the Sabbath. That third proviso covers utensils that serve more than a single function, or that do not ordinarily serve the function of licit utilization on the Sabbath that the householder wishes them to serve on this occasion. The advent of the Sabbath then requires that all tools and other things be regularized and ordered. The rule extends even to utilization of space within the household, space not ordinarily used for a (licit) purpose for which, on the Sabbath, it is needed. If guests come, storage space used for food may be cleared away to accommodate them, the space being conceived as suitable for sitting even when not ordinarily used for that purpose. But one may not clear out a store room for that purpose. One may also make a path in a store room so that one may move about there. One may handle objects that, in some way or another, can serve a licit purpose, in the theory that that purpose inheres. But what is not made ready for use may not be used on the Sabbath. So the advent of the Sabbath not only divides space into public and private, but also differentiates useful tools and objects into those that may or may not be handled within the household.

The prohibition of labor proves equally subtle. It is simply stated: In a normal way *one may not carry out entirely on his own a completed act of constructive labor*, work that produces enduring results. That is what one is supposed to do in profane time. What is implicit in that simple statement proves profound and bears far-reaching implications. No prohibition impedes performing an act of labor in an other-than-normal way, such as in a way that is unusual and thus takes account of the differentiation of time. Labor in a natural, not in an unnatural, manner is prohibited. But that is not all. A person is not forbidden to carry out an act of destruction, or an act of labor that produces no lasting consequences. Nor is part of an act of labor, not brought to conclusion, prohibited. Nor is it forbidden to perform part of an act of labor in partnership with another person who carries out the other requisite part. Nor does one incur culpability for performing an act of labor in several distinct parts, such as over a protracted, differentiated period of time. The advent of the Sabbath prohibits activities carried out in ordinary time in a way deemed natural: acts that are complete, consequential, and in accord with their accepted character.

Taking Account of Activity

On the Sabbath one is liable for the intentional commission of a completed act of constructive labor, such as transporting an object from one domain to the other, if one has performed, in the normal manner, the entire action from beginning to end.

1. If one has performed only part of an action, the matter being completed by another party, he is exempt. If one has performed an entire action but done so in an-other-than-ordinary manner, he is exempt. If one transports an object only to the threshold and puts it down there, he is exempt, even though he later picks it up and completes the transportation outward to public domain.

2. If one performed a forbidden action but did not intend to do so, he is exempt. If one performed a forbidden action but in doing so did not accomplish his goal, he is exempt. If one transported an object or brought an object in, if he did so inadvertently, he is liable for a sin offering. If he did so deliberately, he is subject to the punishment of extirpation.

3. All the same are the one who takes out and the one who brings in, the one who stretches something out and the one who throws (something) in—in all such cases he is liable. By observing Sabbath prohibitions even before sunset (on the sixth day), one takes precautions to avoid inadvertent error.

4. One is liable for constructive but not for destructive acts of labor, and for acts of labor that produce a lasting consequence but not ephemeral ones.

5. One is liable for performing on the Sabbath classifications of labor the like of which was done in the tabernacle. They sowed, so you are not to sow. They harvested, so you are not to harvest. They lifted up the boards from the ground to the wagon, so you are not to lift them in from public to private domain. They lowered boards from the wagon to the ground, so you must not carry anything from private to public domain. They transported boards from wagon to wagon, so you must not carry from one private domain to another.

6. But moving the object must be in the normal manner, not in an exceptional way, if culpability is to be incurred.

7. An entire act of labor must involve a minimum volume, and it must yield an enduring result. An act of destruction is not culpable. Thus, as we recall, he who tears (his clothing) because of his anger or on account of his bereavement, and all those who effect destruction, are exempt.

8. Healing is classified as an act of constructive labor, so it is forbidden; but saving life is invariably permitted, as is any other action of a sacred character that cannot be postponed, such as circumcision, saving sacred scrolls from fire, saving from fire food for immediate use, and tending to the deceased, along with certain other urgent matters requiring a sage's ruling.

This systematic, extensive, and richly detailed account of the activity and labor forbidden on the Sabbath but required on weekdays introduces several considerations, properly classified.

Defining Labor

Preconditions

1. Intentionality: The act must carry out the intention of the actor, and the intention must be to carry out an illicit act of labor.

2. A single actor: Culpability is incurred for an act started, carried through, and completed by a single actor, not by an act that is started by one party and completed by another.

3. Analogy: An act that on the Sabbath may be carried out in the building and maintenance of the tabernacle (temple) may not be performed in the household, and on that analogy the classification of forbidden acts of labor is worked out.

Considerations

1. Routine character: The act must be done in the manner in which it is ordinarily done.

2. Constructive result: The act must build and not destroy, put together and not dismantle; an act of destruction is not culpable.

Consequences

1. Completeness: The act must be completely done, in all its elements and components.
2. Permanent result: The act must produce a lasting result, not an ephemeral one.
3. Consequence: To impart culpability, a forbidden act of labor must involve a matter of consequence, such as transporting a volume of materials that people deem worth storing and transporting, but not a negligible volume.

What is the upshot of this remarkable repertoire of fundamental considerations having to do with activity, in the household, on the holy day? The Halakhah of *Shabbat* in the aggregate concerns itself with formulating a statement of how the advent of the Sabbath defines the kind of activity that may be done by specifying what may *not* be done. That is the meaning of repose, the cessation of activity, not the commencement of activity of a different order. To carry out the Sabbath, one does nothing, not something. And what is that "nothing" that one realizes through inactivity? One may not carry out an act analogous to one that sustains creation. An act or activity for which one bears responsibility, and one that sustains creation, is (1) an act analogous to one required in the building and maintenance of the tabernacle, (2) that is intentionally carried out (3) in its entirety (4) by a single actor, (5) in the ordinary manner, (6) with a constructive and (7) consequential result, one worthy of consideration by accepted norms. These are the seven conditions that pertain, and that, in one way or another, together with counterpart considerations in connection with the transformation of space and time, generate most of the Halakhah of *Shabbat*.

Like God at the completion of creation, the Halakhah of the Sabbath defines the Sabbath to mean to do no more, but instead to do nothing. At issue in Sabbath rest is not ceasing from labor, but ceasing from labor of a quite particular character, labor in the model of God's work in making the world. Then why do the issues of space, time, and activity arise? Given the division of space into public domain, where nothing much can happen, and the private domain of the household, where nearly everything dealt with in the law at hand takes place, we realize that the Sabbath forms an occasion for the household in particular. There man takes up repose, leaving off the tools required to make the world, ceasing to perform the acts that sustain the world.

A further and important component of the definition of the Sabbath as the day to remain in place now requires attention: "Remain every man of you in his place; let no man go out of his place on the seventh day" (Exod 16:29–30). "*His* place" explicitly means private domain. There, the Torah implicitly affirms, people may conduct life in an ordinary way. But "private domain" and householder are not deemed synonymous, and that marks an important judgment. Now "private domain" means "one's place," and that does not have to be the household. Not only so, but an individual is now free to designate his "place" as other than that of his home and extended family, the place where he functions as part of a unit of production.

"Private domain," whether or not the household within its walls, is where an Israelite is supposed to spend the Sabbath, and as the Halakhah clearly indicates, that is the only normal situation for the Sabbath. Spending the Sabbath in public domain, domain not designated for one's place or residence for the holy span of time, means sitting in place and doing nothing. Private domain is where one may do what he likes. It is there that, within the framework of the Sabbath, the people may handle what they wish, carry what they wish from spot to spot, conduct all licit actions, once more, within the limits of the Sabbath: actions that are not constructive with enduring results and that are consonant with the sanctity of the time. Beyond "his place," a householder may not conduct himself as if he owned the territory, meaning, handle whatever he wants, move about what he wishes, do whatever he chooses. On the Sabbath, apart from walking about, for all practical purposes all one may do in public domain by one's mere presence is establish private domain, meaning a space of four cubits; from that point he cannot budge.

If before the Sabbath, however, one has established a place of Sabbath residence, then he may move through private or public domain to a limit of two thousand cubits; but still, in public domain, he may transport nothing. If one's place of Sabbath residence is the household where he normally resides, he need do nothing; but he has the option of selecting some other spot as "his place" for the purpose of the Sabbath, and then he may move about within the range of two thousand cubits from another starting point than the household. Central to the Halakhah is the fusion meal, called an ʿ*erub*, which extends private domain to the outermost possible limits, the walls of the town, real or fictive. The entirety of the private domain, now melded, is held by joint residents of a courtyard or the set of courtyards that lead into an alleyway, or the alleyways that all together comprise a village. That meal of commingling of ownership puts pieces of private domain into one vast, still-private domain ("his place" vastly extended, but also diluted by the commingled ownership of others) and symbolizes relinquishing one's exclusive proprietorship of one's own sector of private domain.

The upshot is, through the medium of an ʿ*erub*, a householder gives up his unlimited power over his own share of private domain in order to acquire limited power over a much-larger share of land that is in that same status. And through that same medium, one may not only commingle his rights of ownership; he may also remove himself from the property that is usually his private domain and establish another domain. It comes down to the same thing. The advent of the Sabbath redefines what is meant by private domain, loosing the individual from the group as much as loosing the proprietary rights of the householder from his own domain, but extending his rights over the domain of others. The Sabbath then brings about a reorganization of the division of property and society alike.

That reorganization involves symbolic commingling, ways in which private ownership for the purposes of creating a common private domain on the Sabbath are shared among householders and their counterparts. This each does by giving up sole ownership rights to his own property to the specified others, but at the same time gaining rights to their property. The ʿ*erub* is the medium for transforming private property into a common domain among householders, as much as it has the power to form a realm of private property within or encompassing also the public domain. The former is accomplished by a meal, the latter by a fence. The ʿ*erub*, whether meal or fence, establishes common ownership for all participants, redefining the meaning of "private property" from what is owned by an individual to what is owned by the resident sector of the community of Israel in a particular here and now. What is at stake in both the formation of a large private domain or establishing private domain out of public domain is the same: the possibility of conducting life on the Sabbath in the normal manner. Now all property is private for the purposes of conducting the required affairs of the household—eating meals, carrying objects from place to place within the designated territory—but privacy of ownership gains a new meaning: no longer individual, but now communal.

A medium of commingling or ʿ*erub* may take the form of a physical line of demarcation, such as a symbolic fence, or it may take the form of a meal shared among householders. In the latter instance, the act of eating together (or more accurately, the possibility of doing so) defines property as shared. That is because, as with God in the temple, nourished by the offerings on the altar, eating defines residence. People who share a common meal, even in theory, then are treated as a cogent social unit, an extended household, possessed of the lands of all adherents thereto.

The paramount question before us is, Why do sages devote their reading of the law of the Sabbath in Mishnah *Shabbat* and ʿ*Erubin* above all to differentiating public from private domain? Why do sages formulate the principle as they do, that the act of labor prohibited on the Sabbath is one that fully constitutes a completed act of labor—beginning, middle, and end—in conformity with the intentionality of the actor?

The answer to both questions derives from the governing theology of the Sabbath. The Written Torah represents the Sabbath as the climax of creation. The theology of the Sabbath put forth in the Halakhah derives from a systematization of definitions implicit in the myth of Eden, which envelopes the Sabbath. In the formation of the normative law defining the matter, sages' thinking about the Sabbath invokes the model of the first Sabbath, the one of Eden. The two paramount points of concern—(1) the systematic definition of private domain, where ordinary activity is permitted, and (2) the rather particular definition of what constitutes a prohibited act of labor on the Sabbath—precipitate deep thought and animate the handful of principles brought to concrete realization in the two tractates. "Thou shalt not labor" of the Ten Commandments refers in a generic sense to all manner of work; but in the Halakhah of *Shabbat*, "labor" bears very particular meanings and is defined in a quite specific, and somewhat odd, manner. We can make sense of the Halakhah of *Shabbat-ʿErubin* only by appeal to the story of creation, the governing metaphor derived therefrom, and the sages' philosophical reflections thereon that transform into principles of a general and universal character the case at hand. What is it about the Sabbath of creation that captures sages' attention?

This brings us to the third tractate of the Mishnah that attends to the Sabbath, besides *Shabbat* and ʿ*Erubin*, and that is the tractate on the Sabbatical year of nature, when the land is given a year of rest on a septennial cycle, tractate *Shebiʿit*.

On the Sabbath that is provided every seventh year for the land of Israel itself, the land celebrates the Sabbath, and then Israel also in its model. The land is holy, as Israel is holy, and the Priestly Code leaves no doubt that, for both, the Sabbath defines the rhythm of life with God: the seventh day for Israel, the seventh year for the land. For both to keep the Sabbath, moreover, is to be like God. And specifically, that is when God had completed the work of creation, pronounced it good, sanctified it—imposing closure and permanence, the creation having reached its conclusion. God observed the Sabbath, which itself finds its definition as the celebration and commemoration of God's own action. This is what God did; this is what we now do. What God did concerned creation; what we do concerns creation. And all else follows. The Sabbath then precipitates the imitation of God on a very particular occasion and for a very distinctive purpose. And given what we have identified as sages' governing theology—the systematic account of God's perfect justice in creation, yielding an account and explanation of all else—we find ourselves at the very center of the system. The meeting of time and space on the seventh day of creation—God having formed space and marked time—finds its counterpart in the ordering of Israelite space at the advent of time, the ordering of that space through the action and inaction of the Israelites themselves.

'Erubin, "commingling," with its sustained exercise of thought on the commingling of ownership of private property for the purpose of Sabbath observance and on the commingling of meals to signify shared ownership, accomplishes for Israel's Sabbath what *Shebi'it* achieves for the land's Sabbath. On the Sabbath inaugurated by the Sabbatical year, the land, so far as it is otherwise private property, no longer is possessed exclusively by the householder. So too, the produce of the land consequently belongs to everybody. It follows that the Halakhah of *'Erubin* realizes for the ordinary Sabbath of Israel the very same principles that are embodied in the Halakhah of *Shebi'it*. That Halakhah defines the Sabbath of the land in exactly the same terms: the land is now no longer private, and the land's produce belongs to everybody. The Sabbath that the land enjoys marks the advent of shared ownership of the land and its fruit. Sharing is so total that hoarding is explicitly forbidden, and what has been hoarded has now to be removed from the household and moved to the public domain, where anyone may come and take it.

Here we find the Sabbath of creation overspreading the Sabbath of the land, as the Priestly Code at Gen 1:1–2:4a and at Lev 25:1–7 define matters. The latter states:

> When you enter the land that I am giving you, the land shall observe a Sabbath of the LORD. Six years you may sow your field and six years you may prune your vineyard and gather in the yield. But in the seventh year the land shall have a Sabbath of complete rest, a Sabbath of the LORD; you shall not sow your field or prune your vineyard. You shall not reap the aftergrowth of your harvest or gather the grapes of your untrimmed vines; it shall be a year of complete rest for the land. But you may eat whatever the land during its Sabbath will produce—you, your male and female slaves, the hired hand and bound laborers who live with you, and your cattle and the beasts in your land may eat all its yield.

The Sabbatical year bears the message, therefore, that on the Sabbath, established arrangements as to ownership and possession are set aside, and a different conception of private property takes over. What on ordinary days is deemed to belong to the householder and to be subject to his exclusive will on the Sabbath falls into a more complex web of possession. The householder continues to utilize his property but not as a proprietor does. He gives up exclusive access thereto, and in exchange he gains rights of access to other people's property. Private property is commingled; everybody shares in everybody's. The result is that private property takes on a new meaning, different from the secular one. So far as the householder proposes to utilize his private property, he must share it with others, who do the same for him. To own then is to abridge ownership in favor of commingling rights thereto; to possess is to share. And that explains why the produce of the land belongs to everyone as well, a corollary to the fundamental postulate of the Sabbath of the land.

Now the Halakhah of *Shebiʿit* appeals to the metaphor of Eden, and along those same lines, if we wish to understand how sages thought about the Sabbath, we have here to follow suit. But that is hardly to transgress the character of the evidence in hand, the story of the first Sabbath as the celebration of the conclusion and perfection of creation itself. Since, accordingly, the Sabbath commemorates the sanctification of creation, we cannot contemplate Sabbath-observance outside of the framework of its generative model, which is Eden. What sages add in the Halakhah of the Oral Torah becomes self-evident: Eden provides the metaphor for imagining the land of Israel, and the Sabbath provides the occasion for the act of metaphorization.

The Halakhah of *Shebiʿit* sets forth in concrete terms what is implicit in the character of Eden. In the Sabbatical year, the land returns to the condition characteristic of Eden at the outset: shared and therefore accessible, its produce available to all. The Sabbatical year recovers that perfect time of Eden, when the world was at rest, with all things in place. Before the rebellion, man did not have to labor on the land; he picked and ate his meals freely. And in the nature of things, everything belonged to everybody; private ownership in response to individual labor did not exist, because man did not have to work anyhow. Reverting to that perfect time, the Torah maintains that the land will provide adequate food for everyone, including the flocks and herds, even if people do not work the land. But that is on condition that all claim of ownership lapses; the food is left in the fields, to be picked by anyone who wishes, but it may not be hoarded by the landowner in particular.

What happens through the *ʿerub*-fence or *ʿerub* meal is the redefinition of proprietorship: what is private is no longer personal, and no one totally owns what is his, but then everyone (who wishes to participate, himself and his household together) owns a share everywhere. So much for the "in his place" part of "each man in his place." His place constitutes an area where ordinary life goes on, but it is no longer "his" in the way in which the land is subject to his will and activity in ordinary time. If constructing a fence serves to signify joint ownership of the village, now turned into private domain, or constructing the gateway of the alleyway and its courtyards, what about the meal? The *ʿerub*-meal signifies the shared character of what is eaten. It is food that belongs to all who wish to share it. But it is the provision of a personal meal, also, that allows an individual to designate for himself a place of Sabbath residence other than the household to which he belongs.

So the Sabbath loosens bonds, those of the householder to his property, those of the individual to the household. It forms communities, the householders of a courtyard into a community of shared ownership of the entire courtyard, the individual into a community other than that formed by the household to which he belongs—now the community of disciples of a given sage, the community of a family other than that in residence in the household, to use two of the examples common in the Halakhah. Just as the Sabbath redefines ownership of the land and its produce, turning all Israelites into a single social entity, "all Israel," which all together possesses the land in common ownership, so the Sabbath redefines the social relationships of the household, allowing persons to separate themselves from the residence of the household and designate some other, some personal, point of residence instead.

Israel on the Sabbath in the land, like God on the Sabbath of Eden, rests from the labor of creation. And that brings us to the question, What about that other principle of the Sabbath, the one set forth by the Halakhah of *Shabbat*? The richly detailed Halakhah of *Shabbat* defines the matter in a prolix yet simple way. It is that on the Sabbath it is prohibited deliberately to carry out in a normal way a completed act of constructive labor, one that produces enduring results, one that carries out one's entire intention: the whole of what one planned, one has accomplished, in exactly the proper manner. That definition takes into account the shank of the Halakhah of *Shabbat* as set forth in the Mishnah tractate, and the amplification and extension of matters in the Tosefta and the two Talmuds in no way revises the basic principles. Here there is a curious, if obvious, fact: it is not an act of labor that itself is prohibited (as the Ten Commandments in Exod 20 and Deut 5 would have it), but an act of labor of a very particular definition.

No prohibition impedes performing an act of labor in an other-than-normal way. In theory, one may go out into the fields and plow, if he does so in some odd manner. He may build an entire house, so long as it collapses promptly. The issue of activity on the Sabbath therefore is removed from the obvious context of work, conventionally defined. Now the activity that is forbidden is of a very particular sort, modeled in its indicative traits after a quite specific paradigm. A person is not forbidden to carry out an act of destruction or an act of labor that produces no lasting consequences. He may start an act of labor if he does not complete it. He may accomplish an act of labor in some extraordinary manner. None of these acts of labor is forbidden, even though, done properly and with consequence, they represent massive violations of the Halakhah. Nor is part of an act of labor that is not brought to conclusion prohibited. Nor is it forbidden to perform part of an act of labor in partnership with another person who carries out the other requisite part. Nor does one incur culpability for performing an act of labor in several distinct parts, such as over a protracted, differentiated period of time. A person may not willingly carry out the entirety of an act of constructive labor, start to finish. Clearly, a definition of the act of labor that is prohibited on the Sabbath has taken over and recast the commonsense meaning of the commandment not to labor on the Sabbath. For considerations enter that recast matters from an absolute to a relative definition. One may tie a knot, but not one that stands. One may carry a package, but not in the usual manner. One may build a wall, but only if it falls down. And as I have stressed, one may do rather much anything without penalty, if he did not intend matters as they actually happened. The metaphor of God in Eden, as sages have reflected on the story of creation, yields the governing principles that define forbidden labor. What God did in the six days of creation provides the model.

What then takes place inside the walls of the Israelite household when the Sabbath's holy time takes over space and revises the conduct of ordinary affairs? Israel goes home to Eden. Israel gives up the situation of mankind in ordinary time and space, destructive, selfish, dissatisfied, and doing. Then on the Sabbath and there in the household, with each one in place, Israel enters the situation of God in that initial, that perfected and sanctified then and there of creation: the activity that consists in sustaining life, sharing dominion, and perfecting repose through acts of restraint and sufficiency.

9

Early Christian Interpretation

Sunday in the New Testament

Bruce D. Chilton

The experience of Jesus' resurrection by his disciples made the first day of the week, Sunday, the day of new creation, also known as the eighth day, the most momentous time in all temporal reckonings: the beginning of the eschatological transformation of all things. For the group that remembered the Twelve gathering around Peter in Jerusalem, the timing of the coming of the Holy Spirit was unequivocal (Acts 2:1–4). The debate regarding how literally this story should be taken has been as brisk as it has been perennial. The present concern is not with the experience behind the text, but how what the text refers to was remembered with a Pentecostal meaning that infused the significance of Sunday as the time beyond the Sabbath.

The stress that the full number of the Twelve (Matthias having replaced Judas; Acts 1:15–26) were together in a single place emphasizes that the gift of the Spirit pertains to Israel. Precisely at Pentecost, the Spirit is portrayed as descending on the twelve apostles, and they speak God's praises in the various languages of those assembled from the four points of the compass for that summer feast of harvest, both Jews and proselytes (2:5–12). The mention of proselytes (2:10) and the stress that those gathered came from "every nation under heaven" (2:5) clearly point ahead to the inclusion of non-Jews by means of baptism within Acts, an inclusion that does not require them to keep the Sabbath.[1]

But even Peter's explanation of the descent of the Spirit voices that inclusive theme (Acts 2:14–37). He quotes from the prophet Joel (2:28–32 in the Septuagint), "And it will be in the last days, says God, that I will pour out from my Spirit upon all flesh."[2] "All flesh," not only historic Israel, is to receive of God's Spirit (Acts 2:37–42): the Twelve are its focus of radiation, not its limit, and Acts speaks of the baptism of some three thousand people in response to Peter's invitation (Acts 2:41).

The outward radiance of Spirit makes Pentecost the most notable feast (in calendrical terms) of Peter and his circle. The distinctively Christian take on Pentecost is easily described on the basis of the New Testament. What is less clear is how that theology developed from Judaic *Shavuot* (or "weeks," as Pentecost is called in the Hebrew Bible). Still, it is worth specifying this Petrine theology before trying to explain it. When Peter is speaking in the house of Cornelius in Acts 10, the Spirit falls upon those who are listening, and those there with Peter who were circumcised were astounded "that the gift of the Holy Spirit has been poured out even upon the nations" (10:44–45). The choice of the verb "to pour out" is no coincidence: it is resonant with the quotation of Joel in Acts 2:17.

Indeed, those in Cornelius's house praise God "in tongues" (10:46) in a manner reminiscent of the apostles' prophecy at Pentecost. (The assumption here and in Acts 2 is that Spirit makes people more articulate than they normally are. That is also the way Paul believes tongues are properly to be conceived, as opposed to those who see the gift of tongues as resulting in incoherence; 1 Cor 14.) Peter directs that this non-Jewish household be baptized "in the name of Jesus Christ" (10:47–48).

That is just the direction Peter gave earlier to his sympathetic hearers at Pentecost (2:37–38). Probably in the case of his speech at Pentecost, and more definitely in the case of his speech in the house of Cornelius, Peter's directions were in Greek, and we should understand that immersion is not for the general purpose of purification; it is immersion "into Jesus' name," which has entered the Greek language (*Iēsous*) as defining the aim of baptism. Christian baptism, immersion into the name of Jesus with reception of the Holy Spirit, was developed within the practice of Peter's circle.

Taken together, the two passages do not suggest any real dispute as to whether the gift of the Spirit followed or preceded baptism into Jesus' name. The point is rather that belief in and baptism into him is connected directly with the outpouring of God's Spirit. The apparent disruption of the usual sequence in Acts 10 is intended to call attention to the artificiality (from the point of view of the emergent Petrine theology) of attempting to withhold baptism from those who believe (as Peter actually says in 10:47).[3]

Still, two questions immediately arise at this point. First, why would it have been natural for Peter to extend baptism to non-Jews on the basis of the outpouring of the Spirit, when he was still sensitive to the scruples of Judaism? (And that sensitivity is recorded by Paul, a contemporary witness; Gal 2:11–14.)[4] Second, from where did Peter understand the new infusion of Spirit to have derived?

Those two questions have a single answer. The source of the Spirit is Jesus as raised from the dead. In Peter's speech at Pentecost, Jesus, having been exalted to the right hand of God, receives the promise of the Holy Spirit from the Father and pours the Spirit out on his followers (2:33). The Spirit that is poured out, then, comes directly from the majesty of God, from his rule over creation as a whole. This is the Spirit as it hovered over the waters at the beginning of creation (Gen 1:2), and not as limited to Israel. Because the Spirit is of God, who creates people in the divine image, its presence marks God's own activity, in which all those who follow Jesus are to be included.

Jesus' own program had involved proclaiming God's kingdom on the authority of his possession of God's Spirit (Matt 12:28). Now, as a consequence of the resurrection, Jesus has poured out that same Spirit upon those who would follow him. For that reason, baptism in the Spirit (Acts 1:4–5) and baptism into the name of

Jesus were one and the same thing. That was why, as Hartman suggests, believing that Jesus was God's Son and calling upon his name were the occasions on which the Spirit was to be received.[5] In the new environment of God's Spirit as signaled by the resurrection, baptism was indeed, as Matt 28:19 indicates, an activity and an experience that involved the Father (the source of one's identity), the Son (the agent of one's identity), and the Holy Spirit (the medium of one's identity).

The timing of Pentecost and the arrival of the Spirit coincided implicitly with the festival calendar of Judaism. In the book of Exodus, it is in the third month, the month when *Shavuot* came, that Moses ascended Sinai (Exod 19:1–25). This association was so strong that during the rabbinic period Eleazar could laconically remark that Pentecost was "the day on which the Torah was given" (*Pesaḥim* 68b in the Babylonian Talmud). The image of all the people gathered at the base of Sinai in Exod 19 may be reflected in the depiction in Acts of Jews (including proselytes) from every point of the compass gathering for Pentecost in Jerusalem (Acts 2:5–11). In the book of Exodus, the Spirit is associated with the mediation of the Torah and its provisions, especially where it concerns preparations for the priests and arrangements for the tabernacle (Exod 31:1–11; 35:30–35).

With all of those commandments received, the book of Numbers portrays Israel as setting out from the wilderness of Sinai on the twentieth day of the second month (Num 10:11–12). After an indeterminate time, but comfortably within range of the usual observation of Pentecost, the people are portrayed as provoking God to anger, so that fire broke out in the camp (11:1–3). Their complaints about provisions lead to Moses' choice of seventy elders, who receive God's Spirit with him at the tabernacle, and they prophesy (11:4–25). Indeed, two people left in the camp, Eldad and Medad, also prophesy, but this brings no objection from Moses. On the contrary, Moses would prefer that all God's people were prophets (11:26–29).

The association of this passage of fire, Spirit, and prophecy makes for a stunning similarity with the scene in Acts, and the specification of seventy elders is also striking, since according to Judaism, seventy is also the number of nations in the world.[6] After all, although those specified as present in Jerusalem are said to be Jews and proselytes, the theme of Acts as a whole is of their prophecy radiating outward to the entire inhabited world.

The association of Weeks (*Shavuot*) with God's covenant with Noah (*Jubilees* 6.1, 10–11, 17–19), the patriarch before the Israelite patriarchs, may help to explain why in the minds of Peter's followers the coming of Spirit then was to extend to humanity at large. Hellenistic Judaism seems especially to have cherished this association with Noah, because he was a paradigm of the righteous and wise non-Israelite. The Sibyl, for example—the premiere prophetess of Greco-Roman culture—is Noah's daughter-in-law in the *Sibylline Oracles* (3.823–827).

Kirsopp Lake called attention to the requirements made of Gentiles within the fourth book of the *Sibylline Oracles* (4.24–34):[7]

> Happy will be those of earthly men who will cherish the great God, blessing before eating, drinking and having confidence in piety. They will deny all temples and altars they see: purposeless transports of dumb stones,

defiled by animates' blood and sacrifices of four-footed animals. But they will behold the great renown of the one God, neither breaking into reckless murder, nor transacting what is stolen for gain, which are cold happenings. They do not have shameful desire for another's bed, nor hateful and repulsive abuse of a male.

What is especially striking about this prophecy is that it is directed to the people of Asia and Europe (*Sib. Or.* 4.1) through the mouth of the Sibyl (4.22–23), the legendary oracle of mantic counsel. Her utterance here is explicitly backed up by the threat of eschatological judgment for all (4.40–48).

Lake's comparison with the Apostolic Council, in which Peter and James both took part (Acts 15:6–29), seems apposite. The Noachian theme certainly cannot be limited to Peter or his circle in any strict sense; the point is rather that the Petrine theology found a deep resonance with the extension of Jesus' movement into a field prepared by Hellenistic Judaism.

A growing body of opinion has found that the emphasis upon prophecy in Luke-Acts accords with the perspectives of Hellenistic historians such as Diodorus Siculus and Dionysius of Halicarnassus.[8] The place of Sibylline prophecies, deriving from a prophetess whose origin "was already lost in the mist of legend by the fifth century" CE,[9] is prominent in both. But while Luke-Acts invokes the motif of prophecy (both literary and contemporary), the Sibyl makes no appearance in a work that is, after all, the longest in the New Testament.

That suggests that the way for the synthesis of Hellenistic oracles and Hebrew prophecy had been prepared by works such as the *Sibylline Oracles* of Hellenistic Judaism, but also that Luke-Acts insists upon the testimony to Jesus' name (directly or indirectly) as an indispensable criterion of true prophecy.[10] This two-volume work is cosmopolitan in its range from the outset (Luke 1:1–4) and yet is also rooted in the particularity of Jesus as he reveals God's Spirit both during his life (Luke 4:18) and as a consequence of his resurrection (Acts 2:32–33).

We have seen that the development of ethical requirements for Gentiles in view of eschatological judgment was part of the ethos of Hellenistic Judaism at the time Luke-Acts was composed. The demands cited by Lake in the fourth book of the *Sibylline Oracles*[11] comport well with the requirements set out in Acts 15, except for the specific proscription of blood. (That, however, is featured prominently with Noah in *Jub.* 6.10.) Still, reciting a blessing before eating might suggest that what is eaten is to be pure, and immersion is mentioned later in the *Sibylline Oracles* (4.165), so the issue is scarcely outside the range of concerns of Hellenistic Judaism.

Indeed, that concern is inherent in the third book of the *Sibylline Oracles*, which Collins dates within the period 163–145 BCE.[12] There, the Sibyl is portrayed as Noah's daughter-in-law (3:823–827), and it was Noah whom God instructed with the commandment not to consume blood or to shed human blood (Gen 9:4–6). Noah receives cognate treatment in books 1 and 2 of the *Sibylline Oracles*.

The dates of that part of the corpus are uncertain, and the Christian additions are evident, but Collins seems on secure ground in his argument that the Judaic redaction was completed before 70 CE in Phrygia.[13] Noah is here made an articulate preacher of repentance to all peoples (*Sib. Or.* 1.128–129), in an elegant expansion of the biblical story (1.125–282) that has the ark make land in Phrygia (1.262). The persistence of such an association between Noah and Asia Minor, where cataclysmic changes in the Black Sea left their mark in primordial memory, is intimated by 1 Pet 3:20, where the number of those in the ark (eight) is stressed, as in the *Sibylline Oracles* 1.281, in comparison to those who were punished.

Pentecost also marked transition, and Christians came to understand this transition eschatologically. The waving of the sheaf before the LORD at the close of Passover anticipated the greater harvest that was to follow in the summer, and that is just what Weeks celebrates (so Lev 23:9–22). So the firstfruits of Passover promised the more plentiful and diverse firstfruits gathered and offered at Weeks (Num 28:26–31). The language of firstfruits is used metaphorically in Paul's theology, to express the gift of Spirit and resurrection (Rom 8:23; 11:16; 1 Cor 15:20, 23). We should expect to hear such connections with the Pentecostal theology of Peter in Paul's preaching, since he was one of Peter's students (Gal 1:18). Likewise, it is predictable that Paul was especially concerned to keep the Feast of Pentecost (1 Cor 16:8; Acts 20:16). Still, that concern would seem to contradict what Paul said about other calendrical observations in his Letter to the Galatians (4:9–10; cf. 2:14). Paul's commitment to the theology and even the calendar of Pentecost is an indication of the deep influence of Petrine theology upon him, and of the penetration of its principal elements within the Hellenistic Church.

The keeping of Pentecost even correlates with the primordially Christian observation of Sundays as a day of gathering in Jesus' name. That custom of meeting on what quickly came to be called "the Lord's day" corresponds to the timing of Jesus' resurrection, surely, but also to priestly teaching concerning the celebration of Pentecost in the temple. This is revealed in a passage of Talmud whose violent language seems humorous, although it reflects a depth of theological animus (*Menaḥot* 65a–b):[14]

> For the Boethusians say, The festival of Pentecost must always coincide with a Sunday [seven full weeks after the offering of the first sheaf of barley grain, which in their view was offered only on a Sunday]. Rabban Yoḥanan ben Zakkai engaged with them and said to them, "You total and complete schmucks! How do you know it?" Not a single one of them could answer, except a doddering old fool, who stumbled and mumbled against him, saying, "Our lord, Moses, loved Israel and knew that Pentecost lasted for only one day, so he therefore made sure to place it on a Sunday, so that Israel would have a two-day vacation." He recited in this regard the following verse: "It is an eleven-day journey from Horeb to Kadesh Barnea by way of Mount Seir" [Deut 1:2]. "Now if our lord, Moses, really loved Israel all that much, why did he delay them in the wilderness for forty years!" He said to him, "My lord, do you think you can get rid of me with that kind of garbage?" He said to him, "You total schmuck! Are you going to treat the complete Torah that is ours like the idle nattering and chattering that is all you can throw up? One verse of Scripture says, 'You shall count

for yourself fifty days' [Lev 23:16], and another verse states, 'Seven weeks shall be complete' [Lev 23:15]. So how about that? The one verse refers to a case in which the festival day coincides with the Sabbath, the other, when a festival day coincides with a weekday. [Pentecost may coincide with any day of the week.]

One plausible reason for Yoḥanan ben Zakkai's vehemence over this issue in the period after 70 CE (when he came to prominence) is that Sunday was being appropriated by a group of Pentecostal *minim* (heretics or sectarians), those who were faithful to the teachings of Peter's circle.

In a recent study of baptism in the New Testament, Lars Hartman has observed that the phrase "into the name of" is not idiomatic Greek, but more probably reflects the Aramaic *lĕshūm* (or Heb. *lĕshēm*). He adduces a passage from the Mishnah (*Zebaḥim* 4:6) in order to explain the meaning of the phrase.[15] There, the phrase clearly refers to those "for the sake of" whom a given sacrifice is offered.[16] Having understood that the generative meaning of the phrase is cultic, Hartman explains the significance of baptism in terms of the new community that is called into being: "Here the people of the new covenant were gathered, cleansed, forgiven, sanctified and equipped with a new spirit. Indeed, the gathering itself can also be regarded as occurring 'into the name of the Lord Jesus.'"[17] Such an emphasis on the role of God's Spirit in baptism is fundamental from the point of view of the New Testament itself, as we have seen. Whether the formulation is of immersion "into" or "in" Jesus' name, the latter simply being better Greek, in either case the point is that Jesus is the occasion and place where the Spirit is encountered. Still, Hartman's study leaves open the question of why a phrase of cultic origin should have been used in connection with baptism.

Now we are in a position to see why it was natural within the Petrine circle to speak of immersion "into the name of Jesus": the cultic language was inspired by the environment of Pentecost. Those who entered into a fresh relationship to God by means of the Holy Spirit were themselves a kind of "firstfruits," because they found their identity in relation to Christ or Spirit as "firstfruit" (so Rom 8:23; 11:16; 16:5; 1 Cor 15:20, 23; 16:15; Jas 1:18; Rev 14:4). The wide range of that usage—a testimony to the influence of this Petrine theology—reflects the deeply Pentecostal character of primitive Christianity. Access to the covenant by means of the Spirit meant that believers entered sacrificially "into the name [*eis to onoma*]" of Jesus in baptism. Also within the Petrine circle, the Eucharist was celebrated in covenantal terms, when one broke bread and shared the cup "into the remembrance of [*eis tēn anamnēsin*]" of Jesus, a phrase associated with covenantal sacrifice (Exod 24:8).[18] In the Petrine understanding, both baptism and Eucharist are sacrificial, and both intimately involve the Spirit of God.

Hartman makes a similar point in regard to the continuing presence of Spirit in his discussion of a famous passage from Paul (1 Cor 12:12–13):

For just as the body is one and has many members, but all the members of the body, being many, are one body, so is Christ. Because by one Spirit we were all immersed into one body, whether Jews or Greeks, whether slaves or free, and we were all made to drink one Spirit.

As Hartman observes: "The last clause of the verse, 'We were all made to drink of one Spirit,' could as well be translated, 'We all had the one Spirit poured over us.' The Spirit not only brought the baptised persons into the body of Christ, but also remains with them as a divine active presence."[19] Spirit is understood to be the continuing medium of faithful existence in Christ, and for that reason it is as natural to associate it with Eucharist as with baptism. After all, Paul could also say that believers, like the Israelites, "drank the same spiritual drink," which came from Christ (1 Cor 10:4),[20] and that the Israelites went through their own immersion (10:2).

Because the Spirit in question is God's and Jesus' at one and the same time, the range of the Spirit's results is extremely broad. It is as manifest as God's own creativity, and as personal as an individual believer's conviction. Charles Gore skillfully brought that out in a study that still merits careful consideration:[21]

> It is true that St. Luke lays stress on the wonderful signs which marked the sudden arrival of the Spirit on, or just before, the day of Pentecost, and on the similar signs which marked the first bestowal of the gift upon the Gentiles, Cornelius and his companions, and again on the twelve men who had been disciples of John the Baptist and were now led on into the faith of Christ.[22] And he delights to recount the miracles of healing wrought by the apostles. But also courage in speaking the word, and wisdom, and faith, and large-hearted goodness are associated with the Spirit's presence,[23] and He is recognized not only as the inspirer of the prophets of old, but also as the present and personal guide and helper of individuals, and of the assemblies of the Church, in all their ways.

Gore's observation is worth stressing, because there is a persistent tendency, even in otherwise well-informed circles, to unduly limit the place of Spirit in earliest Christianity. A recent scholarly book refers to Acts 2, and then to Paul's well-known caution about spiritual gifts in 1 Cor 14, and goes on to state, "We hear nothing further concerning spirit possession in the early Church for another century"![24]

A commonly held view claims that Christianity is not a religion emphasizing the Spirit, so that when people claim that God's Spirit possesses them, that is an unusual occurrence. When a movement is styled "Pentecostal" in the current religious scene, that designation is used to characterize the group concerned as outside of the mainstream of Christianity. But the scene of Pentecost and the scene in the house of Cornelius together demonstrate that possession by God's Spirit was understood to be fundamental to faith in Jesus; it was the principal element in the experience of baptism in the name of Jesus. That is the enduring inheritance of Peter's own Pentecostalism, a celebration of the Spirit of God that is linked inextricably to the practice of worship on Sunday.

PART FOUR

Dietary Purity

10

Scripture's Account

Dietary Purity

Baruch A. Levine

Purity is a pervasive aspect of biblical religion, as it is of ancient religions generally. To interpret it fully would require attention to three major classifications: (1) cultic purity, which is the most extensive category since it affects the sanctuary and priesthood; (2) sexual purity, which is vital to preserving the family structure; and (3) dietary purity, which is basically a domestic regimen. Following upon some general background, the present discussion will be focused on this last category, where we encounter expanding classifications of prohibited foodstuffs that are to be avoided. These are accompanied by specific procedures for maintaining the purity of permitted foods, and of the vessels and instruments involved in their preparation and storage.

On Purity in General

Purity is a state or condition associated with humans and other living creatures, with objects and substances, and with spaces and structures. By extension, human actions and thoughts may be said to be pure or impure. The attainment of purity and its preservation through avoidance of what is regarded as impure are primary goals of the religious life. All ancient Near Eastern religions prescribed purification rites, aimed at remedying existing states of impurity, which was regarded as an active force. Purity was perceived as being in continual conflict with impurity, and these opposites were often personified in polytheistic mythology as warring gods or demons.

The fact that the Hebrew Bible ultimately annunciated a universal, monotheistic belief system does not alter this dynamic. Even in a universe ruled by the supreme God, there was room for active impurity, and it would be incorrect to conclude that, in the biblical view, impurity represented merely the absence or lack of purity, as some have maintained. The extensive procedures and prohibitions prescribed in the Hebrew Bible, aimed at repelling the encroachment of impurity, belie such a conclusion.

Accordingly, it was a primary function of biblical ritual to maintain cultic purity, thereby providing a "safe" terrestrial environment for the Deity, so that he would continue to reside within the human community in purified sanctuaries built to house him. The primal need for the nearness of divine power, and the corollary fear that God would abandon the human community if his purity were compromised—these are the central concerns that drive the effort to retain cultic purity. In the biblical view, sexual purity and a pure diet were also requisite to a holy Israelite community. Their violation would render Israelites impure and ultimately diminish the purity of the sanctuary as well. Infractions of sexual purity would affect the quality of family life, just as neglect of dietary purity would diminish the distinctiveness of Israelite society. Purity is thus to be seen as a precondition of holiness, a phase in the process of its attainment. Because Israel is admonished to become a holy nation, bearing a singular covenant relationship to Yahweh, God of Israel, it was of critical importance to maintain all aspects of purity.

The Language of Purity

Biblical Hebrew expresses purity by forms of the stative verb *ṭāhēr*, "to be pure," conjugated in the *piʿel*, causative stem as *ṭihar*, "to purify," and frequently occurring in the adjectival form *ṭāhôr*, "pure." Cognates of this root are attested in other Semitic languages, including Ugaritic and Punic, as well as in Post-Biblical Hebrew; and less frequently in later dialects of Aramaic; and in Arabic and Ethiopic. It appears to be native to the West Semitic languages. In the lexical vocabularies from Ugarit, *ṭ-h-r* (also *z-h-r*) translates East Semitic Akkadian *ellu*, "pure." Concrete usage of *ṭ-h-r* in Ugaritic relates to the purity of gemstones such as lapis lazuli, and as such connotes a physical property. Similarly, Hebrew *ṭāhôr*, "pure," will be said of gold (*zāhāb ṭāhôr*, "pure gold," Exod 25:17; etc.). In Exod 24:10, describing the ascent of Moses and his associates to the summit of Mt. Sinai, we read:

> Then they beheld the God of Israel, and under his feet there was something resembling a crafted pavement of sapphire, like the very sky for purity [*lāṭōhar*].

These facts of language are more than details. They may well explain why the God of Israel is never referred to in biblical literature as "pure," but most often as *qādôš*, "holy, sacred" (Lev 11:44). To say that Yahweh is "pure" would imply physicality. The most that can be said is that God is "pure of vision" (*ṭehor ʿênayim*), which means, figuratively, that he will countenance no evil (Hab 1:13). The concrete matrix is never lost in Biblical Hebrew, no matter how metaphorical the usage becomes. In contrast, impurity is most often expressed by the adjective *ṭāmēʾ*, "impure," and related forms, which cover a broad "avoidance category," extending from contagious disease to cultic contamination, and convey a sense of harm and danger.

Since late antiquity there has been a trend in the study of religions to associate purity with cleanliness, and to rationalize purity restrictions by assuming that they derive from a concern for health. Though we expect that what is classified as pure, or has been purified, will, in matter of fact, be clean (or at least cleaner!), not everything that is clean is pure. Cleanliness is a hygienic condition, whereas purity is a religious state of being, either intrinsic or attributed. Although we sense a practical link between cleanliness and purity, this falls far short of accounting for the elaborate phenomenology of purity as practically motivated.

Diet as a Category of Purity

As will be clarified in due course, the biblical regimen of dietary purity did not originate in the cult and priesthood, only then to be extended to the society at large. Inevitably, some dietary restrictions overlapped with requirements of the sacrificial cult, whose purity was a major concern. As an example, the classes of land animals and fowl regarded as impure to start with were also unacceptable as sacrificial offerings. And yet, there is every indication that the dietary regimen derives from a complex of socioreligious attitudes rooted in the domestic life of the society and in its eating habits. In identifying the matrix of dietary purity, part of the problem is the nature of the biblical sources themselves. Much of the available information about diet is presented within cultic prescriptions, and there is also the fact that the priesthood progressively imposed certain cultic norms on the domestic dietary regimen over time.

The notion that diet is a matter of religious concern, beyond its relevance to health and nutrition, is common to many cultures, ancient and modern. Israelites may only partake of pure foodstuffs as defined by biblical laws concentrated in the Torah. The first observation to be made concerning the biblical dietary classifications of pure and impure is that they reflect current diet; there was no need to forbid what was not consumed as food. As an example, living creatures whose flesh was not consumed as food in Israelite society are not included in the lists, such as horses, mules, donkeys, and reptiles.

The products of the earth—grains, fruits, and vegetables—are pure in their pristine state, although they can lose their pure status by improper storage and processing. The Hebrew Bible records a dispensation granted to humankind after the flood to consume animals, fowl, and fish as food with the proviso that the blood of animals and fowl may not be consumed (Gen 9:2–6). (Of the role of blood, more is to come.) The Hebrew Bible presumes that before the flood, the proper human diet was vegetarian. The burden of biblical dietary laws is to specify which animals, fowl, and fish (even insects such as locusts) may be consumed by Israelites, and which may not. The Torah preserves two principal codes of law affecting diet, one in Deut 14 and the other in Lev 11. The view adopted here is that Deut 14 is the older of the two texts, whereas Lev 11 extends purity requirements beyond what is addressed in Deuteronomy.

Deuteronomy 14:3–21

By way of introduction, Deut 14:1–2 states that as a holy people, the Israelites are prohibited from adopting certain pagan funerary practices. The theme of Israel's holiness is later resumed in 14:21b, where it is applied to diet, thereby producing an inclusio. What intervenes in 14:3–21a is a code of practice, identifying pure and impure, permitted and forbidden living creatures:

> You may not eat any abomination [tô'ēbâ]. These are the animals that you may eat: the ox, the sheep, and the goat; the deer, the gazelle, the roebuck, the wild goat, the ibex, the antelope, the mountain sheep, and any other animal that has true hoofs that are cleft in two, and that brings up the cud—such may you eat. But the following, which are of those that either bring up the cud or have true hoofs that are cleft through, you may not eat: the camel, the hare, and the daman—for although they bring up the cud, they have no true hoofs, and are impure for you; also the swine, for although it has true hoofs, it does not bring up the cud, and is impure for you. You shall not eat of their flesh nor touch their carcasses.
>
> This you may eat of all that live in water: you may eat anything that has fins and scales. But you may not eat anything that has no fins and scales. Such is impure [ṭāmē'] for you.
>
> You may eat any pure bird. The following you may not eat of them: the eagle, the vulture, and the black vulture; the kite, the falcon, and the buzzard of any variety, and the raven of any variety; and the ostrich, the nighthawk, the sea gull, and the hawk of any variety; the little owl, the great owl; and the white owl; the pelican, and the bustard, and the cormorant; the stork, any variety of heron, the hoopoe, and the bat.
>
> All winged swarming creatures are impure for you; they may not be eaten. You may eat every variety of pure birds.
>
> You may not eat anything that has died a natural death [nĕbēlâ]. Give it to the resident alien in your community to eat, or you may sell it to a foreigner. For you are a holy people to Yahweh, your God. You may not boil a kid in its mother's milk.

The list of dietary restrictions begins by characterizing the forbidden creatures as *tô'ēbâ*, "abomination," a Hebrew term of uncertain etymology. It is applied to several dimensions of human experience: diet (as here), sexual misconduct (Lev 18:22, 24–30; 20:20; Deut 24:4), and pagan worship (Deut 7:25–26; Ezek 33:25–26). As observed, we find a statement at the conclusion of the list to the effect that adherence to the aforementioned dietary restrictions is requisite to becoming a holy people. This highlights the role of dietary practices in the self-definition of social groupings. It is quite telling, in this connection, that Israelites are instructed to dispose of *nĕbēlâ* flesh by selling it to foreigners or giving it away to resident aliens. Distinctive diet serves the objective of social distinctiveness (Lev 20:22–26).

The generic differentiation between pure and impure animals and fowl is first stated in the Yahwist's version of the Flood story (Gen 7:2–3):

Of every pure animal [*mikkōl habbĕhēmâ haṭṭĕhôrâ*] you shall take for yourself seven pairs, males and their mates, and of every animal that is not pure, two, a male and his mate. And as well of the birds of the sky—seven pairs, male and female, to sustain seed upon the earth.

No specifications are stated for differentiating between the pure and impure, but the mere fact that this classification is preserved not in the priestly version of the flood story, as we might expect, but in the writings of the Yahwist (J), further suggests that it did not originate in the sacrificial cult; this helps to refute the contention that the dietary laws initially applied solely to the consecrated priesthood. Rather, the differentiation between pure and impure reflects already-established sociocultural perceptions about the animal world. So it is that after the flood, Noah, when initiating cultic activity, expectedly selected pure animals to sacrifice to Yahweh (Gen 8:20). We are to assume that one was able to distinguish between the pure and the impure on the basis of known criteria. The dietary laws of the Torah proceed to specify these criteria, while the laws of sacrifice, largely concentrated in the priestly writings of the Torah, go even further by designating which of the pure animals and fowl were suitable for use in the cult. As far as we know, fish were not offered as sacrifices in ancient Israel, so that the fact that fish are included in the pure diet argues further against a cultic origin of dietary purity. The same would be true of the varieties of deer, and of wild goats and mountain sheep, acceptable as part of a pure diet, but never prescribed as sacrificial offerings in biblical ritual.

The precise physical criteria for purity have eluded explanation, but certain general observations can be ventured. Two factors are of primary importance: digestion and locomotion. To these should be added a third, interacting factor: the feeding habits and diet of the animals, fowl, and fish themselves. Bringing up the cud is a feature of ruminants; they can be virtually observed chewing food from their double stomach. As for locomotion, animals that have true hoofs were regarded as being domesticated and friendly to humans, whereas paws were associated with hostile beasts. Furthermore, the permitted animals are herbivorous, whereas the forbidden ones are normally not so. A symmetry suggests itself: The pure people consume food taken from creatures that themselves eat what is pure and do not attack humans. This applies to the named impure fowl, which are mostly birds of prey that eat carrion and torn flesh and consume blood. The Torah provides no list of permitted fowl, but some information is available. God provided the Israelites in the wilderness with quail to eat (Exod 16:13; Num 11:21, 31–32; Ps 105:40). By process of elimination, and from information provided in ritual law, we are able to observe that hens, pigeons, doves, and certain kinds of geese, which live in proximity to man and feed on grain, are permissible. The factor of locomotion pertains noticeably to fish; those that have fins and scales were regarded as swimming normally. Forbidden crustaceans, in contrast, were observed scavenging for food and did not appear to be normal in their movements.

It has been observed that disproportionate emphasis is placed on borderline cases, undoubtedly because they exhibited one of the two criteria for animals, but not both, and could be confused with permitted animals. This is true of the camel, the daman, the hare, and the pig, which are singled out. Based on the Torah codes alone, one would not regard the pig, the only forbidden animal with a split hoof, as more significant in dietary prohibitions than the other borderline cases. And yet, both classical and modern scholars have accorded it disproportionate attention. Some have referred, for example, to the Egyptian myth of Horus and Seth, in which the antagonist is a pig who attacks Horus, thereby suggesting that there was something particularly potent about the pig. In some part such speculation is anachronistic and was occasioned by later evidence deriving from the Maccabean period, when refusal to eat pig meat became a test of loyalty to Judaism in the face of religious persecution. In matter of fact, pigs were raised in the Levant, and were part of the diet since early times, as indicated by archaeological finds of pig bones, which also suggest that pigs were utilized as sacrificial animals. It seems that pigs were more often raised in the early stages of settlement, since they did not require grazing land.

As an added stringency, Israelites were forbidden even to touch the carcasses of impure animals (Deut 14:8). All in all, what we have in Deut 14 is a dietary regimen based on the perceived habits of animals, fowl, and fish and certain of their physical characteristics. A society that adhered to this regimen would noticeably differ from other societies who are considered impure, at least partially, as a consequence of their impure diet. Although we remain unable to account for the reasoning behind all of the specifications set forth in Deut 14, certain conclusions would be clearly unwarranted. There is no indication that forbidden animals were part of a taboo system and as such were forbidden precisely because they were revered. If this were true, the flesh of the kid goat (Heb. *śāʿîr*) would be forbidden for normal consumption, because we are told that it was once worshipped, later to be banned as a recipient of sacrifices (Lev 17:7). The ritual of the scapegoat, prescribed in Lev 16, harks back to the cult of the kid goat (Lev 16), just as the widespread utilization of goats as sin offerings was a reflection of that same cult (Lev 23:19; etc.). And yet, goats were permitted as food on the basis of their acceptable physical features. The real taboo in biblical religion is represented by the disposition of blood, a subject to be discussed in due course.

The dietary code of Deut 14 concludes in verse 21 with a post-script that prohibits boiling a kid in its mother's milk, and a fortiori thus forbids consumption of meat prepared in this manner. This same law is cited three times in the Torah. Its earliest occurrence is in Exod 23:19, near the conclusion to the Book of the Covenant, within the context of festival sacrifices. The same cultic context applies to Exod 34:26, which paraphrases Exod 23. The attachment of this regulation to the dietary code of Deut 14 appears to be secondary and is probably attributable to priestly redaction. It was relocated into a noncultic context, that of regular diet, thereby applying cultic norms to household practice. In itself, the prohibition against boiling a kid in its mother's milk recalls the cultic law of Lev 22:27–28 (cf. Exod 22:29):

When an ox or a sheep or a goat is born, it shall stay with its mother for seven days, and only from the eighth day on shall it be acceptable as a burnt offering to Yahweh. However, no animal from the herd or the flock shall be slaughtered on the same day as its young.

We are dealing with apprehension over cultic activity that restrains the dispensation to consume the flesh of animals by reminding the people that animals are living creatures, after all. Finally, the prohibition against touching the carcass of impure animals is to be regarded as preventive, intended to distance Israelites even further from impure foodstuffs. As we shall observe, Lev 11 significantly extends this restriction.

Leviticus 11

A large part of Lev 11 (vv. 1–20) merely repeats Deut 14, at points introducing alternative terminology. Thus, the term *šeqeṣ* replaces *tôʿēbâ* in classifying certain living creatures as "an abomination." Most likely, *šeqeṣ* also replaces *ṭāmēʾ*, "impure." Substantive differences only begin to emerge in verses 21–23 and following, where we have a specification of which "winged, swarming creatures," a general category listed in Deut 14, are permissible and which forbidden:

> But these you may eat from all the winged swarming creatures that walk on [all] fours: all that have jointed legs above their feet to leap with on the ground—of these you may eat the following: locusts of every variety; all varieties of bald locust; crickets of every variety, and all varieties of grasshopper. But all other winged swarming creatures that have four legs shall be an abomination [*šeqeṣ*] for you. (Lev 11:21–23)

Leviticus 11:24–46 contains added regulations that extend the reach of impurity to vessels and to persons. These stipulations are significant, but unanticipated in Deuteronomy.

Regarding land animals, beasts, and swarming creatures (Lev 11:24–31).

> Through the following [animals] you will render yourselves impure; whoever touches their carcass shall remain impure until evening. Likewise, whoever carries any part of their carcass must launder his clothing and remain impure until evening. Through every animal that has true hoofs but without clefts through the hoofs, or does not chew the cud. These are impure for you; whoever touches them becomes impure. Also, all animals that walk on paws, from among those beasts that walk on [all] fours, are impure for you. Whoever touches their carcass shall remain impure until evening. And whoever carries any part of their carcass must launder

his clothing, and will remain impure until evening. These are impure for you.

The following shall be impure for you from among the swarming creatures that swarm on the earth: the mole, the mouse, and the great lizards of every variety; the gecko, the land crocodile, the lizard, the sand lizard, and the chameleon. These are for you the impure among all the swarming creatures. Whoever touches them when they are dead shall remain impure until evening.

This passage identifies forbidden land animals and beasts as those walking on paws, which helps to explain the contrasting criteria for pure land animals. Cleft hoofs represented domestication, whereas paws are characteristic of wild beasts. In substance, this passage adds a prohibition against consumption of specified swarming creatures (Heb. *šereṣ*) that walk on the earth, whereas Deut 14 speaks only of winged, swarming creatures. More significant is the consequence of contact with the carcasses of forbidden creatures. Whereas Deut 14 only prohibits consumption of certain creatures and contact with carcasses of the same, Lev 11 goes further in specifying the consequences of such contact: Touching or carrying such materials renders a person impure until evening, and hence prohibited from access to the sanctuary. Carrying any part of a carcass implicates one's clothing as well, which must be laundered, elsewhere a normal step in cultic purification (Exod 19:10; Lev 13:6, 34; etc.). The extent of impurity for the *šereṣ* is less: one need not launder clothing.

There is still more happening in Lev 11, moreover. Except for the postscript prohibiting the boiling of a kid in its mother's milk, Deut 14 had shown no direct connection to the cult, as explained above. There, the Israelites are declared to be a holy people, to be sure, but throughout, impurity attaches only to forbidden creatures. There is no reference to the effects of consuming such creatures or of contact with them, on persons or vessels. But once dietary impurity is regarded as communicable, persons in an impure state as a consequence of having consumed forbidden foods, or having been in contact with carcasses of impure creatures—such persons would contaminate the sanctuary if allowed to enter its precincts. This is the cultic connection. The effects of contact with the carcasses of permitted animals will be discussed presently.

Regarding the impurity of utensils and the role of water as a conductor (Lev 11:32–38). At this point, the composition of Lev 11 produces ambiguity. Specifically, it is unclear whether the provisions of 11:32–38 cover only the impurity of the *šereṣ* or of all of the living creatures enumerated earlier in Lev 11. Here is the text:

And anything, on which any part of these [*mēhem*] falls when dead, becomes impure; be it any article of wood, or of cloth, or of skin, or of sackcloth—any article that can be put to use, shall be immersed in water, and remain impure until evening. And if any part of these falls into an earthen vessel, everything inside it shall be impure, and [the vessel] itself you shall break. As for any food that is edible, if water falls on it, it becomes impure. And as for any liquid that is drinkable, it becomes impure if it was in any vessel. Everything on which the carcass of any of these falls becomes impure; an oven and a stove must be smashed; they are impure and shall remain impure for you. However, a spring or cistern, serving as a collector of water, shall remain pure, although whoever touches their carcass [inside it] becomes impure. Should any part of their carcass fall on seed that is to be sown, it [the seed] remains pure. But if water is placed on seed, and [then] any part of their carcass falls on it, it becomes impure for you.

Admittedly, the transition from verse 31 to verse 32 is confusing, because the antecedent of *mēhem*, "any part of these," in verse 32 remains unclear. It is improbable, however, that these basic laws governing communicable impurity would be limited to the *šereṣ*, "swarming creature." More likely, they were intended to apply to the carcasses of animal and fowl as well, and to forbidden water creatures: in other words, to all of "these." In sum, the impurity of all of the aforementioned, forbidden substances attaches to persons and vessels. Furthermore, we are introduced to the role of water, which renders seed receptive to impurity, because it softens the seed and leads to its fermentation and/or spoilage.

Regarding the carcasses of permitted animals (Lev 11:39–40).

If an animal that is permitted to you dies, whoever touches its carcass shall remain impure until evening; and one who eats of its carcass must launder his clothing and is impure until evening. And anyone who carries its carcass must launder his clothing ands is impure until evening.

This provision more properly belongs after verse 31. In effect, it merely extends the prohibition against contact with carcasses, creatures that had died or had been slain, to pure animals as well. We may infer from this that a proper method of slaughter was required, although such is not specified (see further).

A repeated ban on swarming creatures, Hebrew šereṣ *(Lev 11:41–43).*

All creatures that swarm on the earth are an abomination [*šeqeṣ*] for you; they may not be eaten. [As regards] any creature that crawls on its belly, or any that walks on [all] fours, including any creature that has many legs, of all swarming creatures that swarm on the earth—you may not eat them, for they are an abomination. You may not make yourselves abominable through any swarming creatures that swarm; you may not defile yourselves by them, thereby becoming impure.

In effect, what began as a dietary code of purity has been expanded by the priests of ancient Israel into a regimen for households and sanctuary alike, requiring priests, Levites, and all Israelites to prepare and store their foodstuffs in pure vessels and to avoid contaminating them during processing. For the rest, Lev 11:44–47 emphasizes the theme of holiness, a state to be attained through the careful differentiation between pure and impure foods.

Methods of slaughter and the disposition of blood. Deuteronomy 12:15–16 ordains that Israelites may slaughter meat for food in a nonsacrificial way wherever they please, so long as they refrain from consuming its blood. They need not be in a state of ritual purity when doing so, as would be the case if they were making sacrifice on the one, designated sanctuary altar. "The impure and the pure may partake of it, as with respect to the deer and stag." This means that slaughtering animals is the same as hunting them, as far as dietary purity is concerned. Leviticus 17:12–14 takes up this comparison and speaks of hunting animals and fowl, requiring only that their blood be poured on the ground and covered before the meat may be consumed. It should be remembered that Deut 14:5 lists seven kinds of deer permitted as food, which were usually killed in the hunt. Birds were often hunted with traps clustered with small stones that were thrown into the air, as we know from Amos 3:5: "Would a bird fall on an earth-trap and not be ensnared? Would a trap rise from the ground and fail to capture?" (cf. Prov 7:23). There is also mention of entrapping birds in nets (Prov 1:17). A method of killing domestic fowl was to pinch the neck (Lev 1:15; 5:8).

As for the slaughter of small and large cattle, and of fowl as well, the usual Hebrew verb is *šāḥaṭ* (occasionally *zābaḥ*). The only clue as to the tool utilized in such operations is provided by the rare term *maʾăkelet*, derived from the verb *ʾākal*, "to eat, consume," which in certain contexts describes the cutting action of a sword (Deut 32:42; 2 Sam 11:25; Nah 2:14). Thus, Abraham took hold of a *maʾăkelet* to slaughter his son, Isaac, in the manner of a burnt offering (Gen 22:6, 10), and the same instrument was used to dismember the concubine in the horrific narrative of Judges (19:29). In Prov 30:14, the plural of *maʾăkelet* is parallel with *ḥărābôt*, "swords." Although it is obvious that some sort of knife was used, it is strange that more is not said on this subject, nor are we told how one is to slaughter properly. Given the prohibition against consuming blood, it is to be assumed that the approved method of slaughter would be one most effective in draining the blood of the animal or bird. Several Torah statements require the salting of sacrificial meat (even of grain offerings, by analogy), which would drain off residual blood (Lev 2:13; Num 18:19).

We would not normally consider the ban on consuming blood as a dietary restriction, although in some cultures blood is consumed as a nutrient. All of the biblical statements forbidding consumption of blood pertain to slaughter of animals and fowl, often to sacrificial slaughter, and shedding their blood is compared to the shedding of human blood. First Samuel 14:32–35 relates an incident after a battle, when the Israelites under Saul's command fell upon the spoils and slaughtered small and large cattle on the ground: "Then the people were eating [the meat] together with the blood [ʿal-haddām]." When informed of this, Saul ordered that everyone produce his livestock at a large stone, on which slaughtering would be carried out in a manner that would drain off the blood into the ground. The stone was not an altar, however, which was only constructed later. This cryptic tale seems to be referring to a quite ancient taboo according to which the blood of animals and fowl was forbidden for human consumption because it was food for the gods and had to be restored to the earth.

In the Israelite cult, this notion was translated into the expiatory role of blood. According to Lev 17:12–14, blood was needed to secure expiation because only the blood of sacrifices could substitute for human life. In this respect, the role of blood resembled that of *ḥēleb*, "fat," which covered the internal organs and was reserved for Yahweh (3:16–17). In summary, the blood taboo affects the preparation of certain foods and as such should be discussed under dietary purity. In its fullness, however, it represents a complex religious "system" that reaches far beyond diet.

Conclusion

Outside of Torah literature, little is said in the Hebrew Bible on the subject of a pure diet, which is strange. Ezekiel (4:14) once insisted that he had never eaten meat torn by beasts, or carcasses, or spoiled sacrificial flesh. Manoah's wife is admonished to refrain from eating anything that is impure or drinking intoxicants before the birth of her son, Samson, who was designated as a Nazirite (Judg 13:14–17). The Nazirite was certainly forbidden to drink intoxicants (Num 6:1–4). Daniel and his three friends refused to eat the royal fare while in Babylon because of what we assume were dietary restrictions (Dan 1:8), and 1 Macc 1:12–63 records that during the persecutions under Antiochus IV (167–164 B.C.E.), the devout suffered death rather than defile themselves by eating the meat of swine.

As has become apparent, much of what we know about domestic diet in biblical times comes from sources dealing with the cult, from which we learn that only pure edibles were offered as sacrifices or consumed by the priesthood. In such terms, the information provided on the cult in Ezek 42–46 is of interest, as is the list of offering materials authorized by Cyrus for delivery to the Judean elders for use in the second temple (Ezra 6:9–10). There we read of small and large cattle, of wheat and salt, and of wine and oil. If it is correct to reason that foodstuffs utilized in the pure temple cult correlated with a pure domestic diet, then cultic information also testifies to what was generally eaten by observant Israelites.

Historically, the function of the domestic dietary regimen expanded proportionately as more Israelites, later Jews, were distanced from the Jerusalem temple and alienated from its public cult. Observing a pure diet and seeing to the proper handling of foodstuffs constituted an available route to religious fulfillment. The elaborations evident in Lev 11 are best understood, therefore, as responses to the demographic changes that occurred after the destruction of the first temple.

In retrospect, two effects of the biblical dietary codes are incontrovertible: The prescribed dietary restrictions functioned to maintain social separation between Israelites and other peoples. That barrier was not arbitrary; it was value based. It expressed a persistent anxiety over the exploitation of living creatures as food, and a sense that some living creatures were dangerous and should not be eaten as food. The life force of both humans and animals was their blood.

11

Rabbinic Reading

Clean and Unclean Foods

Jacob Neusner

The rabbinic reading of scriptural laws that specify what Israelites may eat or must not eat turns the laws into an occasion to make a profound theological statement about the sanctity of Israel, the holy people. Land, temple, and altar all enveloped and contained holy Israel in all its sanctification. Scripture says no less. What makes the rabbinic reading of food taboos consequential is its affirmation that the taboos apply after the destruction of the temple and outside of the land of Israel, and not in connection with the altar alone. That reading addresses the condition of Israel both in the land and outside, both when the temple stood and after its destruction, whether in 586 BCE or in 70 CE (but in context, after 70), both in connection with the holy rites and when they are inoperative. It made the statement that the sanctity of the Israelite people endured everywhere, even outside of the land, and it persisted for all time, even in the condition of estrangement from God represented by the destruction of the temple. This is expressed in the following language:

> Mishnah *Ḥullin* 5:1: [The prohibition against slaughtering on the same day] "it and its young" [Lev 22:28] applies [1] in the Land and outside the Land, [2] in the time of the temple and not in the time of the temple, [3] in the case of unconsecrated beasts and in the case of consecrated beasts.

To make its statement about the eternal sanctification of the people Israel, the Halakhah explicitly responds to three facts: (1) Israelites live not only in the holy land but also abroad, in unclean land; (2) the temple has been destroyed; (3) and consequently, animals are slaughtered not only in the temple in the land but also in unconsecrated space and abroad, and the meat is eaten not only in a cultic but also in a profane circumstance. Here one finds an answer if wondering whether the Halakhah that applied to the temple and the home when the temple was standing and Israel was in the land of Israel—whether it continues to apply with the temple in ruins and Israel in exile. Although the sanctity of the temple stands in abeyance, the sanctity of the Israelite table persists; although Israel is in exile from the Holy Land, Israel remains holy; although rules of uncleanness are not now kept in the temple, they continue in force where they can be observed. When prepared for the Israelite table, birds and animals that flourish outside of the land are regulated by the same rules that apply in the land and even (where relevant) at the altar. So Israel, the people, not only retains sanctity but also preserves it outside of the land, and the sanctity of Israel transcends that of the temple and its altar.

Temple and altar, land and produce, and the people, Israel—all are holy. But the sanctification of each is autonomous of that of the other, so that even though the one is separate from the other, each retains its condition of holiness. Then how are the several realms of sanctification interrelated? That is the question taken up in Mishnah-Tosefta-Bavli tractate Ḥullin, which deals with secular meals outside the temple and not on a continuum with the altar, predictably in humble and workaday terms. Certainly one of the most profound and subtle of the compositions of the Halakhah, Ḥullin takes as its problem the comparison and contrast of the same act—in itself governed by rules of sanctification—performed in different circumstances, specifically the preparation of food with special reference to the spilling of blood for the sustenance of man. The Torah repeatedly asserts that "the blood is the life," making provision for the disposition of blood produced in slaughtering an animal. If killed for God, that is to say, in the temple courtyard, the animal yields blood for the altar, to be sprinkled at the corners in an act of expiation; it further produces the sacrificial parts to be burned up in smoke on the altar fires and thence to ascend to God's nostrils; the beast may also yield meat for the priests and their families to eat. If killed for man's needs, the animal yields blood to be covered with dust, returned to the earth. God and man therefore stand in alignment with one another. It is that alignment, expressed in the language of man's being created "in our image, after our likeness," that defines the logic of the Halakhah before us.

But that equation serves only the situation in which the temple stands, Israel is located in the land of Israel, and beasts are subject to the blood and altar rite. What happens when the fires have gone out on the temple altar, Israel locates itself outside of the land of Israel, and animals no longer are consecrated for divine service? Then the balance is lost, the perfect match of slaughter for the altar and slaughter for everyday food. If we read the Torah's requirements in connection with taking an animal's life for God's and man's use as a set of interdependent and categorical actions, then what law persists in this time? That is the question answered in the depths of the law of Ḥullin, certainly the high point of the entire Halakhic system.

The Halakhah takes up only one component of the larger task of sustaining the life of the holy people in a sanctified manner. Food is prepared for use at home in accord with diverse bodies of Halakhah, scattered among the topical tractates or category formations. Thus we find one set governing taking out of the food what is owing to the priesthood, the poor, or other scheduled castes, and another set concerning the preparation of meat for the Israelite table. The former, while dealing with dietary rules observed in the home, not only in the temple, finds its place in the larger framework of sharing with God the produce of the land. The latter fits well into the present rubric, the consecration of the Israelite household.

The subject of tractate *Ḥullin*, secular food, is the proper modes of killing and dividing the animals used for meat at home. The first four chapters deal with that subject. Most of the rules for slaughtering an animal for God's table apply also to slaughtering one for the Israelite's table. If we control for the fixed differences—the infinitely more elevated level of sanctification that applies to the holy space of the temple and the holy caste of the priests—we can account for the few consequential differences. But the story does not end with the legal narrative that requires beasts for ordinary Israel to be slaughtered and evaluated as to use, as though for use on the altar.

Other food taboos pertinent to preparation of meat meals cover the next eight chapters, in each instance spelling out regulations set forth in the Torah. These cover the law against slaughtering the dam and her young on the same day, the requirement to cover up the blood of the slaughtered beast, the taboo against the sciatic nerve and cooking meat with milk, food uncleanness with special reference to connection, two chapters on what is owing to the priest from the meat of animals slaughtered at home for secular purposes, then the gift of first fleece to the priest, and finally the law of letting the dam go from the nest when one takes the eggs.

Since the main point of the act of slaughter is deliberately to take the life of the living beast, rather than allowing the animal to die of natural causes and only then to use its meat, a category between suitable and unsuitable has to take account of an interstitial case. A suitable act of slaughter kills the beast and attends to its blood. An unsuitable act of slaughter does not. But what about a beast that has not died on its own, but that also has not been slaughtered in the ordinary manner, out of the fullness of life? Such an interstitial case is taken up under the word *terefah* (*ṭěrēpâ*). That word, at Exod 22:30, refers to a beast clawed by a wild animal: "You shall be men consecrated to me; therefore you shall not eat any flesh that is born by beasts in the field; you shall cast it to the dogs." *Ṭěrēpâ* then pertains to carrion, a beast that dies without a proper act of slaughter. Thus Exod 22:30 refers to a beast that has not yet died but that cannot survive. This yields the notion that beasts that bear some imperfection capable of causing death cannot be eaten by Israelites. Hence, both beasts that die on their own, as carrion, and those that are going to die by reason of wounds or imperfections are prohibited as *ṭěrēpâ* beasts.

The governing problematic derives from the premise that the altar and the table compare, belonging to a single continuum of sanctification and conforming to a single set of cogent rules. So the generative issue throughout is, How is the table like the altar? And that draws in its wake the complementary issue: How is it different? Then how the circumstance of the one imposes a different rule from that of the other will demand detailed attention. Since the table compares with the altar, how and where and why is it subject to a different rule from that pertaining to the altar? So the process is the familiar one, that work of comparison first, then contrast, that animates the Mishnah's intellectual program.

The requirements for the two settings exhibit striking differences, as is to be expected. In the temple, priests ordinarily slaughter the beast and are the only ones who can sprinkle the blood on the altar. In the household, any Israelite performs the act of slaughter, and as to the blood, anyone may cover up the blood as well. Temple rites take place in daylight; the counterpart act of slaughter in the household may be done at night, and so on. The main point, however, is not to be missed: any Israelite (here including a Samaritan or an apostate) may perform the act of slaughter, and it may be carried out at any time, day or night. Then how are the two settings comparable? The actual act is the same: with a knife, applied to the throat, drawn across the two organs of the throat, windpipe and gullet (*m. Ḥullin* 2:3). Therefore, a beast is slaughtered for the altar and for the household in exactly the same way. Since that is not the case for killing fowl, the point should not be missed. The rule joining household to altar goes a step further. The act of slaughter for domestic use must be intentional and carried out by man, just as in the case of the altar: "[If] the knife fell and effected the act of slaughter, even if it effected the act of slaughter properly, it is invalid. As it is said, 'And you will slaughter . . . and you will eat' [Deut 12:21]—just as *you* effect the act of slaughter, so do *you* eat." The introduction of the issue of correct intentionality underscores that the altar and the table form a single genus, the operative traits being dictated by the altar.

Just as in the temple, offerings may be presented in behalf of Gentiles, so an Israelite may slaughter a Gentile's beast in behalf of the Gentile. But if the intent is improper, the act is null, just as it would be if the officiating priest declared an improper intentionality in connection with a critical component of the rite, such as tossing the blood with the wrong purpose in mind. So the law (cf. *m. Ḥullin* 2:7) is explicit: "He who slaughters a beast [intending] to toss its blood for the purposes of idolatry and to burn its fat for the purposes of idolatry, lo, this is meat of the sacrifices of corpses." And again, for intentionality in more general terms: "He who slaughters [1] for the sake of mountains, [2] for the sake of valleys, [3] for the sake of seas, [4] for the sake of rivers, [5] for the sake of deserts—his act of slaughter is invalid." As in the temple, so at home, the blood must be collected, not allowed to run out into a stream, and it is then covered with dirt, that is, given burial. On the other hand, slaughtering an unconsecrated beast outside of the temple with the intent of offering up a sacrifice produces carrion. So a clear distinction differentiates slaughtering in the household for its purposes from slaughtering in the temple for its appropriate considerations. But what links the two venues proves equally striking: what renders an animal unfit for the altar invalidates it for the table as well. And conversely, what the altar will not accept the household table cannot receive either. So to state matters simply, when Israel eats meat, it eats the meat of the same classification and character that God consumes at the altar.

Accordingly, beasts are slaughtered for the altar and the domestic table in accord with one and the same protocol, and the critical consideration that pertains to the altar—the attitude of the officiating priest—also pertains to the table: the attitude of the person who carries out or supervises the act of slaughter (as the case requires). But there is a striking difference between the household and the temple. The Halakhah encompasses the Israelite household both in the Holy Land and abroad, and these rules transcend boundaries of space, time, and circumstance. Rules pertaining to vegetables and fruits grown in the land, by contrast, apply only to what is produced in the land; tithes and heave offerings are required only there. So the Halakhah of *Ḥullin* establishes a fundamental distinction between meat and grain and other produce. Preparation of meat, whether for the altar or for the table, is subject to the same rules, which is why those rules extend the sanctity of the altar to the home. Preparation of fruits and vegetables, in which God has a different interest—these are for the priesthood and the poor, not consumed by God at the altar—does not.

The topical program of the Halakhah is in two parts: first what pertains to preparation of meat, covering up the blood, the prohibition of the sciatic nerve, separation of meat from dairy products ("cooking meat in milk"), and the cultic uncleanness of food; second, what involves gifts of meat or animal by-products to the priests. Letting the dam go from the nest when taking the young is placed at the end, because it has no bearing on the altar at all (relating "to unconsecrated birds but not to consecrated ones"). That general uncleanness should enter the picture presents no surprise; the Halakhah takes for granted that Israelites will eat their meat not only in accord with the requirements of the Torah, such as are specified, but also in accord with the rules of cultic cleanness that govern, to begin with, in the temple itself.

What about cultic cleanness in the household? The Halakhah does not state that meat even consumed at home is to be eaten in the state of cultic cleanness as it is in the temple (whether by the altar, whether by the priests), but the exposition at *m. Ḥullin* 9 rests on that premise. The rule we expect to find would state: "The rules of cultic cleanness even for meat eaten at home apply [1] in the Land of Israel but not outside of the Land [where by definition everything suffers from corpse-uncleanness], [2] in the time of the temple and not in the time of the temple, [3] to unconsecrated animals and to Holy Things. It applies [1] to domesticated cattle and to wild beasts, [2] to all parts of the beast, and it does apply [3] to a bird."

But the Halakhah addresses a different matter, which is the comparison and contrast of two categories of uncleanness that affect meat: food uncleanness and carrion. Food contracts uncleanness from various specified sources, such as a corpse or a dead creeping thing. What we have, therefore, is a tertiary exercise in sorting out two sources of uncleanness affecting food, each with its own consequences for the status and handling of said food. Meat untouched by a corpse or dead creeping thing falls into one category, meat classified as unclean, as carrion into another. The consequences of the one kind of uncleanness differ from those of the other. The Halakhah, generated as it is by the labor of hierarchical classification that defines the work of the Mishnah, exhibits a systematic concern for asking how different species of the same genus (two different sources of uncleanness affecting meat) join together or function together to produce the same result—if they do.

The Halakhah everywhere takes for granted that considerations of uncleanness pertain, not only those of suitability (proper slaughter and the like). So the picture is clear and one-sided: the Halakhah makes sense only if its fundamental premise, comparing the altar to the table, extends even to imposing cleanness taboos of the former upon the latter. And that carries us deep into the religious conception of the Halakhah at hand, one that is hardly unfamiliar: the sanctity that encompasses

Israel, which is distinct from the sanctity that permeates the land of Israel, which itself forms a category separate from the sanctity that is embodied in the temple and upward to its altar. Granted, the one is holier than the other. But how do the realms of the holy relate—and interpenetrate? That is what the Halakhah at hand addresses, with the outcome stated at the outset: Israel's sanctity prevails over all circumstance.

The Halakhah states in so many words what it wants to know, which is as observed at the outset: whether (1) the destruction of the temple and cessation of the offerings, (2) the degradation of the land of Israel, and (3) the exile of the holy people, Israel, from the Holy Land—whether these events affect the rules of sustenance in the model of nourishing God in the temple, in the land, among the holy people. The answer is, whatever the condition of the temple and its altar, whatever the source—the Holy Land or unclean Gentile lands—of animals, and whatever the location of Israel, whether in the land or not, one thing persists. The sanctification of Israel, the people, endures (1) in the absence of the cult, (2) in alien and unclean territory, and (3) whatever the source of the food that Israel eats. Israel's sanctity is eternal, noncontingent, absolute. The sanctification that inheres in Israel, the people, transcends the land and outlives the temple and its cult. Since the sanctity of Israel, the people, persists beyond the temple and outside of the land, that sanctity stands at a higher point in the hierarchy of domains of the holy that ascend from earth to heaven and from man to God.

The Halakhah, with its capacity not only for classification but consequently also for hierarchization, does not treat as an all-or-nothing proposition either sanctification or cultic cleanness. That is the advantage of seeing all things as matters of degree, location within a continuum. In the present case, the Halakhah works out in detail the general theory of the gradations of sanctification matched by those of uncleanness. We can understand the Halakhah of *Ḥullin* only within the nurturing context of the general theory of sanctification, spatial (locative), temporal, and circumstantial, involving answers to the questions of where, when, and whom.

Why turn in particular to the Halakhah of *Ḥullin* to make that statement that Israel is holier than the land and than the temple and endows with sanctity the animals slaughtered to nourish the people? Because the Torah supplies a law containing the entire message: it imposes the same requirements that pertain to slaughtering an animal sacrifice for Jerusalem's altar to killing an animal for Israel's use at home. Thus the meat that Israel eats is subject to the same regulations applying to meat that God receives on the altar fires. The same law is explicit that meat for those who are not holy, for Gentile idolaters, is not subject to the same rules (Exod 22:30; Deut 14:21). So the point cannot be missed: food for God and for Israel must be prepared in comparable manner, which does not apply to food for Gentiles.

How does that principle affect animals raised abroad? The laws of *Ḥullin* apply to them, because the laws apply to unconsecrated animals as much as consecrated ones. The destiny—nourishing Israel—is what counts, that alone. The beast intended for Israelite consumption at the table even in a foreign country must be prepared as though for God on the altar in Jerusalem. This can only mean that because the beast is intended (by the act of correct slaughter) for Israel, the use of the beast by

Israel sanctifies the beast and necessitates conformity with the rules of slaughter for God in the temple. Israel, even abroad, renders the food that it eats comparable to food for the altar.

What has food preparation to do with the consideration of location? The rule that permits slaughter of meat outside of the temple (Deut 12:20–24) is explicit: that rule speaks of Israel outside of the temple in Jerusalem. So even if the act of slaughter does not take place in Jerusalem, the act must conform, because the focus is on Israel, wherever Israel is located—even far from Jerusalem, as Scripture states explicitly. The Halakhah before us simply carries to its logical next step that same conception: even so far from Jerusalem as territory that is laden with corpse uncleanness, that is foreign soil; even in an age in which the Jerusalem temple is no more; and even in connection with a beast that has not been consecrated for the altar.

Since Scripture itself has separated the act of slaughter from the rite of sacrifice in the temple, the Halakhah has done little more than explore the consequences of that rule when it states that the requirements of slaughter in the cult pertain also outside of the cult, and thus wherever Israelites are located, and whenever the act takes place—even outside of the land altogether, even during the time that the temple is no longer standing. Since the logic set forth by the Torah at Deut 12:20–24 contains an Israel in the land but outside of Jerusalem, then the next step, and it is not a giant step, is to contemplate an Israel outside of the land altogether, or even a temple in ruins. The integral connection of slaughter of animals and sacrifice at the altar was broken when Deuteronomy focused all cultic activity within Jerusalem. All that the Halakhah has done is to address in so many words the extreme consequences of that situation: if the rules apply even to unconsecrated beasts, even to the land beyond Jerusalem, and even outside of the temple, then by the same token, logic dictates a utopian consequence.

So the Torah in any event set the stage when it took up the situation of slaughter not in behalf of the transaction at the altar and not in the setting of the holy place at all. And consequently, the Halakhah worked out in the critical detail of sustaining life the conviction that Israel the people forms the locus of sanctification. Then all else follows. That is why, as I claim, it is particularly through this repeated formulation and only through these laws in the Halakhah of *Ḥullin*—the repetition of the same formula making certain that one does not miss the point—that sages can have made their statement. That allegation about the enduring, ubiquitous sanctification inherent in Israel the people—even outside of the land, even in the time of the temple's destruction and the altar's disuse—pervades the exposition of the laws in detail. It is an amazing statement in its insistence upon the priority and permanence of that act of sanctification—the sanctity of Israel—whatever may become of the holiness of the altar and of the land!

12

The New Testament's Interpretation

Eucharist as Holy Food, Mimesis of Sacrifice

Bruce D. Chilton

Each act of Eucharist is a mimetic moment, involving ritual gestures, a defined liturgical group, and an agreed field of the meaning of what is done.

By conceiving of the Eucharist within the New Testament in mimetic terms, we can overcome two impediments to understanding that have emerged repeatedly in the critical literature. The first of these has been the tendency to reduce all eucharistic acts to a single origin—usually a heroic, mythologized account of "the Last Supper." The desire to distance criticism from that mythology has produced the second impediment: efforts to locate the genesis of Eucharist apart from Jesus (in the influence of Paul, for example) prevent us from accounting for the generality of the practice within earliest Christianity. Mimesis is sufficiently varied *and* sufficiently general to steer us between Charybdis and Scylla, provided that we absolve Jesus from having to explain *all* Christian practices and that we allow for the mimetic recollection of Jesus as a unifying theme within the varieties of that practice.

Over the past decade, I have developed an account of the evolution of eucharistic practice within Christianity, beginning with the contributions of Jesus as a conscious practitioner of Judaism. My first book that explored this issue engaged explicitly with the work of anthropologists of sacrifice, including René Girard, in order to assess Jesus' position in relation to the sacrificial cult in Jerusalem.[1] When I initially researched the book, the Eucharist was not foremost on my mind. My principal concern was to evaluate Jesus' attitudes toward the temple and his actions within the temple itself. But in the course of that work, I saw the direct connection between Jesus' last meals with his followers and his action in the temple. The Eucharist emerged as a mimetic surrogate of sacrifice. Encouraged by several scholars, notably Bernhard Lang, I then undertook a strictly exegetical study[2] to detail the evolution of the texts within the typical practices of the first Christians.

Here I wish briefly to explain the six types of Eucharist attested within the New Testament, as I have identified them on exegetical grounds. These types are mimetic moments characterizing the particular groups that produced them. In the way of mimesis, the types attest fluidity in their ritual acts, their constituent communities, and their accounts of meaning. Even Jesus, in my reading, developed not just one but actually two types of Eucharist during his life. At the end of this chapter, I wish to return to a theoretical question, in order to be more precise about the moment Eucharist emerged as a mimetic surrogate of sacrifice within Jesus' practice: that appears to have been the moment generative of the subsequent types, and therefore of Christianity's emergence as a religion separate from Judaism. In the sense of recent sociological discussion, I will suggest that at this generative moment, Jesus' practice may usefully be said to have been magical.

Six Types of Eucharist in the New Testament

The Mishnah, in an effort to conceive of a heinous defect on the part of a priest involved in slaughtering the red heifer, pictures him as intending to eat the flesh or drink the blood (*m. Parah* 4:3). Because people had no share of blood, which belonged uniquely to God, even the thought of drinking it was blasphemous. To imagine drinking human blood, consumed with human flesh, could only make the blasphemy worse. So if Jesus' words are taken with their traditional, autobiographical meaning, his Last Supper can only be understood as a deliberate break from Judaism. Either Jesus himself promulgated a new religion, or his followers did so in his name and invented "the Last Supper" themselves. Both those alternatives find adherents today among scholars, and the debate between those who see the Gospels as literally true reports and those who see them as literary fictions shows little sign of making progress. But in either case, the nagging question remains: if the generative act was indeed antisacrificial (whether that act was literal or literary), how did the cycles of traditions and the texts as they stand come to their present, sacrificial constructions?

There is another, more critical way of understanding how the Eucharist emerged in earliest Christianity, an approach taking account of the cultural changes that the development of the movement involved and allowing for the consistent concern for effective sacrifice across the cultures involved. Interest in the social world of early Judaism, and interest in how Christianity as a social movement emerged within Judaism and then became distinct from it within the Hellenistic world—all this has been growing for a hundred years.

We are no longer limited to the old dichotomy between the "conservative" position that the Gospels are literal reports and the "liberal" position that they are literary fictions. Critical study has revealed that the Gospels are composite products of the various social groups that were part of Jesus' movement from its days within Judaism to the emergence of Christianity as a distinct religion. When we place eucharistic practices within the social constituencies that made the Gospels into the texts we can read today, we can understand the original meaning Jesus gave to the Last Supper and how his meaning generated other meanings.

First Type: Sanctification of the Kingdom

The Last Supper was not the only supper, just the last one. In fact, "the Last Supper" would have had no meaning apart from Jesus' well-established custom of eating with people socially. There was nothing unusual about a rabbi making social eating an instrument of his instruction, and it was part of Jesus' method from the first days of his movement in Galilee.

Meals within Judaism were regular expressions of social solidarity and of common identity as the people of God. Many sorts of meals are attested in the literature of early Judaism. From Qumran we learn of banquets at which the community convened in order of hierarchy; from the Pharisees we learn of collegial meals shared within fellowships (*chaburoth*, *ḥăbûrôt*), at which like-minded fellows would share the foods and the company they considered pure. Ordinary households might welcome the coming of the Sabbath with a prayer of sanctification (*kiddush*, *qiddûš*) over a cup of wine, or open a family occasion with a blessing (*berakhah*, *běrākâ*) over bread and wine.

Jesus' meals were similar in some ways to several of these meals, but they were also distinctive. He had a characteristic understanding of what the meals meant and of who should participate in them. For him, eating socially with others in Israel was an enacted parable of the feast in the kingdom that was to come. The idea that God would offer festivity for all peoples on his holy mountain (Isa 2:2–4) was a key feature in the fervent expectations of Judaism during the first century, and Jesus shared that hope, as may be seen in a saying from the source of his teaching conventionally known as Q (Matt 8:11 = Luke 13:28–29):[3]

> Many shall come from east and west,
> and feast with Abraham, Isaac, and Jacob
> in the kingdom of God.

Eating was a way of enacting the kingdom of God, of practicing the generous rule of the divine king. As a result, Jesus adamantly accepted as companions people such as tax agents and others of suspect purity, and he received notorious sinners at table. The meal for him was a sign of the kingdom of God, and all the people of God, assuming they sought forgiveness, were to have access to it.

Jesus' practice of fellowship at meals caused opposition from those whose understanding of Israel was exclusive. To them, he seemed profligate, willing to eat and drink with anyone, as Jesus himself was pictured as observing in a famous saying also from Q (Matt 11:19 = Luke 7:34):[4]

> A man came eating and drinking, and they complain:
> Look, a glutton and drunkard,
> a fellow of tax agents and sinners.

Some of Jesus' opponents saw the purity of Israel as something that could only be guarded by separating from others, as in the meals of their fellowships (*ḥăbûrôt*).

Jesus' view of purity was different. He held that a son or daughter of Israel, by virtue of being *of Israel*, could approach his table or even worship in the temple. Where necessary, repentance beforehand could be demanded, and Jesus taught his followers to pray for forgiveness daily, but his understanding was that Israelites as such were pure and were fit to offer purely of their own within the sacrificial worship of Israel.

As long as Jesus' activity was limited to Galilee, he was involved in active disputes, but essentially inconsequential ones. (Slightly deviant rabbis in Galilee were far from uncommon.) To some extent, Jesus' practice coincided with that of a *ḥăbûrâ*, although his construal of purity was unusual. Given the prominence accorded wine in his meals,[5] we might describe the first type of his meals—the practice of purity in anticipation of the kingdom—as a *Kiddush* ("sanctification") of the kingdom. Indeed, there is practically no meal of Judaism with which Jesus' meals do not offer some sort of analogy, because the meal was a seal and an occasion of purity, and Jesus was concerned with what was pure. But both the nature of his concern and the character of his meals were distinctive in their inclusiveness: Israel as forgiven and willing to provide of its own produce was for him the occasion of the kingdom. That was the first type in the development of the Eucharist.

Second Type: Mimetic Surrogate of Sacrifice

Jesus also brought his teaching into the temple, where he insisted on his own teaching (or *hălākâ*) of purity. The incident that reflects the resulting dispute is usually called the Cleansing of the Temple (Matt 21:12-13 = Mark 11:15-17 = Luke 19:45-46 = John 2:13-17). From the point of view of the authorities there, what Jesus was after was the opposite of cleansing. He objected to the presence of merchants, who had been given permission to sell sacrificial animals in the vast, outer court of the temple. His objection was based on his own, peasant's view of purity:[6] Israel should offer, not priest's produce for which they handed over money, but their own sacrifices that they brought into the temple. He believed so vehemently what he taught that he and his followers drove the animals and the sellers out of the great court, no doubt with the use of force.

Jesus' interference in the ordinary worship of the temple might have been sufficient by itself to bring about his execution. After all, the temple was the center of Judaism for as long as it stood. Roman officials were so interested in its smooth functioning at the hands of the priests whom they appointed that they were known to sanction the penalty of death for sacrilege. Yet there is no indication that Jesus was immediately arrested. Instead, he remained at liberty for some time and was finally taken into custody just after one of his meals, "the Last Supper." The decision of the authorities of the temple to move against Jesus when they did is what made this supper his last.

Why did the authorities wait, and why did they act when they did? The Gospels portray them as fearful of the popular backing that Jesus enjoyed, and his simultaneously inclusive and apocalyptic teaching of purity probably did bring enthusiastic followers into the temple with him. But in addition, there was another factor: Jesus could not simply be dispatched as a cultic criminal. He was not attempting an onslaught upon the temple as such; his dispute with the authorities concerned purity within the temple. Other rabbis of his period also engaged in physical demonstrations of the purity they required in the conduct of worship. One of them, for example, is said once to have driven thousands of sheep into the temple, so that people could offer sacrifice in the manner he approved (see *b. Beṣah* 20a–b). Jesus' action was extreme, but not totally without precedent, even in the use of force.

The delay of the authorities, then, was understandable. We may also say that it was commendable, reflecting continued controversy over the merits of Jesus' teaching and whether his occupation of the great court should be condemned out of hand. But why did they finally arrest Jesus? The texts of the Last Supper provide the key; something about Jesus' meals after his occupation of the temple caused Judas to inform on Jesus. Of course, "Judas" is the only name that the traditions of the New Testament have left us. We cannot say who or how many of the disciples became disaffected by Jesus' behavior after his occupation of the temple.

However they learned of Jesus' new interpretation of his meals of fellowship, the authorities arrested him just after the supper we call last. Jesus continued to celebrate fellowship at table as a foretaste of the kingdom, just as he had before. But he also added a new and scandalous dimension of meaning. His occupation of the temple having failed, Jesus said of the wine, "This is my blood," and of the bread, "This is my flesh" (Matt 26:26, 28 = Mark 14:22, 24 = Luke 22:19–20 = 1 Cor 11:24–25 = Justin, *1 Apol.* 66.3).

In Jesus' context, the context of his confrontation with the authorities of the temple, his words had one predominant meaning. He did not mean to say, "Here are my personal body and blood"; that interpretation only makes sense at a later stage. Jesus' principal point was rather that, in the absence of a temple that permitted his view of purity to be practiced, wine was his blood of sacrifice, and bread was his flesh of sacrifice. In Aramaic, "blood" and "flesh" (which may also be rendered as "body") can carry such a sacrificial meaning, and in Jesus' context, that is the most natural meaning. The meaning of the Last Supper, then, actually evolved over a series of meals after Jesus' occupation of the temple. During that period, Jesus claimed that wine and bread were a better sacrifice than what was offered in the temple: at least wine and bread were Israel's own, not tokens of priestly dominance.

No wonder the opposition to him, even among the Twelve (in the shape of Judas, according to the Gospels), became deadly. In essence, Jesus made his meals into a rival altar; we may call such a reading of his words a ritual or cultic interpretation. This second type of Eucharist offered wine and bread as a mimetic surrogate of sacrifice.

The cultic interpretation has two advantages over the traditional, autobiographical interpretation as the meaning Jesus attributed to his own final meals. The first advantage is contextual: the cultic interpretation places Jesus firmly with the Judaism of his period and the final dispute of his life and at the same time accounts for the opposition of the authorities to him. The second advantage is the explanatory power of this reading: the cultic interpretation enables us to explain

136   *Dietary Purity*

sequentially four later developments in the understanding of Eucharist within early Christianity.

Third Type: The Blessing of Bread at Home

The third type is that of Petrine Christianity, when the blessing of bread at home, the *berakhah* (*běrākâ*) of Judaism, became a principal model of Eucharist. A practical result of that development was that bread came to have precedence over wine, and Acts refers to the ritual as the "breaking" of bread (2:42–47). More profoundly, the circle of Peter conceived of Jesus as a new Moses, who gave commands concerning purity as Moses did on Sinai, and who also expected his followers to worship on Mount Zion. As compared to Jesus' practice (in its first and second stages), Petrine practice represents a double domestication. First, adherents of the movement congregated in the homes of their colleagues rather than seeking the hospitality of others. Second, the validity of sacrifice in the temple was acknowledged. Both forms of domestication grew out of the new circumstances of the movement in Jerusalem and fresh opportunities for worship in the temple; they changed the nature of the meal and the memory of what Jesus had said at the "Last Supper." The application of the model of a *berakhah* to Eucharist was a self-conscious metaphor, because the careful identification of those gathered in Jesus' name with a household was itself metaphorical.

Fourth Type: Eucharist as a Seder

The fourth type of Eucharist, the contribution of the circle of James, pursued the tendency of domestication further. The Eucharist was seen as a Seder (*sēder*, order), in terms of its meaning and its chronology (Mark 14:12–16, and the contradictory timing of 14:1–2). So understood, only Jews in a state of purity could participate fully in Eucharist, which could be truly recollected only once a year, at Passover in Jerusalem among the circumcised (so Exod 12:48; Deut 16:6). The Quartodeciman controversy (concerning the timing of Easter) of a later period, fierce though it appears, was but a shadow cast by a much more serious contention concerning the nature of Christianity. The Jacobean program was to integrate Jesus' movement fully within the liturgical institutions of Judaism, to insist upon the Judaic identity of the movement and upon Jerusalem as its governing center. Nonetheless, there is never any doubt but that Eucharist is not portrayed as a literal replacement of all the Seders of Israel, and the Jacobean "Last Supper" does not supplant the other types of Eucharist in the New Testament. For those reasons, the language of metaphor is appropriate here, as well as at the Petrine stage, in order to convey the type of mimetic activity involved.

Fifth Type: Eucharist as a Sacrifice for Sin

Paul and the Synoptic Gospels represent the fifth type of Eucharist. Paul vehemently resists Jacobean claims by insisting that Jesus' last meal occurred on the night in which he was betrayed (1 Cor 11:23), not on Passover. He emphasizes the link between Jesus' death and the Eucharist, and he accepts the Hellenistic refinement of the Petrine type that presented the Eucharist as a sacrifice for sin associated with the temple (see, e.g., Rom 3:25).

In the Synoptic Gospels, the heroism of Jesus is such that the meal is an occasion to join in the solidarity of martyrdom.[7] By various wordings the Synoptics insist that Jesus' blood is shed in the interests of their communities in the cities in which which those Gospels were probably composed, for the "many" in Damascus (Matt 26:28) and Rome (Mark 14:24), on behalf of "you" in Antioch (Luke 22:20). The Synoptic strategy is not to oppose the Jacobean program directly; in fact, the Passover chronology is incorporated (producing internal contradictions). But any limitation of the benefits of Eucharist to circumcised Israelites is superseded by the mimetic imperative to join Jesus' martyrdom and its sacrificial benefits.

Sixth Type: Eucharist as Sacrament

The Synoptic tradition also provides two stories of miraculous feeding—of five thousand and of four thousand—which symbolized the inclusion of Jews and non-Jews within Eucharist, understood as in the nature of a philosophical symposium (Mark 6:32–44; 8:1–10; and parallels). This willingness to explore differing meanings within Eucharistic action attests that any such meaning, taken individually, was understood metaphorically, and that it was reproduced mimetically.

The feeding of the five thousand—understood as occurring at Passover—is taken up in John 6 in a fully Paschal sense. Jesus identified himself as the *manna*, miraculous food bestowed by God upon his people. The motif was already articulated by Paul (1 Cor 10:1–4), but John develops it to construe the Eucharist as a mystery, in which Jesus offers his own flesh and blood (carefully defined to avoid a crude misunderstanding; John 6:30–58, 61–65). That autobiographical reading of Jesus' words—as giving his personal body and blood in Eucharist—had no doubt already occurred to Hellenistic Christians who followed Synoptic practice and appreciated its sacrificial overtones.

The Johannine practice made that meaning as explicit as the break with Judaism is in the Fourth Gospel. Both that departure and the identification of Jesus himself (rather than his supper) as the Paschal Lamb are pursued in the book of Revelation (5:6–14; 7:13–17). This sixth type of Eucharist can only be understood as a consciously non-Judaic and Hellenistic development. It involves participants in joining by oath (Latin *sacramentum*, corresponding to the Greek *mystērion* of primitive Christianity;[8] Matt 13:11; Mark 4:11; Luke 8:10; cf. John 6:60–71) in the sacrifice of the mysterious hero himself, separating themselves from others. Eucharist has become sacrament and involves a knowing conflict with the ordinary understanding of what Judaism might and might not include, as well as an amendment of Jesus, teaching in regard to oaths (Matt 5:33–37; 23:16–22; James 5:12).[9]

The Last Supper is thus neither simply Jesus' "real" Seder nor simply a symposium of Hellenists to which the name of Jesus happens to have been attached.

138   *Dietary Purity*

Such reductionist interpretations, which will have the Gospels be only historical or only fictive, starve the reader of the meanings that generated the texts at hand. The engines of those meanings were diverse practices, whose discovery permits us to feast on the richness of tradition. A generative exegesis of eucharistic texts may not conclude with a single meaning that is alleged to have occasioned all the others. One of the principal findings of such an approach is rather that meaning itself is to some extent epiphenomenal, a consequence of a definable practice with its own initial sense being introduced into a fresh environment of people who, in turn, take up the practice as they understand it and produce their own meanings. The sense with which a practice is mediated to a community is therefore one measure of what that community will finally produce as its practice, but the initial meaning does not determine the final meaning.

The meanings conveyed by words must be the point of departure for a generative exegesis, because those meanings are our only access to what produced the texts at hand. But having gained that access, it becomes evident that Eucharist is not a matter of the development of a single, basic meaning within several different environments. Those environments have themselves produced various meanings under the influence of definable practices. Eucharist was not simply handed on as a tradition. Eucharistic traditions were rather the catalyst that permitted communities to crystallize their own practice in oral or textual form. What they crystallized was a function of the practice that had been learned, palpable gestures with specified objects and previous meanings, along with the meanings and the emotional responses that the community discovered in Eucharist. There is no history of the tradition apart from a history of meaning, a history of emotional response, a history of practice: the practical result of a generative exegesis of eucharistic texts is that practice itself is an appropriate focus in understanding the New Testament.

The Moment of Magical Surrogacy

The cultic sense of Jesus' last meals with his disciples is the generative moment that permits us to explain its later meanings as eucharistic covenant, Passover, heroic symposium, and mystery. These four types of Eucharist, developed within distinct circles of practice and belief within the primitive church, evolved from the initial two types, eschatological banquet and surrogate of sacrifice, which Jesus developed. In that evolution, Jesus' insistence on the mimetic surrogacy of his meals is evidently the key element. If Jesus is seen as generating Eucharist as a surrogate of sacrifice, a question emerges: Why did he undertake such an action, with such an understanding? In terms of circumstances at the time, his failed occupation of the temple provides an adequate occasion, but not a sufficient cause from the point of view of later developments. How did the framing of a meal as a mimetic surrogate of sacrifice lead to the emergence of a new sacrament in a religious system distinct from Judaism?

Since the work of Morton Smith, the identification of Jesus as a magician has featured in the critical literature.[10] Ralph Schroeder has made an especially interesting contribution from this point of view by actively criticizing the work of Max Weber.[11] Schroeder explains:

> The most undifferentiated form of magic, in Weber's view, is where magical power is thought to be embodied in a person who can bring about supernatural events by virtue of an innate capacity. This belief is the original source of charisma. "The oldest of all 'callings'" or professions, Weber points out, "is that of the magician" (1981a:8). From this point, charisma develops by a process of abstraction towards the notion that certain forces are "behind" this extraordinary power—although they remain within the world (1968:401).[12]

Schroeder complains that Weber's perspective leads to an analysis of magic as static, while from a sociological perspective religion is notable for its capacity to change and to cause change.[13] What Schroeder does not say, and yet may easily be inferred from his study, is that magic should not be seen as the changeless foundation of religion, but as a specific manifestation of religion, when the entire system is held to be concentrated in an individual or individuals. Magic expresses more the crisis of a system than the presupposition of a system. For precisely that reason, magicians are easily seen as threats, because they embody crisis, and are typically blamed for crises (see Acts 8:9, 11; 13:6, 8; 19:19). But in invoking miracle to combat magic, Christianity reveals its properly magical origins.

Such a description accords well with some of the figures whom Josephus calls false prophets. There has been a tendency to class John the Baptist with these leaders, whom their followers presumably called prophets. In fact, Josephus simply calls John a good man (*Antiquities* 18.5.2 §117) and describes Bannus's similar commitment to sanctification by bathing him in approving terms (*Life* §11). Nothing they did (as related by Josephus) can be compared with what Josephus said the false prophets did: One scaled Mount Gerizim to find the vessels deposited by Moses (*Ant.* 18 §§85–87); Theudas waited at the Jordan for the waters to part for him, as they had for Joshua (20 §§97–98);[14] the Egyptian marched from the Mount of Olives in the hope that the walls of Jerusalem might fall at his command (20 §§169–172) so that he could conquer Jerusalem (*Jewish War* 2 §261–263). If there is an act in the Gospels that approximates such fanaticism, it is Jesus' entry into Jerusalem and his occupation of the temple. Against all the odds, he apparently expected to prevail in insisting upon his own understanding of what true purity at the temple was, in opposition to Caiaphas himself, despite the imposing authority of a high priest sanctioned by Rome. When Jesus is styled a "prophet" in Matt 21:11, 46, that may have something to do with the usage of Josephus, but to portray John the Baptist in such terms is less apposite.

These acts of magic are not spontaneous or heroic foundations of new religions by means of Weberian charisma. Rather, each instantiates a response to a sense of crisis, the conviction that the entire religious system has gone wrong and may only be retrieved by a magician who takes that system onto himself. Finding Moses' vessels, parting the Jordan, taking Jerusalem, occupying the temple—these are all examples of the attempt to right the system by seizing and manipulating its most central symbols. They are instances of magic as theurgy, the access of divine power in order to change and mold the ordinary structures of authority, whether social or natural.

Seen in this light, Jesus' mimetic surrogacy of sacrifice, as well as his occupation of the temple, represents a distillation of principal elements of his own religious system into his actions and his person. Raw materials of Christology, as well as of eucharistic theology, were generated by this deliberate—and in Schroeder's terms magical—concentration. But the directions of those streams were no more determined by their source than a thunderstorm can be thought to guide a river in the twists and turns of its environment. In the manner of a magician, Jesus concentrated the sacrificial ideology of Israel in his own meals with his disciples—and released forces whose results he could scarcely have calculated.

PART FIVE

Sexual Purity

13

Scripture's Account

Sexual Purity

Baruch A. Levine

Sexual purity is an aspect of the general category of purity, a subject that is introduced in the chapter entitled "Dietary Purity." The societies of the ancient Near East, like all others, showed intense concern for the continuity and stability of the group, at a time when its very survival over generations could be in doubt, and when fertility was less potent than in modern times. Life expectancy was shorter, and the childbearing years of women were more limited than in our own day. Infant mortality was at a high rate, and poor nutrition was widespread

Throughout history, the primary vehicle of group continuity has been the family, nuclear, extended, or otherwise composed. As a consequence, sexual behavior has been carefully channeled, controlled, and monitored by law and custom, so as to assure the organic structure of the family. Since it was the family (or the clan) that served as the basic economic unit, laws governing inheritance and ownership were aimed at retaining operative control of the group's assets, primarily its land. This concern impacted the legitimacy of children, especially sons born to the family, who were normally the heirs. Such sociological observations are particularly relevant to the ethos of ancient Israelite society, given the overbearing emphasis on "seed," on future descendants, that informed the biblical mentality (Gen 15:5 et passim; Lev 18:21; etc.).

Ancient peoples developed special ways of expressing their deep anxiety over sexuality, and their fear of losing fertility as a consequence of sins or offenses against divine powers, in the present case, against the God of Israel. However, even in the monotheistic outlook of Israelite religion, there was place for demonic forces that attack humans and rob them of their potency, or take the lives of their infants. In ancient Israel, as in many other cultures, sexual misconduct was conceptualized as impurity and defilement, and both magical and ritual acts were undertaken so as to avert its ill effects. These acts were institutionalized as purification, preventive and corrective; they were intended both to ward off potential threats to purity in advance and to attain and subsequently maintain purity. As a category, impurity resulted both from guilt-ridden acts, such as incest, as well as from natural conditions, such as menstruation and parturition in females, that did not involve impropriety or guilt but were nonetheless believed to be fraught with danger. Declaring such conditions impure assured that they would receive the full attention of the priesthood and the community.

Still another factor in understanding the regulation of sexual purity in biblical Israel is the fact that ancient peoples knew much less than we do about human reproduction. They did not know, for instance, that mature females contribute eggs, which are fertilized by male sperm, to produce the embryo. In their view, the womb served only as a nurturing receptacle for the growth of the embryo, which was solely the product of male sperm. They did not fully understand the physiology of ovulation and were apprehensive over the periodic discharge of menstrual blood. The sanguinity of parturition only intensified the expected fears over what is in fact a critical juncture in the reproductive process, so that childbirth called for specific rites of purification.

We may also infer that ancient peoples may not have understood that human cells reproduce themselves. They may have thought that each adult male possessed a fixed amount of sperm, which if wasted through masturbation or otherwise unproductive sexual activity, would limit his fertility or terminate it altogether. In brief, whenever blood issued naturally from the female body, or semen from the male body, there was need for purification of some sort, ranging from simple bathing to the performance of expiatory sacrifices. To all of the above may be added an intense fear of contagion, so that some health conditions were thought to be contagious even though they were not actually so.

Against this background, several categories of sexual purity operative in biblical religion can be investigated.

Incest

The principal Torah statement on incest is found in Lev 18, more precisely in 18:6–18:

No one (of you) shall be intimate with any of his "flesh" relatives by uncovering nakedness [= by having sexual intercourse]; I am Yahweh.

You shall not uncover the nakedness [that is exclusively] your father's, that is, your mother's nakedness. She is your mother; you must not uncover her nakedness. You shall not uncover the nakedness of your father's wife; that nakedness is [exclusively] your father's.

The nakedness of your sister, whether the daughter of your father, or the daughter of your mother, [namely,] whether born into the household or born outside it—you shall not uncover their nakedness.

The nakedness of your son's daughter, or of your daughter's daughter—you shall not uncover their nakedness, for they were born of your nakedness.

The nakedness of the daughter of your father's wife, who was born into your father's household—as she is your sister, you shall not uncover her nakedness.

The nakedness of your father's sister you shall not uncover. She is your father's "flesh" relative. You shall not uncover the nakedness of your mother's sister, for she is your mother's "flesh" relative. You shall not uncover the nakedness [exclusive] to your father's brother, [which is to say,] you shall not be intimate with his wife. She is your aunt.

You shall not uncover the nakedness of your daughter-in-law. She is your son's wife; do not uncover her nakedness. The nakedness of your brother's wife you shall not uncover; that nakedness is [exclusively] your brother's.

The nakedness of (both) a woman and her daughter you shall not uncover, nor shall you marry her son's daughter or her daughter's daughter, uncovering her nakedness. They are her [flesh] relatives; it is depravity. Do not marry a woman as a rival to her own sister and uncover her nakedness during the other's lifetime.

With few exceptions, which will be duly noted, incest regulations, as well as other aspects of sexual behavior, are addressed to the Israelite man, the progenitor, who marries and sets about creating a family. He is the starting point of legislation and the person primarily responsible for adhering to the law, although women who participate in sexual offenses also incurred punishment. Incest restrictions effectively define the immediate family, on the principle that it is unnatural for a man to marry a close female relative. Hence appears the need to specify those who are close relatives, and to differentiate between them and clan relatives, members of the same *mišpāḥâ*, who actually were desirable mates (see further). Defining family relationships is potentially more complex where polygamous marriage was practiced, such as in biblical Israel, because each wife would bring into the family additional women who would become relatives of the progenitor.

Two Hebrew terms of reference are central to defining who belongs to the immediate family: *šĕʾēr* (literally, "flesh"), a family relation whom we might call consanguineous (related by blood). This status contrasts with that of an affinal relative who married into the family, such as one's wife. In the context of the ban on priestly defilement, Lev 21:2–3 lists six *šĕʾēr* relations as exceptions to the ban: one's mother and father, one's son and daughter and brother and unmarried sister. Ezekiel 44:25 contains a similar list, whereas to the category of "flesh" relatives, Lev 18:12–13 adds the sister of one's father or mother. Understandably, only females are relevant regarding prohibited sexual unions, which is the subject of Lev 18.

A second term, one of fluid meaning, is Hebrew *ʿerwâ*, literally "nakedness," a euphemism for sexual intercourse. It typically occurs in the formula *gillâ ʿerwâ*, "to uncover nakedness." At times, however, this same term is best understood as connoting exclusive sexual access. Thus the statement "that is, your father's nakedness," explaining the prohibition of intercourse with one's own mother, does not refer to the father's "nakedness," but rather to his exclusive access to his wife's nakedness.

In effect, marriage with a female relative is deemed incestuous for either of two reasons: (1) It is incestuous because of the woman's direct relationship to the male progenitor (as in the case of his sister), or because the woman in question was in a "flesh" relationship with another member of the inner circle (as in the case of one's mother's sister). In two statements, the code of law goes beyond the family to extend the circle of incest. Thus, a man may not marry his wife's sister during his wife's lifetime, because of the sisters' preexisting closeness to each other, which would induce rivalry. Similarly, one may not marry both a woman and her daughter, or granddaughter, because of their preexisting closeness to each other. (2) Marriage is incestuous because the "nakedness" of the woman taken in marriage: her sexuality was reserved exclusively for another of the progenitor's *šĕʾēr* relatives (as in the case of one's father's wife, his stepmother).

Leviticus 20 parallels Lev 18 in its overall content but is formulated casuistically. It employs different terminology and specifies penalties, often capital punishment, in the manner of a code of law. Deuteronomy 23:1 prohibits marriage with one's father's wife, his stepmother. Within a series of execrations, Deut 27:20–23 condemns anyone who has sexual intercourse with certain relatives, specifically, his father's wife; his sister, born of his father or mother; and his mother-in-law. Once again, different terminology is employed. Deuteronomy 25:5–10 introduces an exception to the ban on marriage with one's brother's wife. In cases where a man died and left no son to carry on his name, the brother-in-law in question, called *yābām* (Latin *levir*), is obligated to take his *yebāmâ*, "brother's wife," as his own. This is known as levirate marriage. If he refuses, he must release his sister-in-law by undergoing a humiliating ceremony. In different ways, this theme underlies the narratives of the book of Ruth and of Gen 38, the tale of Judah and Tamar, his daughter-in-law (see further). Together these narratives dramatize the ill effects of failure to carry on the family name. The custom of levirate marriage illustrates how the urge to preserve the family over generations may at times override the anathema of incest.

Other information provided by the Hebrew Bible diverges from the structured regulations just surveyed. All Torah sources specifically prohibit marriage with half-sisters (Lev 18:9; 20:17; Deut 27:22), and yet 2 Sam 13:13 has Tamar saying to her half brother, Amnon, about to rape her, that David, their common father, would not have denied her to him as a wife. In Gen 20:12, Abram insists that his wife, Sarai, was, in fact, his half sister. In both cases, we are dealing with children of the same father. Furthermore, both Lev 18:12–14 and 20:19–20 prohibit marriage with any of a man's three possible aunts, and yet Amram, father of Moses and Aaron, married Yochebed, his aunt (Exod 6:20), as is recorded in a priestly genealogy. A glaring discrepancy is provided by Gen 29:21–30, which relate that Jacob married two sisters, Leah and Rachel, thereby contradicting Lev 18:18, which prohibits this practice. We observe that no Torah legislation forbids marriage with cousins of the patrilineal clan; in fact, such marriages were encouraged, and some important cases are recorded (e.g., Rebecca to Isaac in Gen 22–23; 24:24; Rehoboam to his cousin Maachah in 2 Chr 11:20). Similarly, we find no prohibition of marriage to one's nieces, and yet Gen 11:29 records that Abram's brother Nahor married Milcah, his brother Haran's daughter. In light of these indications, it is safe to conclude that customs varied over time and within different tribes and clans, but that as a rule, endogamy within the clan was meritorious, undoubtedly because it preserved the patrilineal chain of inheritance. Thus, the daughters of Zelophehad, a man who died without leaving sons, would inherit their father's land only if they married within their father's clan (Num 36).

Leviticus 18, speaking for the priestly tradition, characterizes incest as impurity (expressed by forms of Heb. *ṭāmēʾ*, "to be impure") and as "abomination" (Heb. *tôʿēbâ*). Thus Lev 18:24:

> Do not render yourselves impure [*tiṭṭammĕʾû*] by means of all of the above, for by means of all of these had all of the nations whom I am driving away before you become impure [*niṭmĕʾû*]. (cf. Lev 18:30)

Some have suggested, although never demonstrated conclusively, that Hebrew *tôʿēbâ* derives from an Egyptian verb *wᶜbw*, "to purify," and reflects the semantic phenomenon of "opposition formation," whereby a verb or other lexeme comes to express an opposite meaning through usage. In the present case, what in the pagan Egyptian religion constituted purification would, in Israelite monotheism, connote defilement.

In the verses that follow, it is explained that Israel's right to the promised land is contingent on avoidance of such severe sexual immorality. Elsewhere, partaking of forbidden foods and pagan worship are also classified as *tôʿēbâ* (cf. Deut 12). There is logic to this triple classification, because all three kinds of offenses were perceived, whether correctly or not, as characteristic of the former inhabitants of the promised land, the Canaanites, or variously of the Egyptians. A people must avoid such practices if it is to attain and retain purity

It is somewhat surprising that the Torah codes do not define the status of children born out of incest, or from adultery and harlotry, as we shall see presently. Deuteronomy 23:3 excludes a *mamzēr*, "bastard," or his direct descendants from marrying within the community (Heb. *qāhāl*) of Israel. One would assume that children born of incest and adultery would be so classified, as rabbinic tradition ordains (*m. Qiddušin* 3:12). The status of children born of harlotry is more difficult to define because harlotry, itself, is less clearly defined in legal terms.

Adultery, Harlotry, Rape, and the Importance of Virginity

The best-known biblical prohibition against adultery is stated apodictically in both versions of the Decalogue: "You shall not commit adultery [*lōʾ tinʾāp*]" (Exod 20:13; Deut 5:17). This prohibition immediately follows the commandment against murder. The Decalogue proceeds to admonish every Israelite against coveting his neighbor's wife, or anything else that belongs to his neighbor (Exod 20:14; Deut 5:18). It is reasonable to expect that adultery will result from covetousness, and this is precisely what developed in the adulterous relationship between David and Bathsheba (2 Sam 11–12.), which led to tragedy. Biblical redactors never allowed the reader to forget this lapse on David's part (1 King 15:5; Ps 51:2). Deuteronomy 22:22 states the matter casuistically:

> If a man is found lying with a woman married to another man [literally, "mated to a husband"], both of them shall meet death; the man who lies with the woman, as well as the woman. Thus shall you drive out evil from Israel.

The priestly tradition preserves both formulations:

> Do not inseminate the wife of your fellow citizen and become impure through her. (Lev 18:20)
> Any man who commits adultery with a married woman, who commits adultery with his neighbor's wife, shall surely be put to death—both the adulterer and the adulteress. (Lev 20:10)

Conforming to the priestly reformulation of law, adultery is classified as impurity in Leviticus, whereas Deuteronomy calls adultery "evil." In biblical law, it is the status of the female partner that consistently determines whether or not a sexual relationship is adulterous or otherwise improper. It is adulterous whenever the female partner is married, whether or not the male partner is married, a disparity that generates a double standard. A married man is effectively free to engage in extramarital sex with certain responsibilities imposed, whereas a married woman is most definitely not free to do so. The legal status of a woman in biblical society was restricted; she was under the legal control of a man most of the time, either her father (or brothers), or subsequently her husband. Divorce or widowhood usually brought a woman back to her family or made a welfare case of her. It is important, therefore, to clarify who was regarded as a married woman, legally speaking.

In ancient Israel, marriage involved two sequential stages: (1) Betrothal, a status often conveyed by forms of the verb ʾēraś, "to request in marriage," with a betrothed woman designated as mĕʾōrāśâ, "pledged, promised, spoken for" (cf. Deut 20:7); and (2) the "taking" (the verb lāqaḥ) of the woman in final marriage. Betrothal constituted quasi-marriage, so that once pledged, a woman was forbidden to have sexual intercourse with any other man in the interim, just as if she were finally married. As for her relations with her fiancé, custom varied, in some instances allowing a one-time consummation at the time of betrothal, but most often putting the young woman in limbo, sexually speaking, until final marriage. Thus, according to Deut 22:23–24, consensual sex between a man and a young woman pledged to another is regarded as adulterous and brings the death penalty for both partners. Deuteronomy refers to that act as the violation of "the wife of one's neighbor." However, if a woman in the same interim status is raped, only the man is to be condemned to death. The pledged woman (or married woman, a fortiori), was a helpless victim.

For its part, the priestly source addresses the interim situation in Lev 19:20–22:

> If a man lies with a woman thereby inseminating [her—one who is] a slave woman assigned in advance to another man, but who has not been redeemed or given her freedom, there shall be an indemnity. They shall not be put to death because she had not been manumitted.

This stipulation is to be understood against the background of Exod 21:7–11, referring to the practice of selling one's daughter into slavery to another Israelite while she was prepubescent. When the girl reached marriageable age, her master, though not permitted to sell her to a non-Israelite, could sell her to another Israelite, who would redeem her by paying an indemnity and then take her as wife. Our passage addresses the time span between pledging and indemnification, when still another man had sexual intercourse with the young woman. We are told that this act would not qualify as adultery because the young woman's marriage had not yet been finalized by payment.

It would be of interest to refer to another interim situation, that of a woman awaiting a levirate union, as in the case of Judah's daughter-in-law, Tamar (Gen 38). After her husband died without sons, and Judah's second son, Onan, refused to inseminate Tamar rather than fulfill his levirate duty, there remained a third son of Judah, Shelah, still too young for marriage. Judah neglected to arrange for union of Shelah and Tamar when the time came. So Tamar took matters into her own hands and, disguising herself, had sexual intercourse with her father-in-law, Judah, unbeknownst to himself, and became pregnant. While bound to her levir, her status was akin to being pledged to another man, and Judah immediately condemned her to a fiery death as an adulteress. When he learned that he himself had been her sexual partner, he repealed the sentence and admitted his culpability. All the same, the predicates of this narrative confirm that a woman bound to levirate marriage was in a sense married, just like a woman who had been pledged (cf. Deut 25:5–10).

Before discussing harlotry, which has much in common with adultery, we should mention the ordeal of a wife suspected by her husband of adultery, as set forth in Num 5:11–31. Briefly stated, a husband who had reason to suspect his wife of adultery, most likely because he could not account for her pregnancy, but who lacked acceptable legal evidence to this effect, could compel his wife to undergo an ordeal to determine her guilt or innocence. If the ordeal, composed of both magical and sacrificial acts, cleared the wife, she was declared pure (*tĕhōrâ*), but if she showed the deleterious bodily effects induced by the bitter potion, "she was declared impure [*niṭmĕʾâ*]" and was permanently disgraced. Once again, marital fidelity is defined as purity, whereas infidelity is classified as impurity.

Like adultery, harlotry also represents illicit sexual activity, which had the potential of producing stigmatized progeny. It is, however, an activity that is more difficult to define distinctly and appears at times to overlap with adultery. Given the biblical mentality, we must differentiate between harlotrous behavior on the part of women, and the behavior of men who consorted with harlots. Once again, we observe a double standard. A woman labeled *zônâ*, "prostitute, wayward woman," is in the first instance an unmarried woman regularly paid for her sexual services. Thus Deut 23:18–19:

> There shall be no *qĕdēšâ* from among the daughters of Israel, and there shall be no *qādēš* from among the sons of Israel. You shall not bring the prostitute's hire, nor the pay of a dog [male prostitute], into the house of Yahweh, your God, in fulfillment of any vow, for both of them are an abomination to Yahweh, your God.

The Holiness Code, in Lev 19:29, admonishes the Israelite father from turning his daughter into a harlot:

> Do not degrade your daughter by making her a harlot, lest the land become harlotrous, and filled with depravity.

It is generally accepted that the designations *qādēš* and *qĕdēšâ*, which simply mean "priest" and "priestess," function contextually as terms for male and female prostitutes, respectively. Thus, the disguised young woman encountered by Judah on the road, in truth his daughter-in-law, is once referred to as *zônâ* (Gen 38:15) but later as *qĕdēšâ* (38:21–22). To explore fully the often-suggested but enigmatic relationship of such practitioners to sacred prostitution would carry us beyond the present subject. In Deut 23, just cited, the immediate context is that of prostitution. It would appear that the *qādēš*, in particular, engaged in both homosexual and heterosexual activity (see further).

Many biblical sources refer to the professional prostitute (Rahab of Jericho, who hid the spies: Josh 2:1; 6:17, 22, 25; Samson's sexual partner: Judg 16:1; Judah's sexual partner, in reality his daughter-in-law, Tamar: Gen 38:15; etc.). Especially illuminating is the case of Jephthah, whose mother was a prostitute and who was consequently driven out of his home by the legitimate sons of his father's wife (Judg 11:1–3). Ostracism would often be the fate of a prostitute's children, who would not be cared for by their Israelite relations. Observe, however, that in the narrative of Judah and Tamar (Gen 38), no particular sin or penalty attached to an Israelite man who took recourse to a prostitute. Judah's sin was not that he sought out a prostitute, but that he had failed to fulfill the levirate mandate.

Nonetheless, Prov 7 counsels the proverbial "son" to beware of the *zônâ*, there characterized as hateful and reprehensible, who would lure him to her home on the pretext that her husband was away on a distant journey. He might end up with an arrow in his gut! What is most interesting is the nature of the brazen streetwalker's enticements. She says that she would be feasting on parts of the offerings that she had brought in fulfillment of her vows, rendering her at least implicitly in violation of Deut 23:19. Although parts of such votive offerings could be eaten at home, this prostitute presumably paid for them from her harlot's hire! As viewed from the man's perspective, the difference between adultery and harlotry, though blurred to an extent, is nevertheless legally substantive. An adulterer possessed another man's wife, which is a criminal act destructive of the family of at least one of the partners, whereas consorting with harlots was extramarital in effect.

In terms of sexual purity, Lev 21:7 prohibits marriage between a priest and "a degraded harlot" (cf. 21:9), as well as marriage to a divorced woman, on the grounds that the priest is specially consecrated (Heb. *qādōš*). Taking a prostitute as wife would clearly threaten a priest's sacred status, and given that sexual misconduct on the part of a married woman served as the principal grounds for divorce, the purity of a divorcée was highly suspect (cf. Deut 24:1–4; see below). We also read that the daughter of a priest who defiles herself through harlotry in effect disgraces her father and is to be condemned to death by fire (Lev 21:9)—recalling Judah's initial verdict on Tamar, his daughter-in-law (Gen 38:24). The high priest, just as he is forbidden to defile himself at the death of even his closest relatives, is also forbidden to marry a widow or divorcée or certainly a degraded prostitute. He is restricted to a virgin bride (Lev 21:10–15). Throughout the provisions of Lev 21, the nexus of sexual conduct and purity is emphatically evident, as is the interrelatedness of funerary defilement and sexual impurity in defining the closest family relationships.

This leads us directly to the actual law of divorce in Deut 24:1–4, already mentioned above:

> In the case where a man takes a woman as wife and has intercourse with her: If it happens that she fails to please him because he has discovered in her a matter of sexual misconduct [ʿ*erwat dābār*], he should write her a bill of divorcement and place it in her hand and expel her from his household. If, after exiting his household, she proceeds to become the wife of another man—and the latter man [similarly] rejects her, writes her a bill of divorcement, places it in her hand, and expels her from his household—or if the latter man dies, her first husband, who had expelled her, may not again take her to be his wife, since she had been defiled [*huṭṭammāʾâ*]; for that would be an abomination in the presence of Yahweh. You must not bring sin upon the land which Yahweh your God is granting to you as a territory.

The key construction in this legal passage is ʿ*erwat dābār*, whose meaning remains elusive. It only occurs once more, in Deut 23:11–15, a passage that commands Israelites to preserve a holy military encampment in which Yahweh is present. Soldiers should relieve themselves outside the encampment, covering up their excrement. Those experiencing nocturnal emissions must depart the encampment until evening, and then bathe before being allowed to reenter it at sundown. The passage concludes: "Let him [Yahweh] not find anything improper [ʿ*erwat dābār*] among you and turn away from you" (Deut 23:15). This appears to express an extended meaning, however. As mentioned in the discussion of incest, in the context of sexual behavior, the Hebrew ʿ*erwâ* is either a euphemism for sexual intercourse or a way of referring to exclusive sexual access. Here it functions as the grounds for divorce, which is hard to explain, because reference cannot be to adultery on the wife's part, which held the penalty of death. At the same time, it would seem inevitably to designate a sexual offense of some sort and means the same as *dĕbar ʿerwâ*, "a matter of sexual misconduct." We are left, therefore, without a clear notion of the woman's alleged misdeeds.

This brings us to a discussion of virginity in the female as a dimension of sexual purity. The ideal bride was a virgin, especially in ancient societies where marriage, or at least betrothal, usually came at an early age, not too long after the onset of puberty. A young woman who had lost her virginity in the few years following puberty was stigmatized, at the very least, which explains the early law of Exod 22:15–16:

> If a man seduces a virgin who had not been pledged in marriage, and had intercourse with her, he must make her his wife by payment of the *mōhar*. If her father definitely refuses to give her to him, he [the seducer] must weigh out silver in the amount of the *mōhar* for virgin brides.

In other words, even in cases of consensual sex, the loss of virginity was detrimental to the young woman's father, who would henceforth not receive payment if and when his daughter ever married another man. It was certainly also detrimental to the young woman's own marriage prospects. As for the male partner, he was relieved of culpability by paying the *mōhar*, usually translated "bride price," but more accurately to be understood as "indemnification for the right of connubium." By marrying the young woman, he would be affording her an acceptable status. One who raped a virgin, who had not been pledged to another in marriage, was necessarily obliged to marry her and would never be allowed to divorce her, because he had disgraced her irreparably. He must compensate the young woman's father for his loss, in the amount of fifty shekels (Deut 22:28–29). It is somewhat ironic that though the rapist was responsible for remedying the predicament of his female victim and her father, he bore no specific penalty for his actual violence toward the young woman. Once again, we observe that the primary concern was for the family's stability, which occasioned a policy of protecting young women from losing out on marriage.

The most poignant statement on the importance of virginity in the society of biblical Israel comes in Deut 22:13–21, which deals with a situation in which a bridegroom claimed that he was the victim of misrepresentation. As a pretext, he charged that his chosen wife was not a virgin when he married her; yet in reality he had come to despise her and wanted out of the marriage. If evidence of the young woman's virginity at the time of consummation could be produced to the satisfaction of the elders, and the bridegroom's charges shown to be false, that man was fined 100 shekels, payable to the young woman's father. He would be compelled to keep her as his wife and could never divorce her. "For the man has defamed a virgin in Israel." The text continues:

> If, however, the charge proved to be true, and evidence of virginity could not be found, they shall bring the young woman to the entrance of her father's house, and the citizens of her town shall stone her to death, for she

committed an atrocity in Israel by whoring [*liznôt*] while in her father's household.

The remedy for the young woman who had been falsely charged was to bind her husband to her for keeps, so that she stayed married. Although hardly romantic, this fate was more favorable than never marrying at all. In this instance, the young woman had committed no offense and was the victim of defamation. However, in a case where the charge was true, the young woman, who was betrothed by the young man in question, had committed adultery because she was in effect already his wife. What is most interesting is that her adulterous behavior is described by the verb *zānâ*, "to be wayward, sexually unfaithful," the same verb that is used to describe harlotry, indicating that the meaning of Hebrew *zānâ* shifted, at times suggesting actual adultery.

A proper discussion of adultery and harlotry would be inadequate without reference to the widespread metaphor of Israel's infidelity in its covenant relationship with Yahweh, where Israel is identified as the bride, loved and chosen by God, but who is ungratefully faithless, straying after pagan gods. A survey of the operative Hebrew verbs *zānâ*, "to be wayward, harlotrous," and less frequently *nā'ap*, "to commit adultery," initiates us into a major theme of biblical prophecy and in its own way testifies to the strong emphasis on sexual purity in Israelite society. Only an ethos that rigidly insisted on marital fidelity and enacted strict laws to control sexuality and reproduction could generate such dramatic metaphors of infidelity. Perhaps the most powerful set of marital metaphors is to be found in Jer 3, against the background of Jer 2:2–3:

> Thus said Yahweh:
> I accounted to your favor the devotion of your youth,
> Your love as a bride;
> That you followed me in the wilderness,
> In an unsown land.

Israel's devotion of earlier times was soon to falter, however, and Jer 2 moves directly to a denunciation of the people's faithlessness, which soon progresses to the marital metaphor, reaching its most explicit form in Jer 3:1:

> If a man divorces his wife, and she leaves him and is married to another man, can he ever go back to her? Would not such a land be defiled? Now, you have whored with many lovers; can you return to me, says Yahweh?

It cannot escape our notice that this prophetic utterance resonates with the formulation of the law of divorce in Deut 24:1–4, discussed above. In fact, Jer 3 develops the theme of expulsion and return, modulating it by application to Israel's waywardness. In so doing, the text of Jeremiah demonstrates the nexus of purity and national destiny. Two earlier prophets express the same sentiment. Thus Hos 4, as part of an overall condemnation of northern Israelite society's sad state in the third quarter of the eighth century BCE, includes a detailed description of harlotry, half realistically and half metaphorically, as a concomitant of pagan worship. It is that prophet who alludes to a cultic role for prostitutes: "For they sequester themselves with prostitutes [*hazzōnôt*], and offer sacrifices with *qĕdēšôt*" (Hos 4:14b). Hosea 9:1–2 carries this theme forward:

> Rejoice not, O Israel, as other nations exult;
> For you have strayed [*kî zānîtā*] away from your God.
> You have loved the harlot's hire,
> At every granary floor.

Isaiah (1:21) assumes a moral posture in the years immediately following the Assyrian blockade of Jerusalem in 701 BCE:

> See how she has become a harlot [*zônâ*],
> The (once) faithful city!
> That was filled with justice,
> Where righteousness dwelt.
> But now—murderers!

It was Ezekiel, however, a Judean prophet of the exilic transition, who most dramatically elaborated the metaphor of harlotry (and of adultery) in reviewing the history of Israel's inconstant relationship with God. In Ezek 16 we read of an infant girl, abandoned in the open field and waddling in blood, who was rescued by a caring God. When she reaches puberty and the age of lovemaking, Yahweh bathes her and washes off her menstrual blood. He clothes her in finery and adorns her with gems, so that she is suited for royalty. But, alas, Israel the bride exploits her beauty to become a harlot and adulteress. Israel is called both whore and adulteress (Ezek 16:30–32).

Homosexuality, Bestiality, and Transvestism

Leviticus 18:22–23 issues a combined statement on homosexuality and bestiality:

> Do not have sexual intercourse with a male as one has sexual intercourse with a woman; it is an abomination. Do not lie with any type of animal, rendering yourself impure through her, and no woman may approach an animal to be mated with her; it is perversion.

Leviticus 20:13, 15 repeat these prohibitions in casuistic formulation, mandating the death penalty. The prohibition against bestiality also occurs in an earlier text, Exod 22:18: "Anyone who lies with an animal shall surely be put to death." It remains uncertain whether women are included in this prohibition, because an elliptic third-person verb, Hebrew *šōkēb*, in the masculine could be generic in its reference and include all persons.

Two features of these regulations have aroused particular interest: In the first place, there is no prohibition of lesbian sexual activity to parallel the prohibition of male homosexuality. Then too, the prohibition of bestiality is the only law in the codes of Lev 18 and 20 that is addressed to both Israelite men and Israelite women. It is usually thought that lesbian sexual behavior was a matter of relative indifference because it did not, in fact, involve the wasting of sperm, as did male homosexuality. Add to this the overall tendency to address the men of the community on matters of proper behavior; they were held responsible for what went on within the household. The exceptional inclusion of women in the bestiality law is explicable in realistic terms, because women worked in the fields and tended to livestock, whereas a married woman's opportunities for human sexual encounters were severely limited.

The combination of male homosexuality with bestiality, like its immediate contexts elsewhere, reflects the intensity of homophobia in the biblical ethos, which went beyond the concern for conserving sperm. Homosexuality is associated with the erstwhile inhabitants of Canaan in the postscript to Lev 18 (vv. 24–30). Their loss of the land is attributed to such practices, along with idolatry, and the same fate could befall Israel. In 1 Kgs 14:22–24, within an etiological passage, Judah under Rehoboam is condemned for tolerating the practice of male prostitution, along with decrying pagan worship. All of these sins are classified as the abominations characteristic of the earlier inhabitants of Canaan. In contrast, pious Judean kings, like Asa (1 Kgs 15:12), Jehoshaphat (22:47), and Josiah (2 Kgs 23:7) banished the *qĕdēšîm* and closed down their places of operation. The narrative of Lot in Sodom (Gen 19) is usually cited as an epitome of Canaanite homophobia, along with zenophobia, but this is not explicit in the biblical text.

A corollary of the prohibition against homosexuality is that of transvestism. Thus, Deut 22:5:

> A man's item of clothing shall not be worn by a woman, nor shall a man wear the garment of a woman, for anyone who does this is an abomination to Yahweh, your God.

Here women are also addressed in the prohibition of dressing like the opposite sex, a practice understandably associated with homosexual behavior.

Menstruation and Parturition (F), Seminal Emissions (M), and Heterosexual Intercourse (M + F)

Up to this point, discussion has centered on sexual behavior that threatened the purity of those who engaged in it, which is to say, with persons who had sexual intercourse with forbidden partners and/or under prohibited circumstances. There is, however, another kind of sexual impurity that relates to conditions of a sexual nature, which caused concern and anxiety but did not involve any impropriety. We might call them "natural." As already recognized, the ancient Israelites, like their contemporaries, knew much less than we do about human physiology and health care. They classified as impure certain conditions such as illness and disease, as well as those associated with human reproduction.

The first subject to be discussed under this heading is menstruation. There is a blanket prohibition of sexual intercourse with a menstruating woman in Lev 18:19, within the code of incest and other sexual offenses:

> And do not be intimate with a woman during the impurity of her menstrual flow, to uncover her nakedness.

A similar prohibition against intercourse with a menstruating woman occurs in Ezek 18, within a lengthy parable, virtually a canonical list of the differences between the righteous and the wicked, which resonates with Lev 18:

> If a man is righteous and does what is just and right: If he has not eaten *(flesh) with its blood in it,* nor lifted his eyes to the fetishes of the house of Israel; if he has not defiled his neighbor's wife, nor been intimate with a menstruating woman . . . (Ezek 18:5–6)

Similar images are evoked in Ezek 22:10. The key term is Hebrew *niddâ*, functionally understood as "menstruation, a menstruating woman." Its etymology has occasioned some debate, but it probably derives from the verb *nādâ*, cognate with Akkadian *nadû*, "to cast off, hurl," a phonetic variant of *nāzâ*, "to spatter," elsewhere employed to describe the sprinkling of sacrificial blood (Lev 4:6, 17; 5:9). On this basis, we would understand this term as referring to the flow of menstrual blood. In Lev 12:2, within the ritual prescriptions affecting a woman after childbirth, we encounter the notion that a menstruating woman is infirm or ill (cf. Lev 15:33; 20:18; Isa 30:22). This mentality reflects the widespread notion that menstruation is an infirmity in women, a reaction that may be attributable to the belief that blood emitting from the body is inevitably a symptom of illness, or the result of a wound, and to the discomfort often experienced by women in connection with menstruation.

An elaborate statement on the restrictions occasioned by the monthly cycle appears in Lev 15:19–24 (with omissions):

> And when a woman has a bloody discharge, her discharge being blood from her body, she shall remain in her menstrual impurity seven days. Whoever touches her shall remain impure until evening. Anything that she lies on during her menstrual impurity shall become impure, and as well, anything she sits on shall become impure. . . . If a man lies with her, her menstrual impurity is transmitted to him, and he shall remain impure for seven days, and any bedding on which he lies shall become impure.

In the deleted section, the text details how contact with the woman's impure bedding or clothing renders a person impure until evening, and requires one to bathe. The text later deals with abnormal discharges, which—unlike regular menstruation, which only requires bathing at the end of the period—also required ritual purification at the termination of the discharges (Lev 15:25–30). It is to be understood that all impure persons were barred from the sanctuary during the applicable period, including a menstruating woman. What we encounter is heightened aversion to the phenomenon of menstruation, although there is nowhere any requirement to segregate women in this condition, or to have them reside in special quarters during the applicable time frame.

As was true of harlotry, which became a metaphor for Israel's infidelity (see above), so too did the phenomenon of menstruation become a metaphor for all that was impure, especially Israel's noticeable tendency toward paganism. Thus, we read in 2 Chr 29:5 that Hezekiah instructed the Levites:

> Consecrate the House of Yahweh, God of your ancestors, and remove what is abhorrent [ʾet-hanniddâ] from the sanctuary.

In the near exilic and exilic periods, usage of this metaphor is more pronounced, so that *niddâ* becomes a replacement for *ṭumʾâ*, "impurity," and *ḥaṭṭaʾt*, "sinfulness" (Zech 13:1; Ezra 9:11). Thus, in Ezek 36:17, the house of Israel is condemned for defiling the land of its habitation, for "their way was like the impurity of menstruation in my presence." Similarly, Ezekiel warns Israel that God will render their gold and silver, out of which they had fashioned fetishes, impure, a condition conveyed by the term *niddâ* (Ezek 7:19–20). Best known, perhaps is the depiction of a destroyed Jerusalem in Lam 1:8–9 (with omissions):

> Jerusalem has committed an offense, and for that reason she has become impure [*niddâ*]. All those who esteemed her now demean her, for they have seen her nakedness.... Her impurity is in the folds of her garments.

The etymology of Hebrew *niddâ*, "to cast off, hurl," allows for the figurative meaning "abandoned, rejected," which reflects the avoidance of physical contact with menstruating women and conveys the sadness associated with exile.

What in the course of time became codified in priestly law had been known as a theme in biblical literature. An allusion to menstruation is the pretext offered by Rachel, who had hidden her father's teraphim under her cushion, that she could not rise to honor him "because I am having the way of women" (Gen 31:33–35). In 2 Sam 11:4 we read that when David had adulterous intercourse with Bathsheba, "she had just consecrated herself after her impurity," a reference to bathing after menstruation. A similar reference to bathing after menstruation occurs in Ezek 16:9, where we read that God bathed Israel, the foundling child who had reached puberty, washing away her blood. More to the point is the comment that when Sarah grew old, "she had ceased having the 'way' of women" (Gen 18:11) and could not bear children. This statement makes it clear that the ancients realized the connection between menstruation and parturition, both of which involved the observable discharge of blood from the female body, although their knowledge of the reproductive process in the female was limited in many respects.

Moving to parturition, we find the principal code of priestly law on the subject of childbirth in Lev 12:

> When a woman is inseminated and bears a male [child], she becomes impure for seven days; in the same manner as [during] the days of her menstrual infirmity shall she be impure. On the eighth day the flesh of his foreskin shall be circumcised. For thirty-three days she shall remain in a state of blood purification. She may not touch any consecrated article nor enter the sanctuary until her period of purification is completed. If she gives birth to a female [child], she becomes impure for two weeks, in the same manner as her menstruation, and for sixty-six days she shall remain in a state of blood purification. (Lev 12:2–5)

The brief text of Lev 12 goes on to prescribe sacrificial offerings by a priest, required in securing expiation on her behalf "from her flow of blood" (12:7). Provisions are made for less-costly offerings in cases of need. It is significant that a sin offering is included, and that the verb *kippēr*, "to expiate, cleanse of offenses," is employed, as if the woman involved had committed some offense! The explanation for such features brings us back to what was said at the outset: Impurity functioned as a broad category, encompassing illness and other physical conditions where no guilt or impropriety obtained, but which nonetheless evoked a sense of danger and vulnerability. One of the ways to protect vulnerable persons was to declare them impure, and the new mother, who required special care in recovering from childbirth, is a prime example. At the time of birth, the child is in no way impure, and neither is the father. Only the mother is, for a specific period of time. The circumcision of male infants is thus not a rite of purification in the accepted sense, but rather a covenantal initiation. We are at a loss to account for the doubling of the period when a woman who has given birth to a daughter is excluded from the sanctuary. Logically, it may have had something to do with the belief that the birth of a daughter rendered the new mother more vulnerable.

It has been suggested that there is a demonic basis for the exclusion of the new mother from the sanctuary and for her designation as impure. It was believed that demonic forces are most attracted by fertility, so that the presence in the sanctuary of a fertile woman who has just given birth, together with her infant, would have magnetized demons, thereby defiling the sanctuary. This may help to explain why there was no cultic celebration of birth in Israelite religion, nor of death, for that matter. Just as Lev 21 prohibits priests from contact with the dead, so Lev 12 prohibits the new mother from entering the sanctuary.

The Hebrew Bible provides little information on the practical health care of newborn infants or their mothers. Ezekiel 16, already discussed in connection with the theme of harlotry, supplies some details as part of its description of an abandoned infant who has not received proper care:

> As for your birth, when you were born your navel cord was not cut, and you were not bathed in water to smooth you; you were not rubbed with salt, nor were you swaddled. . . . On the day you were born, you were left lying, cast off, in the open field. When I passed by you and saw you wallowing in your blood, I said to you: "Live in spite of your blood!" (Ezek 16:4–6, with omissions)

From blood in the female we proceed to discuss sperm in the male, and it becomes necessary to repeat what was said in the introduction to this chapter on sexual purity. Given the fact that the ancients had not yet identified the female egg, it was vital to control the supply of sperm, which was probably thought to be nonrenewable. What Onan did, as reported in Gen 38:8–9, was to practice coitus interruptus, thereby preventing his sperm from inseminating his levirate wife by ejaculating on the ground. Traditionally, Onan's actions have been understood as masturbation, but this is not necessarily accurate.

What we do find are several statements on the matter of involuntary seminal emissions. The first occurs in Deut 23:11, within a passage already referred to above, prescribing that the Israelite military encampment be holy and free of "anything evil":

> If there is in your midst a man who has been rendered impure as a result of a nocturnal emission, he must depart the encampment; he may not reenter the encampment. Toward evening, he must bathe himself in water, and at sundown he may reenter the encampment.

In Lev 15:16–18 we find a more definitive statement:

> Any man from whom there emits a layer of semen must bathe his entire body in water and remain impure until evening. And any garment [of cloth] or any of leather which has a layer of semen on it must be laundered in water and remains impure until evening. If a man penetrates a woman with a layer of sperm, both must bathe in water, and they remain impure until evening.

The upshot of the above statements is that the only approved, voluntary use of sperm was to inseminate the female through heterosexual intercourse, under proper circumstances. Such sexual activity constituted a fulfillment of God's first blessing to humankind: "Be fruitful and multiply, and fill the earth and subdue it!" (Gen 1:28).

14

Rabbinic Reading

Sexual Purity

Jacob Neusner

The ordeal spelled out at Num 5:1–31 provides the Halakhah of rabbinic Judaism with its opportunity to make its statement on sexual purity: the sanctification of a woman to her husband. That statement would underscore the considerations of justice for all concerned. While the rite imposed on the woman suspected of adultery in Scripture places the burden of proof on the woman, the rabbinic sages accorded to women what Scripture had denied. The injustice done to the innocent wife, who by the husband's whim is required to undergo the humiliating ordeal of the bitter water, serves as the Halakhah's occasion to make its definitive statement that God's justice is perfect: the wicked receive their exact punishment, the righteous receive their precise reward.

For the sages it is not enough to show that sin or crime provokes divine response, that God penalizes evildoers. Justice in the here and now counts only when the righteous also receive what is coming to them. Scripture's casual remark that the woman found innocent will bear more children provokes elaborate demonstration, out of the established facts of history that Scripture supplies, that both righteous and wicked are subject to God's flawless and exact justice. Then sages surely liberate women from a procedure lacking in all juridical protections and accord to the accused woman the rights that they could devise, within their framework, to secure justice for her.

What have the sages done? First of all, the Halakhah takes the ordeal and encases it in juridical procedures, rules of evidence, guidelines meant to protect the woman from needless exposure to the ordeal. The Halakhah radically revises the entire transaction when it says that if the husband expresses jealousy by instructing his wife not to speak with a specified person, and the wife spoke with the man, there is no juridical result: she still is permitted to have sexual relations with her husband and is permitted to eat priestly rations if he is a priest. But if she went with him to some private place and remained with him for sufficient time to become unclean, she is prohibited from having sexual relations with her husband, and if the husband is a priest, she is prohibited from eating priestly rations.

The Halakhah thus conceives of a two-stage process, two kinds of testimony. In the first kind, she is warned not to get involved, but she is not then prohibited to the husband. In the second kind of stage, witnesses attest that she can have committed adultery. Not only so, but the Halakhah wants valid evidence if it is to deprive the wife of her marriage settlement. If a single witness to the act of intercourse is available, that does not suffice. People who ordinarily cannot testify against her do not have the power to deprive her of her property rights in the marriage, such as her mother-in-law and the daughter of her mother-in-law, her cowife, the husband's brother's wife, and the daughter of her husband. She still collects her alimony. But because of their testimony, she does not undergo the rite; she is divorced in course, and the transaction concludes there.

Before the ordeal is invoked, the Halakhah therefore wants some sort of solid evidence (1) of untoward sexual activity and also (2) of clear action on the part of the wife: at least the possibility, confirmed through a specific case, that adultery has taken place. Scripture leaves everything to the husband's whim, the "spirit of jealousy." So here if the husband gives his statement of jealousy and the wife responds by ignoring the statement, the ordeal does not apply. By her specific action the wife has to indicate the possibility that the husband is right. This is a far cry from Scripture's "spirit of jealousy." For the Torah, the ordeal settles all questions. For the Halakhah, the ordeal takes effect only in carefully defined cases where (1) sufficient evidence exists to invoke the rite, but (2) insufficient evidence makes it unnecessary: well-established doubt, so to speak.

The Halakhah further introduces the clarification that the marriage must be a valid one; if the marriage violates the law of the Torah, such as the marriage of a widow to a high priest or a divorcée to an ordinary priest, the rite of the ordeal does not apply. The rite does not apply at the stage of betrothal, but only in a fully consummated marriage. If the fiancé expressed jealousy to the betrothed or the levir to the deceased childless brother's widow, no rite is inflicted. Sages severely limited the range of applicability of the rite. Not only so, but also the marriage may well be severed without the ordeal's being inflicted if the wife confesses, if there are witnesses to the act, if the wife declines to go through the ordeal, if the husband declines to impose it, or if the husband has sexual relations with her en route to the performance of the ordeal. In such cases the marital bond is called into question, so the wife loses her status as wife of a priest, should the husband be a priest. If in the preliminaries to the ordeal she confesses, she is given a writ of divorce, losing her marriage settlement. Only if she continues to plead purity is the ordeal imposed. The details of the rite are meant to match the sequence of actions that the unfaithful wife has taken with the paramour, beautifully expounded at Mishnah Soṭah 1:7 and its accompanying Tosefta-composite, cited presently.

The Halakhah makes provision for the cancellation of the rite, down to the point at which the scroll is blotted out, with the divine names inscribed therein. At that point the accused wife can no longer pull out of the ordeal. That moment matches, in effect, the moment of death for the sacrificer, when we have to dispose of the animals that he has sanctified for his offering. But if at that point she confesses, the water is poured out, and she loses her marriage settlement but otherwise is left alone. So too, if witnesses come or if she refuses to drink or if the husband pulls out, the meal offering is burned. If I had to summarize in a single sentence the main thrust of the Halakhah of *Sotah*, it is to create the conditions of perfect, unresolved doubt, so far as the husband is concerned, alongside perfect certainty of innocence, so far as the wife is concerned. Despite the humiliation that awaits, she is willing to place her marriage settlement on the line, so sure is she that she is innocent. His doubt is well-founded but remains a matter of doubt, so uncertain is he of her status. Then and only then, the ordeal intervenes to resolve the exquisitely balanced scale of her certainty against his doubt.

The exposition of the topic lays heavy emphasis upon how, measure for measure, the punishment fits the crime—but the reward matches the virtue. What the guilty wife has done, the law punishes appropriately; but also, they point to cases in which acts of merit receive appropriate recognition and reward. In this way sages make the point that, within the walls of the household, rules of justice prevail, with reward for goodness and punishment for evil the standard in the household as much as in public life. Why sages have chosen the Halakhah of the accused wife as the venue for their systematic exposition of the divine law of justice is not difficult to explain.

If we turn from the treatment of sexual purity by the Halakhah to the reflection on the matter by the Haggadah, we find precisely the same focus on how God's perfect justice is embodied in the very rite of the accused wife. What we note is sages' identification of the precision of justice, first in the process of the accused wife, the exact match of action and reaction, each step in the sin, each step in the response, and above all, the immediacy of God's presence in the entire transaction. They draw general conclusions from the specifics of the law that Scripture sets forth, and that is where systematic thinking about something takes over from exegetical learning about cases, or in our own categories, philosophy grows from history, as observed earlier:

> Mishnah *Sotah* 1:7: By that same measure by which a man metes out [to others], do they mete out to him: She primped herself for sin, the Omnipresent made her repulsive. She exposed herself for sin, the Omnipresent exposed her. With the thigh she began to sin, and afterward with the belly, therefore the thigh suffers the curse first, and afterward the belly. But the rest of the body does not escape [punishment].
>
> Tosefta *Sotah* 3:2: And so you find that with regard to the accused wife: With the measure with which she measured out, with that measure do they mete out to her. She stood before him so as to be pretty before him, therefore a priest stands her up in front of everybody to display her shame, as it is said, "And the priest will set the woman before the LORD" [Num 5:18].
>
> Tosefta *Sotah* 3:3: She wrapped a beautiful scarf for him, therefore a priest takes her cap from her head and puts it under foot. She braided her

hair for him, therefore a priest loosens it. She painted her face for him, therefore her face is made to turn yellow. She put blue on her eyes for him, therefore her eyes bulge out.

Tosefta *Sotah* 3:4: She signaled to him with her finger, therefore her fingernails fall out. She showed him her flesh, therefore a priest tears her cloak and shows her shame in public. She tied on a belt for him, therefore a priest brings a rope of twigs and ties it above her breasts, and whoever wants to stare comes and stares at her [*m. Sotah* 1:6C–D]. She pushed her thigh at him, therefore her thigh falls. She took him on her belly, therefore her belly swells. She fed him goodies, therefore her meal-offering is fit for a cow. She gave him the best wines to drink in elegant goblets, therefore the priest gives her the bitter water to drink in a clay pot.

We begin with sages' own general observations based on the facts set forth in Scripture. The woman accused of adultery has a course for responding to drinking the bitter water that is supposed to produce one result for the guilty, another for the innocent, as described in Scripture in this language:

If no man has lain with you, . . . be free from this water of bitterness that brings the curse. But if you have gone astray, . . . then the Lord make you an execration . . . when the Lord makes your thigh fall away and your body swell; may this water . . . pass into your bowels and make your body swell and your thigh fall away. (Num 5:20–22)

This language is amplified and expanded, extended to the entire rite, where the woman is disheveled; then the order, thigh, belly, shows the perfect precision of the penalty. What Scripture treats as a case, sages transform into a generalization, so making Scripture yield governing rules. The same passage proceeds to further cases that prove the same point: where the sin begins, there the punishment also commences; but also, where an act of virtue takes its point, there divine reward focuses as well. Merely listing the following names, without spelling out details, for the cognoscenti of Scripture will make that point: Samson, Absalom, Miriam, Joseph, and Moses. Knowing how Samson and Absalom match, also Miriam, Joseph, and Moses, would then suffice to establish the paired and matched general principles.

Justice requires not only punishment of the sinner or the guilty but also reward of the righteous and the good, and so sages find ample, systematic evidence in Scripture for both sides of the equation of justice:

Mishnah *Sotah* 1:9:
A. And so is it on the good side:
B. Miriam waited a while for Moses, since it is said, "And his sister stood afar off" [Exod 2:4], therefore, Israel waited on her seven days in the wilderness, since it is said, "And the people did not travel on until Miriam was brought in again" [Num 12:15].

Mishnah *Soṭah* 1:10:
A. Joseph had the merit of burying his father, and none of his brothers was greater than he, since it is said, "And Joseph went up to bury his father, ... and there went up with him both chariots and horsemen" [Gen 50:7, 9].
B. We have none so great as Joseph, for only Moses took care of his [bones].
C. Moses had the merit of burying the bones of Joseph, and none in Israel was greater than he, since it is said, "And Moses took the bones of Joseph with him" [Exod 13:19].
D. We have none so great as Moses, for only the Holy One, blessed be He, took care of his [bones], since it is said, "And he buried him in the valley" [Deut 34:6].
E. And not of Moses alone have they stated [this rule], but of all righteous people, since it is said, "And your righteousness shall go before you. The glory of the LORD shall gather you [in death]" [Isa 58:8].

Scripture provides the main probative evidence for the anticipation that when God judges, he will match the act of merit with an appropriate reward and the sin with an appropriate punishment. The proposition begins, however, with general observations as to how things are (*m. Soṭah* 1:7), and not with specific allusions to proof texts; the character of the law set forth in Scripture is reflected upon. The accumulated cases yield the generalizations.

Sipre on Numbers, a systematic exegesis of the biblical book of Numbers, takes up the Mishnah's proposition concerning Num 5:23–31, that when God punishes, he starts with that with which the transgression commenced, which sages see as a mark of the precision of divine justice:

Sipre on Numbers 18:1.1:
A. And when he has made her drink the water, [then, if she has defiled herself and has acted unfaithfully against her husband, the water that brings the curse shall enter into her and cause bitter pain,] and her body shall swell, and her thigh shall fall away, [and the woman shall become an execration among her people. But if the woman has not defiled herself and is clean, then she shall be free and shall conceive children] [Num 5:23–28].
B. I know only that her body and thigh are affected. How do I know that that is the case for the rest of her limbs?
C. Scripture states, "... The water that brings the curse shall enter into her."
D. So I take account of the phrase, "... The water that brings the curse shall enter into her."
E. Why [if all the limbs are affected equally] then does Scripture specify her body and her thigh in particular?
F. As to her thigh, the limb with which she began to commit the transgression—from there the punishment begins.

But the sages represented by *Sipre on Numbers*, exegetes of Scripture, and the

Mishnah, like the commentators whom we shall meet in the Tosefta that follows, wish to introduce their own cases in support of the same proposition:

G. Along these same lines:
H. "And he blotted out everything that sprouted from the earth, from man to beast" [Gen 7:23].
I. From the one who began the transgression [namely] Adam, the punishment begins.

Adam sinned first, therefore the flood began with Adam. Now comes a different sort of proportion: the exact match. The Sodomites are smitten with piles:

J. Along these same lines:
K. "... And the men who were at the gate of the house they smote with piles" [Gen 19:11].
L. From the one who began the transgression the punishment begins.

In the third instance, Pharaoh is in the position of Adam; with him the sin began, with him the punishment starts:

M. Along these same lines:
N. "... And I shall be honored through Pharaoh and through all of his force" [Exod 14:4].
O. Pharaoh began the transgression, so from him began the punishment.
P. Along these same lines:
Q. "And you will most certainly smite at the edge of the sword the inhabitants of that city" [Deut 13:16].
R. From the one who began the transgression, the punishment begins.
S. Along these same lines is the present case:
T. The limb with which she began to commit the transgression—from there the punishment begins.

Here comes a point important to the system: God's mercy vastly exceeds his justice, so the measure of reward is far greater than the measure of punishment—and if possible, it is still more prompt:

U. Now does this not yield an argument a fortiori?
V. If in the case of the attribution of punishment, which is the lesser, from the limb with which she began to commit the transgression—from there the punishment begins;
W. in the case of the attribute of bestowing good, which is the greater, how much the more so!

Punishment is rational in yet a more concrete way: it commences with the very thing that has sinned, or with the person who has sinned. So the principles of reason and good order pervade the world. We know that fact because Scripture's account of all that matters has shown it. But the exposition of justice commences with the topic at hand.

The Tosefta contributes further cases illustrating the exact and appropriate character of both divine justice and divine reward. What is important here is what is not made explicit; it concerns a question that the Mishnah does not raise: What about the Gentiles? Does the principle of world order of justice apply to them, or are they subject to chaos? The answer given through cases here is that the same rules of justice apply to Gentiles, not only to Israelites such as are listed in the Mishnah's primary statement of the principle. That point is made through the cases that are selected: Sennacherib, who besieged Jerusalem after destroying Israel, comprised by the northern tribes; Nebuchadnezzar, who took and destroyed Jerusalem in the time of Jeremiah. Now the sin is the single most important one, arrogance or hubris, and the penalty is swift and appropriate: the humbling of the proud by an act of humiliation:

Tosefta *Soṭah* 3:18:
A. Sennacherib took pride before the Omnipresent only through an agent, as it is said, "By your messengers you have mocked the LORD, and you have said, 'With my many chariots I have gone up the heights of the mountains. . . . I dug wells and drank foreign waters, and I dried up with the sole of my foot all the streams of Egypt'" [2 Kgs 19:23–24].
B. So the Omnipresent, blessed be He, exacted punishment from him only through an agent, as it is said, "And that night the messenger of the LORD went forth and slew a hundred and eighty-five thousand in the camp of the Assyrians" [2 Kgs 19:35].
C. And all of them were kings, with their crowns bound to their heads.

Tosefta *Soṭah* 3:19:
A. Nebuchadnezzar said, "The denizens of this earth are not worthy for me to dwell among them. I shall make for myself a little cloud and dwell in it," as it is said, "I will ascend above the heights of the clouds; I will make myself like the Most High" [Isa 14:14].
B. Said to him the Omnipresent, blessed be He, "You said in your heart, 'I will ascend to heaven, above the stars of God I will set my throne on high'—I shall bring you down to the depths of the pit" [Isa 14:13, 15].
C. What does it say? "But you are brought down to Sheol, to the depths of the pit" [Isa 14:15].
D. Were you the one who said, "The denizens of this earth are not worthy for me to dwell among them"?
E. The king said, "Is not this great Babylon, which I have built by my mighty power as a royal residence and for the glory of my majesty?" While the words were still in the king's mouth, there fell a voice from heaven, "O King Nebuchadnezzar, to you it is spoken, The kingdom has departed from you, and you shall be driven from among men, and your dwelling shall be with

the beasts of the field, and you shall be made to eat grass like an ox" [Dan 4:27–32].

F. All this came upon King Nebuchadnezzar at the end of twelve months [Dan 4:25–26, 30].

As in the Mishnah, so here too we wish to prove that justice governs not only to penalize sin but also to reward virtue. To this point we have shown the proportionate character of punishment to sin, the exact measure of justice. The first task in this other context is now to establish the proportions of reward to punishment.

Is reward measured out with the same precision? Not at all; reward many times exceeds punishment. So if the measure of retribution is exactly proportionate to the sin, the measure of reward exceeds the contrary measure by a factor of five hundred. Later we shall see explicit argument that justice without mercy is incomplete; to have justice, mercy is the required complement. Here we address another aspect of the same matter, that if the measure of punishment precisely matches the measure of sin, when it comes to reward for merit or virtue, matters are not that way:

Tosefta *Soṭah* 4:1:
A. I know only with regard to the measure of retribution that by that same measure by which a man metes out, they mete out to him [*m. Soṭah* 1:7A]. How do I know that the same is so with the measure of goodness [*m. Soṭah* 1:9A]?
B. Thus do you say:
C. The measure of goodness is five hundred times greater than the measure of retribution.
D. With regard to the measure of retribution, it is written, "Visiting the sin of the fathers on the sons and on the grandsons to the third and fourth generation" [Exod 20:5].
E. And with regard to the measure of goodness, it is written, "And doing mercy for thousands" [Exod 20:6].
F. You must therefore conclude that the measure of goodness is five hundred times greater than the measure of retribution.

Having made that point, we revert to the specifics of cases involving mortals, not God, and here we wish to show the simple point that reward and punishment meet in the precision of justice.

Before proceeding to the Tosefta's extension of matters in a quite unanticipated direction, let us turn to further amplifications of the basic point concerning the exact character of the punishment for a given sin. The fact is, not only does the sinner lose what he or she wanted, but the sinner also is denied what formerly he or she had possessed, a still more mordant and exact penalty indeed. At Tosefta *Soṭah* 4:16, the statement of the Mishnah, "Just as she is prohibited to her husband, so she is prohibited to her lover" [*m. Soṭah* 5:1], is transformed into a generalization, which is spelled out and then demonstrated by a list lacking all articulation; the items on the list serve to make the point. The illustrative case—the snake and Eve—is given at Tosefta *Sotah* 4:17–18. The list then follows at 4:19.

> Tosefta *Sotah* 4:16:
> A. Just as she is prohibited to her husband, so she is prohibited to her lover:
> B. You turn out to rule in the case of an accused wife who set her eyes on someone who was not available to her:
> C. What she wanted is not given to her, and what she had in hand is taken away from her.

The poetry of justice is not lost: what the sinner wanted, the sinner does not get; and what the sinner had, the sinner loses:

> Tosefta *Sotah* 4:17:
> A. And so you find in the case of the snake of olden times, who was smarter than all the cattle and wild beasts of the field, as it is said, "Now the serpent was smarter than any other wild creature that the Lord God had made" [Gen 3:1].
> B. He wanted to slay Adam and to marry Eve.
> C. The Omnipresent said to him, "I said that you should be king over all beasts and wild animals. Now that you did not want things that way, 'You are more cursed than all the beasts and wild animals of the field'" [Gen 3:14].
> D. "I said that you should walk straight-up like man. Now that you did not want things that way, 'Upon your belly you shall go'" [Gen 3:14].
> E. "I said that you should eat human food and drink human drink. Now: 'And dust you shall eat all the days of your life'" [Gen 3:14].

> Tosefta *Sotah* 4:18:
> A. "You wanted to kill Adam and marry Eve? 'And I will put enmity between you and the woman'" [Gen 3:15].
> B. You turn out to rule: What he wanted was not given to him, and what he had in hand was taken away from him.

Through classification and hierarchization to uncover patterns, sages' mode of thought does not require the spelling out of the consequences of the pattern through endless cases. On the contrary, sages are perfectly happy to list the other examples of the same rule, knowing that we can reconstruct the details if we know the facts of Scripture that have been shown to follow a common paradigm:

> Tosefta *Sotah* 4:19:
> A. And so you find in the case of Cain, Korah, Balaam, Doeg, Ahithophel, Gahazi, Absalom, Adonijah, Uzziah, and Haman, all of whom set their eyes on what they did not have coming to them.

B. What they wanted was not given to them, and what they had in hand was taken away from them.

If we were given only Tosefta *Sotah* 4:19A, a construction lacking all explanation, we should have been able to reach 4:19B! Here is a fine example of how a pattern signals its own details, and how knowing the native categories allows us to elaborate the pattern with little further data. But whether we should have identified as the generative message, "What he wanted was not given to him, and what he had in hand was taken away from him," is not equivalently clear, and I am inclined to think that without the fully exposed example, we could not have done what the compositor has instructed us to do: fill out the et cetera. What a passage of this kind underscores is sages' confidence that those who would study their writings saw the paradigm within the case and possessed minds capable of generalization and objective demonstration.

As to Tosefta *Sotah* 4:1, which we considered above, sages both distinguish the realm of the Torah from the realm of idolatry, Israel from the Gentiles, but also treat the two realms as subject to one and the same rule of justice. But then what difference does the Torah make for holy Israel, the Torah's sector of humanity? As the Tosefta's passage that we first met just now proceeds, discussion shades over into a response to this very question. The point concerning reward and punishment is made not at random but through the close reading of Scripture's record concerning not only the line of Noah—the generation of the flood, the men of Sodom and Gomorrah, the Egyptians—but also the founder of God's line on earth: Abraham. Abraham here, often as head of the line with Isaac and Jacob, is deemed the archetype for Israel, his extended family. What he did affects his heirs. His actions form models for the right conduct of his heirs. What happened to him will be recapitulated in the lives and fate of his heirs.

So from retributive justice and the Gentiles, the discourse shifts to distributive reward, shared by the founder and his heirs later on. Reward also is governed by exact justice; the precision of the deed is matched by the precision of the response:

Tosefta *Sotah* 4:1:
G. And so you find in the case of Abraham that by that same measure by which a man metes out, they mete out to him.
H. He ran before the ministering angels three times, as it is said, "When he saw them, he ran to meet them" [Gen 18:2], "And Abraham hastened to the tent" [Gen 18:6], "And Abraham ran to the herd" [Gen 18:7].
I. So did the Omnipresent, blessed be He, run before his children three times, as it is said, "The LORD came from Sinai, and dawned from Seir upon us; he shone forth from Mount Paran" [Deut 33:2].

Justice extends beyond the limits of a single life, when the life is Abraham's. Now justice requires that Abraham's heirs participate in the heritage of virtue that he has bequeathed. Point by point, God remembers Abraham's generous actions in favor of Abraham's children into the long future, an intimation of a doctrine involving a heritage of grace that will play a considerable role in the theological system. Here, point by point, what Abraham does brings benefit to his heirs:

Tosefta *Sotah* 4:2:
A. Of Abraham it is said, "He bowed himself to the earth" [Gen 18:2].
B. So will the Omnipresent, blessed be He, respond graciously to his children in time to come, "Kings will be your foster-fathers, and their queens your nursing mothers. With their faces to the ground they shall bow down to you and lick the dust of your feet" [Isa 49:23].
C. Of Abraham it is said, "Let a little water be brought" [Gen 18:4].
D. So did the Omnipresent, blessed be He, respond graciously and give to his children a well in the wilderness, which gushed through the whole camp of Israel, as it is said, "The well which the princes dug, which the nobles of the people delved" [Num 21:18], teaching that it went over the whole south and watered the entire desert, "which looks down upon the desert" [Num 21:20].
E. Of Abraham it is said, "And rest yourselves under the tree" [Gen 18:4].
F. So the Omnipresent gave his children seven glorious clouds in the wilderness, one on their right, one on their left, one before them, one behind them, one above their heads, and one as the Presence among them.

The same theme is expounded in a systematic way through the entire account; it is worth dealing with the complete statement:

Tosefta *Sotah* 4:3:
A. Of Abraham it is said, "While I fetch a morsel of bread that you may refresh yourselves" [Gen 18:5].
B. So did the Omnipresent, blessed be He, give them manna in the wilderness, as it is said, "The people went about and gathered it . . . and made cakes of it, and the taste of it was like the taste of cakes baked with oil" [Num 11:8].

Tosefta *Sotah* 4:4:
A. Of Abraham it is said, "And Abraham ran to the herd and took a calf, tender and good" [Gen 18:7].
B. So the Omnipresent, blessed be He, rained down quail from the sea for his children, as it is said, "And there went forth a wind from the LORD, and it brought quails from the sea, and let them fall beside the camp" [Num 11:31].

Tosefta *Sotah* 4:5:
A. Of Abraham what does it say? "And Abraham stood over them" [Gen 18:8].
B. So the Omnipresent, blessed be He, watched over his children in Egypt, as it is said, "And the LORD passed over the door" [Exod 12:23].

Tosefta *Soṭah* 4:6:
A. Of Abraham what does it say? "And Abraham went with them to set them on their way" [Gen 18:16].
B. So the Omnipresent, blessed be He, accompanied his children for forty years, as it is said, "These forty years the LORD your God has been with you" [Deut 2:7].

The evidence is of the same character as that adduced in the Mishnah: cases of Scripture. But the power of the Tosefta's treatment of Abraham must be felt: finding an exact counterpart in Israel's later history to each gesture of the progenitor, Abraham, shows the match between the deeds of the patriarchs and the destiny of their family later on. Justice now is given dimensions we should not have anticipated, involving not only the individual but also the individual's family, meaning the entire community of holy Israel. Once more, we observe, a systematic effort focuses upon details. Justice is not a generalized expectation but a quite particular fact, bread/manna, calf/quail, and so on. There is where sages find the kind of detailed evidence that corresponds to the sort suitable in natural history.

The focus now shifts from how justice applies to the actions of named individuals—Samson, Absalom, Sennacherib, and Nebuchadnezzar—to the future history of Israel, the entire sector of humanity formed by those whom God has chosen and to whom he will give eternal life. It is a jarring initiative. The kinds of instances of justice that are given until that point concern sin and punishment, or the reward of individuals for their own actions. And these cases surely conform to the context: justice as the principle that governs what happens to individuals in an orderly world. But now we find ample evidence of the fundamental position in the sages' system, the generative character in their consideration of all issues that, as the first principle of world order, justice governs.

For sages not only accept the burden of proving, against all experience, that goodness goes to the good and evil to the wicked. They have also alleged, and here propose to instantiate, that the holy people Israel itself, its history, its destiny, conform to the principle of justice. And if the claim that justice governs in the lives and actions of private persons conflicts with experience, the condition of Israel, conquered and scattered, surely calls into question any allegation that Israel's story embodies that same orderly and reasonable principle. Before us the sages take one step forward in their consideration of that very difficult question: How shall we explain the prosperity of the idolaters, the Gentiles, and the humiliation of those who serve the one true God: Israel? That step consists only in matching what Abraham does with what later happens to his family.

If sages had to state the logic that imposes order and proportion upon all relationships—the social counterpart to the laws of gravity—they would point to justice: what accords with justice is logical, and what does not is irrational. In the sages' view, ample evidence derives from Scripture's enormous corpus of facts to sustain that the moral order, based on justice, governs the affairs of humans and nations. But justice begins in the adjudication of the affairs of men and women in the Israelite household and from there radiates outward, to the social order of

Israel, and thence to the world order of the nations. It is from the Halakhah before us that sages commence their exposition of God's perfect justice, in rewarding the innocent and punishing the guilty, because only there could they state their deepest conviction concerning justice: all things start in the Israelite household, the smallest whole social unit of creation. That is why the law of the accused wife forms the ideal occasion, within the Halakhic system, to underscore the requirements of justice.

15

Christian Interpretation

Sexuality and Family in Christianity

Bruce D. Chilton

During the nearly two millennia of its development, Christianity has insisted upon quite different standards in the comportment of the sexes and in the ordering of families. That is natural in a religious perspectivethat has been involved in the drastic social changes that Christianity has seen. But the fact that Christian views of sexuality and family have changed in no way diminishes Christianity's categorical insistence upon sexuality and family as vital aspects of how the people of God are to live within the Spirit of God. In this topic more than in others, Christianity presents a paradox: changes of standards on the one hand, and categorical insistence upon current standards, on the other hand.

To understand this paradox, we will consider four representative—and at one time or another dominant—models of sexuality and family. Our survey will by no means be comprehensive, but it should give us a sense of the range of models involved. Arranged by their emergence in time, the four models are these:

1. Opposition to the conventional family and recognition of women (in Jesus' teaching and primitive Christianity).
2. The embrace of family, the silence of women (in early Christianity).
3. The transformation of sexuality into gender (in Orthodox Christianity).
4. The contention over gender (in later Christianity).

During the survey, we will pay especial attention to how a given model was generated by its underlying vision of human life unfolding in the presence of God. That will permit us, in the conclusion, to see how the paradox of constant change in this realm, together with categorical insistence upon the centrality of sexuality and family, in fact represent a coherent feature of Christianity.

Opposition to the Conventional Family and Recognition of Women

As we examine primitive Christianity and Jesus' teachings, we find clear indications that Jesus and his family were on strained terms. Within Mark, for example, we encounter the following scene (3:31–35):

> And his mother and his brothers come and standing outside, they sent a delegation to him, calling him. And a crowd sat around him, and they say to him, "Look, your mother and your brothers and your sisters seek you outside." He replied and says, "Who are my mother and my brothers?" He looks around at those sitting in a circle about him, and says, "Look: my mother and my brothers. Whoever does the will of God, he is my brother and sister and mother."

Here we have not a picture of family bliss, but an echo of the earlier statement (3:21) that there were those associated with Jesus who tried to prevent him from engaging in exorcism. They said he was "beside himself." Now he says they are not true family.

The assertion involved in Mark 3:31–35 insists upon an explicit principle: the bonds of family are to come second to the will of God. This is much more than an anecdote concerning a particular dispute; instead, it reflects an emerging principle. We find the principle clearly expressed (in Jesus' name), for example, in the Gospel according to Matthew (10:34–41):

> Do not presume that I came to put peace on the earth! I did not come to put peace—but a sword! Because I came to separate man against his father, and daughter against her mother, and a bride against her mother-in-law, and the man's enemies will be his house members! The one who loves father or mother more than me is not worthy of me, and the one who loves son or daughter more than me is not worthy of me, and whoever does not take his cross and follow behind me is not worthy of me. The one who has found his life will forfeit it, and the one who has forfeited his life for my sake will find it. The one who receives you receives me, and the one who receives me receives the one who delegated me. The one who receives a prophet in the name of a prophet will receive a prophet's reward, and the one who receives a righteous man in a righteous man's name will receive a righteous man's reward.

This is a well-crafted speech, which represents the perspective of the church after the resurrection: the picture is for people to follow Jesus in the way of the cross, and to put the fellowship of those sent in his name—the name of a prophet and righteous man—ahead of any other call upon loyalty.

Jesus understood the kingdom of God as a divine power that was in the process of transforming the world as it can be seen and known, and he conveyed that vision to Christianity. Part of the transformation included the dissolution of the ordinary bonds of family, which were widely experienced as a fundamental category of social life.

Jesus' radical challenge of the place of loyalty to family explains another famous aspect of his message. He insisted upon including women among his followers, and authorizing their participation in the process of learning (so Luke 10:38–42):

> As they traveled, he entered a certain village; a certain woman named Martha received him. And her sister, called Miriam, sat at the Lord's feet and heard his word. But Martha was distracted with much serving, approached and said, "Lord, does it not matter to you that my sister has left me alone to serve? Speak to her, then, so that she comes to my aid!" But the Lord answered and said to her, "Martha, Martha, you care and worry and fret about many things, but one is necessary. For Miriam has chosen the good part, which will not be removed from her."

The word of the kingdom is such that, in the brilliance of its vision of God, it dissolves the usual constraints, including the constraints of family and sexuality. If God is in the process of transforming the world and us with it—which is Jesus' understanding of the kingdom[1]—then nothing must stand in the way of the transformation.

More than twenty years after Jesus' execution, Paul—in his letter to the Galatians (written around 53 CE)—insisted upon a cognate principle (Gal 3:28):

> There is neither Jew nor Greek, neither slave nor free, neither male nor female, because you are all one in Jesus Christ.

That widening of the principle, to include the removal of ethnic and economic boundaries, as well as of sexual boundaries, has provided Christianity with a strong sense of the autonomy of human conscience, collective and individual, in the ordering of society. That helps to explain the revolutionary developments in the understanding of sexuality and family which have been characteristic of Christian thought.

The Embrace of Family, the Silence of Women

In early Christianity, the second Christian century was a time of profound ferment within the church. The definition of Christianity as distinct from Judaism was widely agreed, on the part of Jews and Christians and representatives of the Roman Empire, and that made for a sense of beleaguered cohesion. Christians could no longer claim the right as Jews not to take part in the (for them) idolatrous worship of the image of Caesar, and that made for a persistent environment of persecution. On the other hand, the definition as being apart from Judaism pressed Christians into the arena of philosophical debate with many other ways of looking at God

(Judaism included), a debate then very popular.[2] They gave accounts to outsiders and to one another of how their way was the way the one God would have humanity live.

No work was more popular among Christians at this time than the *Shepherd of Hermas*. Jaroslav Pelikan is representative of scholarship in his description of the apocalypticism of the *Shepherd of Hermas*:[3]

> The author (or authors) of the *Shepherd* used the format of an apocalyptic summons to call the readers to repentance. The vividness of its eschatological language is exceeded only by the decisiveness of its plea. The Lord had not yet returned, and therefore the work of judgment was not yet complete; but it would soon be finished, and then the consummation would come.

As Pelikan points out, his use of the word "apocalyptic" here does not refer to the hard and fast distinction between this world and the world to come. Rather, a process started within the world points toward its eschatological completion. In fact, the line of demarcation between the present and the future is less sharply drawn in Hermas than it is, say, in the Revelation of John in the New Testament (written around 100 CE).

In the first vision of *Hermas* (chap. 1), an angelic Lady appears to Hermas and accuses him of sin (specifically, of impure thoughts about a woman, whom the angelic Lady resembles). She succinctly analyzes the rewards that attend righteousness, and therefore also the punishments that await evil:

> For the righteous man has righteous designs. As long as his designs are righteous, his repute stands fast in heaven, and he finds the Lord ready to assist him in all his doings. But they who have evil designs in their hearts bring upon themselves death and captivity, especially those who obtain this world for themselves, and glory in their wealth, and do not lay hold of the good things which are to come.

The apocalyptic perspective of the angelic promise and threat is evident in the wording of this citation. "The good things which are to come" refers to the heavenly treasure, which was commonly held by Christians to be stored for them until the day of judgment (1 Pet 1:3–5).

The apocalyptic convictions of the *Shepherd of Hermas* are evident and amply support the scholarly reading of the document, which has become a matter of consensus. But it is equally apparent that there is another sort of conviction at work. Hermas is assured that the righteous person "finds the Lord ready to assist him in all his doings." The promise is for support in the present, not only in the final judgment which is to come. Similarly, the fate of the wicked is "death and captivity," not a purely eschatological threat.

The social setting of the *Shepherd of Hermas* makes the promise and the threat all the more striking. On the basis of earlier materials, "Hermas" finally composed the *Shepherd* around the year 150 CE, just when intellectuals reached a crescendo in their attacks on Christians. Fronto, tutor of the emperors Antoninus and Marcus Aurelius (and consul under Hadrian), charged that Christians worshipped an ass's head, sacrificed children, and encouraged promiscuity during worship.[4] Under such circumstances, to imagine oneself as assisted and punished by the Lord takes on a particular meaning.

The righteous who "finds the Lord ready to assist him in all his doings" discovers support, then, in the midst of suspicion, but not so much prosperity that he becomes one of those who "obtain this world for themselves, and glory in their wealth." Just as Christians tried to walk a fine line between the Roman hostility, which would destroy their lives, and accommodation to Rome, which would destroy their souls, so Hermas is called to a life of just getting along with divine support. In that position, he is to escape both the wrath of God and death at the hands of Caesar.

Hermas, as the author is usually called, lays out his chief concern as the problem of sin. Given that, as he is told, the righteous are only as righteous as their intentions, Hermas panics, "If this sin is recorded against me, how shall I be saved?" (*Shepherd* 1.2.1). In another vision, the grounds of his fear are only confirmed. A great and old woman appears, seated on a throne of snow-white wool. That description echoes the appearance of God himself in the vision of Dan 7:9, and Hermas is eventually told that the venerable matron is the church (*Shepherd* 2.4.1). It is she who underscores what Hermas has already learned (1.2.4):

> For it is an evil and mad purpose against a revered spirit and one already approved, if a man desire an evil deed, and especially if it be Hermas the temperate, who abstains from every evil desire and is full of all simplicity and great innocence.

The authority of the church, then, only reinforces the desperate predicament of all who are like Hermas. Because the issue is one's intentions and desires, not only one's actions, the problem seems here to be set up as impossible to solve. And since the issue is the lack of complete control over what he thinks, Hermas's predicament seems to be universal.

Here *Shepherd of Hermas* identifies, with the greatest precision of any extant document from the early church, how the problem of sin was seen to threaten the integrity of the faith overall. As compared to the social issue of how to conduct oneself as a disciple in an inhospitable environment, the deeper incongruity of being held responsible for whatever one might think and feel was a far more fundamental problem. After all, that concern could feed the response of a dualistic Gnosticism, which would make the nature of one's desire a symptom of whether one was spiritual in one's own constitution. A counsel of despair is an obvious response to the command to control one's desire. If Hermas must determine his desires in order to be saved, the most rational course might be to admit that he is not saved and cannot be.

The *Shepherd of Hermas* resolves the dilemma in what the angelic representation of the church goes on to say. God's anger against evil intents is confirmed, but the grounds of his anger are said to be other than the issue of intents (*Shepherd* 1.3.1): "But it is not for this that God is angry with you, but in order that you should convert your family, which has sinned against the Lord, and against you, their parents." The answer to the dilemma of human intention is given: it is the mercy of divine restraint. Although God would justly be angered by the failure of good intent among the righteous, he is compassionate enough to provide a remedy. If at least they will see to the nurture of their families, he will not be angry.

The symmetry of God's willingness to accept the nurture of one's family in the place of intentional perfection is simply stated. In the social realm, one can act with greater conscious control than in the purely personal realm (*Shepherd* 1.3.2): "For as the smith, by hammering his work, overcomes the task which he desires, so also the daily righteous word overcomes all wickedness." The *Shepherd* comes to a confidence in reasoned behavior, as influenced by the "Word" of God, which corresponds to Clement of Alexandria's much more philosophical theology of Christ, also developed in the second century. Clement's approach was inventive, and a continuation of the identification between Jesus and the Word of God made in the Gospel according to John (1:1–18) and by Justin Martyr (another second-century thinker). Clement insisted that the Word was influential even on one's passions. But Clement's thought, the *Shepherd* shows us, is also representative of popular Christian belief. The "daily righteous word" of God, God's accessibility through reason and speech and deliberate action, was widely understood to "overcome all wickedness," whether in the world or (if only eventually) in one's heart.

The family is a vital sphere of Christian action in the *Shepherd of Hermas*, because it is the one place where it is assumed that Hermas exerts influence. "The affairs of daily life" in the world are assumed to corrupt families, and Hermas is instructed to correct his own family, especially his children (*Shepherd* 1.3.1–2). Later, the same principle will include Hermas's wife within his family, and it will be extended to the church at large (*Shepherd* 2.2).

The placement of the family at the center of action marks a signal development in Christian theology. The position attributed to Jesus in the primitive church envisaged the renunciation of family for the sake of the gospel (Matt 19:27–30; Mark 10:28–31; Luke 18:28–30). That position was modulated within early Christianity as represented within the New Testament: the relationships of family were portrayed as providing an opportunity for enacting the love one had learned in Christ (1 Pet 2:18–3:7). By the time of the *Shepherd of Hermas*, however, a deeper transformation in the evaluation of family had occurred. It was now the sphere of first recourse in working out one's constitutional inability to offer God the perfection he required. Here, in fact, is the source of the vital concern for family within classical Christianity. It is not merely a "value" or a place of affection: family is where salvation is ordinarily worked out.

The imperative to Christian leaders sums up the ethical perspective on salvation that is developed in the *Shepherd of Hermas* (2.2.7): "You, therefore, who do righteousness, remain steadfast and do not be double-minded, that your way might be with the angels." By this point in *Hermas*, it has already been shown that an individual cannot avoid being double-minded to some extent: aspects of the imagination simply evade complete control. But one can be dedicated to the rational, deliberate task of nurturing one's family and the family of the church: that is what God demands by way of repentance.

A remarkable tension has been evident within Christianity from its classical formulations during the course of the second century. On the one hand, family and sexual relations have been viewed as pertaining to a condition of flesh that is to be overcome; on the other hand, such relationships have been held up as the normative field within which salvation may be worked out. The *Shepherd of Hermas*, precisely because it is a relatively unsophisticated document, represents the tension quite clearly (2.2.3):

> But make these words known to all your children and to your wife, who shall in future be to you as a sister. For she does not refrain her tongue, with which she sins; but when she has heard these words, she will refrain it and will obtain mercy.

Sexual relations are blandly put aside, when they are typified as incestuous (relations with a "sister"). By contrast, inappropriate speech is given labored attention. Christianity constructed for itself the image of the perfect woman, obedient, celibate, and silent, because it located the struggle for salvation within social and human terms.

The Transformation of Sexuality into Gender

In Orthodox Christianity, Augustine of Hippo (354–430) is a pivotal figure; he lived during a time of trial for Christianity, in certain ways as severe as the persecution of the time before Constantine. In 410 CE, Alaric sacked the city of Rome itself. That event was a stunning blow to the Christian Empire generally, but it was a double blow to Latin Christianity. First, the pillage occurred while the empire was Christian; two centuries earlier, Tertullian had argued that idolatry brought about disaster (see *Apology* 41.1), and now Christianity could be said to do so. Second, Latin Christianity, especially in North Africa, had been particularly attracted to a millenarian eschatology. How could one explain that the triumphant end of history, announced by Eusebius and his followers in connection with Constantine's accession to power, seemed to be reversed by the Goths?

The explanation of that dilemma occupied Augustine in his *City of God*, a tremendous work of twenty-three books, written between 413 and 426. From the outset, he sounds his theme: the city of God is an eternal city, which exists in the midst of the city of men; those two cities are both mixed and at odds in this world, but they are to be separated by the final judgment (*City of God* 1.1). That essentially simple thesis is sustained through an account of Roman religion and Hellenistic philosophy, including Augustine's critical appreciation of Plato (books 1–10).

In the central section of his work, Augustine sets out his case within a discussion of truly global history, beginning with the story of the creation in Genesis.

From the fall of the angels, which Augustine associates with the separation of light and darkness in Gen 1:4, he speaks of the striving between good and evil. But the distinction between those two is involved with the will of certain angels, not with any intrinsic wickedness (*City of God* 11.33). People, too, are disordered in their desire, rather than in their creation by God (12.8).

The result of perverted will, whether angelic or human, is to establish two antithetical regimes (14.28):

> So two loves have constituted two cities—the earthly is formed by love of self even to contempt of God, the heavenly by love of God even to contempt of self. For the one glories in herself, the other [one] in the Lord. The one seeks glory from man; for the other [one], God, the witness of the conscience, is the greatest glory. . . . In the one the lust for power prevails, both in her own rulers and in the nations she subdues; in the other all serve each other in charity, governors by taking thought for all and subjects by obeying.

By book 18, Augustine arrives at his own time and repeats that the two cities "alike enjoy temporal goods or suffer temporal ills, but differ in faith, in hope, in love, until they be separated by the final judgment and each receive its end, of which there is no end" (18.54).

That commits Augustine to speak of eschatological issues, which he does until the end of the work as a whole. Christianity's commitment to the creation as God's work inevitably involves the hope of the transcendence of evil. It is in his discussion of eschatology that Augustine frames classic and orthodox responses to some of the most persistent questions of the Christian theology of his time. He adheres to the expectation of the resurrection of the flesh, not simply of the body (as had been the manner of Origen during the third century). In so doing, he refutes the Manichaean philosophy, which he had accepted before his conversion to Christianity. In Manichaeanism, named after a Persian teacher of the third century CE named Mani, light and darkness are two eternal substances that struggle against one another, and they war over the creation they have both participated in making. As in the case of Gnosticism, on which it was dependent, Manichaeanism counseled a denial of the flesh. By his insistence on the resurrection of the flesh, Augustine revives the strong assertion of the extent of God's embrace of his own creation in the tradition of Latin Christianity.

For the logic of his own argument, Augustine is required to confront the particular issue of sexual differences between people (*City of God* 22.17):

> Some believe that women will not rise in female sex, but that all will be males, since God made only man from clay, and the woman from the man. But they seem wiser to me who do not doubt that both sexes will arise. For there will be no lust there, which is the cause of shame. For before they sinned they were naked, and the man and the woman were not ashamed. So all defects will be taken away from those bodies, but their nature will

be preserved. The female sex is not a defect, but a natural state, which will then be free from intercourse and childbirth. There will be female parts, not suited to their old use, but to a new beauty, and they will not arouse the greed of the beholder, for there will be no greed, but they will inspire praise of the wisdom and goodness of God, who both created what was not, and freed from corruption what he made.

His assumption, following the line of his *City of God* as a whole, is that the depiction of humanity's fall as a result of love of self can be reversed to understand how the love of God will transform us.

Part of that transformation, in Augustine's vision, is to include male and female, no longer as instruments of intercourse and childbirth, but as in the image of God, created male and female (so Gen 1:27).[5] Throughout, it is plain that Augustine casts human sexuality as a problem, beset by the corruption of greed (the debased product of self-love). For that reason, writing as a male, he casts the problem as a whole as that of men wanting women for their own use, and he acknowledges his personal difficulty in just that regard (*City of God* 22.22–24). That particular association of females with sexuality is typical of late antiquity and is especially prominent in gnostic writings, where women's desire to be as creative as men leads them to literally hysterical reproduction (see, e.g., *On the Origin of the World*).[6] What is crucial in Augustine's analysis, however, is the simple and revolutionary statement "The female sex is not a defect, but a natural state" (*City of God* 22:17). That denies that femininity is to be described as the privation of the masculine, but must rather be seen as engendered by God as part of creation, and not simply for the practicalities of reproduction.

Augustine imagines gender, which is engendered by God in God's image, as distinct from sexuality, a characteristic of the corrupt state of humanity. For him, people are raised with their created and natural gender, and are raised sufficiently recognizably that they are present to one another in the resurrection. In his adherence to a kind of millenarianism and to the resurrection of the flesh in the Latin tradition, Augustine is very much a product of North Africa and Italy, where he was active (chiefly as a teacher of rhetoric) before his conversion and his return to North Africa. In every time and in every place, in his vision, there is the possibility that the city of God will be revealed and embraced; now, in the church, we at last know its name and can see the face of that love which would transform us all. Part of that transformation is the insight that female and male are not only sexual roles, but are also two sides of engendered humanity in the image of God.

The Contention over Gender

In the period since the end of the Second World War, feminism has been among the most important influences within the development of contemporary Christianity. Feminists have revolutionized both the self-understandings of women and men, and also the critical appreciation of the sources of Christianity. By way of definition, we consider feminism here as the effort to evaluate femininity within its own terms of reference, and not merely as a function of sexual utility or attraction.

A good description of feminist interpretation as widely practiced is offered in a recent book, a collaborative effort edited by Elisabeth Schüssler Fiorenza and others:[7]

> Rather than focusing only on the women's passages, it generally seeks to analyze writings in their entirety. This method is used in order to assess how much the texts religiously advocate and foster all women's and marginalized men's subordination and exploitation and how much they transgress the kyriarchal boundaries of their time.

The adjective *kyriarchal* is derived from *kyrios* in Greek, which means "lord." the concern here is with a lordship of dominance and a dynamic of what Schüssler Fiorenza calls transgression, but which might more naturally be described as liberation:

> Its contributors "search the scriptures" in a double sense. They scrutinize and interrogate the scriptures to uncover their "crimes" of silencing and marginalization. Moreover, most of them also seek to bring to the fore and make audible again the subjugated voices and suppressed traditions that have left traces in ancient writings.

In such work the assumption is that what has been subjugated and suppressed in the past might instruct us, that it is coherent enough to provide alternatives, and in some sense better alternatives, to the dominant emphasis of the lords of this world and of Christianity.

The emphasis upon the evaluation of documents in their entirety is in fact characteristic of feminist concerns, because context has long been an emblematic-concern within feminism. Only within her context can one evaluate a person and assess the degrees to which she might be exploited and/or empowered to express who she is. When that insight is applied to texts, the result is to resist the atomizing of passages, which has been characteristic of conventional scholarship. Instead, one tends to seek the meaning of wholes, and of wholes in relation to one another. It is no coincidence that the period of the influence of feminism has also evidenced a greater interest in the social contexts of Christianity.

In the same volume which Schüssler Fiorenza edited, Turid Karlsen Seim analyzes a classic passage in Luke's Gospel (10:38–42). In a sensitive reading, she emphasizes that empowerment or liberation is the emphasis:[8]

> Mary sitting at the Lord's feet and listening to his words is portrayed in the typical position of the pupil (cf. Acts 22:3). This description of a teacher-pupil relationship is an important feature of the text. The role as student in which Mary is positioned goes beyond the normal opportunity for women to hear the word in the context of worship. Moreover, the text alludes to

terms that in rabbinic tradition are connected to teaching institutions. It also echoes other sayings about "hearing the word" as the decisive criterion for discipleship directed to both women and men (see Luke 6:46ff.; 8:15, 21; 11:28).

But alongside this liberating tendency of the text, Seim also explores what she calls the "passivity and silence" of Mary. After all, she merely listens, and Martha does not even speak to her, but to Jesus. While men who listen "may become public preachers, women are never given any explicit commission to preach."[9]

What increased attention to context has enabled Seim to do is expose the ambivalence of Luke's Gospel in its presentation of women. She also refers to Acts in this regard, which was written as a sequel to follow Luke (see Acts 1:1–5), and that reference strengthens her analysis. But in that regard, there is a connection she does not make that proves interesting. In Acts 6, the apostles are portrayed as refusing "to abandon the word of the Lord and serve tables" (6:2). That is what prompts them to appoint people later in church history called "servants" (*diakonoi*, "deacons"), who administer nourishment to the community while the apostles continue in prayer and the service of the word (see 6:1–6).

Seim is helpful in calling attention to the absence of any explicit authorization that Mary should preach, but it is also appropriate to observe the resonance of Mary with the place of the apostles. Her silence is not well characterized as a mere matter of passivity, because she demonstrates the continuing attendance to the word, from which the apostles were distracted prior to the appointment of deacons. Her "good part" is not merely to be like the apostles, but to be better than they in her constant commitment to the word. That creates a tension in Luke-Acts: women are indeed assigned places, and on the whole they are well described as marginalized, but at the same time the positive but partial correspondence between what women do and what fully empowered men do invites a development beyond the text. In just that sense, feminist interpretation may legitimately claim to speak of what texts are pointing to more faithfully than other forms of interpretation.

Conclusion

At first, the variety of Christian models of gender and familial relationship may seem bewildering. But the four distinctive models we have considered in fact relate to each other closely. Feminist confidence that gender is contextual, and to be assessed contextually in regard to its repression and liberation, is not based upon an objective standard of truth, but upon conviction. That conviction is that gender is not merely functional or instrumental, whether for reproduction or of pleasure. Rather, gender is understood to be engendered, part of the meaningful configuration of humanity as shaped by God, which includes relationships that become "family" only in the metaphorical sense of which Jesus spoke. In that sense, feminist interpretation develops naturally from the analysis of Augustine.

Yet Augustine, for all his brilliance, surely worked in no vacuum. The bold conviction of the *Shepherd of Hermas* may seem to be crudely expressed as compared to the vast learning and elegant exposition of *City of God*, but those two works share the confidence that how people relate to one another in social terms represents and develops how they relate to God. Whether it is a question of family or of society, how we behave toward our neighbor is the measure of how God engages us (see also Matt 25:31–46). And that is true only because the insight of Jesus is taken to be axiomatic: if God is our truest parent, then our relations need continually to be worked out as sisters and brothers.

Sisters and brother are related throughout life, and beyond life. Their gender, along with many other elements, is naturally a part of them, and yet they relate to one another, not sexually first of all, but as different members of the same family. Christian attitudes toward gender and family, and even Christian definitions of what those are, have varied quite widely. But throughout there is an underlying coherence. Our most powerful and significant relationship is with God, our common parent. That, for every Christian and for all Christians, is the fully engaged relationship from which meaning is generated. In relation to God, we know who we are, become what we are, understand how we are to be. But all that is for the most part understood, not in the abstract realm, but in how we engage with other children of God. Within that family, relationships are engendered in which we find our gender, our truest expression of the natures given us in creation.

PART SIX

Lex Talionis

16

Scripture's Account

Lex Talionis

Baruch A. Levine

The English term *retaliation* derives from the Latin noun *talio*, as in the term *lex talionis*, "the law of retaliation." This principle operated in Roman criminal law and in ancient Near Eastern legal systems generally, including in biblical law. It requires not only that the punishment fit the crime, but also that it match the crime in measure and kind. Retaliation is a form of retribution. The most prevalent application of lex talionis is capital punishment, where one who takes another human life is condemned to death, thereby paying with his own life. As we shall see, capital punishment, although carefully applied, was crucial to the biblical penal system and a major component of the Israelite ethos. As in other ancient systems, the principle of retaliation was also applied to corporal punishment, whereby the guilty party would suffer bodily mutilation in kind. A proverbial example is when a person who plucks out the eye of another is punished by having his own eye gouged out.

Considerable discussion, much of it apologetic, has focused on the literalness of the prescribed retaliatory punishment in biblical Israel, especially as regards bodily mutilation. Was "an eye for an eye" ever carried out in practice, or was it tacitly understood that compensation was the penalty originally intended? It would be methodologically inaccurate to question the realism of the laws a priori; it is better to allow the sources themselves to speak. As will be shown, mutilation was at home in the culture of ancient Israel, as it was elsewhere in the ancient Near East, and it persists to this day in certain societies.

The starting point for a discussion of retaliation as an action-response, what we will refer to as "initiatory retaliation," is the acknowledgement that it did not originate in law. Retaliation exhibits a metalegal matrix, embodying attitudes that are rooted in myth and ritual, with magical overtones. Law by its very character is contingent; but the exercise of retaliation, unless restricted by law, is unaffected by contingencies. Once set in motion, it will be acted out unconditionally, often resulting in the unjust killing of those who only accidentally brought about the death of another. This dynamic is best demonstrated by the age-old practice, acknowledged in the Hebrew Bible, whereby a person avenges the slaying of a clan relative by seeking out and slaying his killer (Num 35:9–34; Deut 19:1–13; cf. Exod 21:12; see below). Not only would the avenging relative be within his traditional rights to do so, without prior recourse to judicial process, and regardless of the original killer's intent or lack thereof; he would be duty-bound to do so and could not shirk this responsibility.

The relevant biblical laws deal precisely with problems generated by initiatory retaliation in a society that, once it took form, held to rules of evidence and operated through the judicial process. The right of retaliation, which is never challenged in principle, collided with notions of justice that go beyond remedying the consequences of a crime to weighing the possible mitigating conditions of its original commission. It would be well, therefore, to look into the core concepts expressed in retaliation first, and then review how biblical legislation sought to rein it in and adapt it to prevailing notions of justice in ancient Israel.

Modern scholarship has devoted considerable resources to the study of biblical criminal law in comparative perspective, bringing to light compelling parallels with Mesopotamian legal systems, in particular. Comparative evidence demonstrates, first and foremost, that biblical criminal law is realistic and not merely programmatic. What is legislated in the Hebrew Bible, and reflected in narrative and prophecy, was practiced, at least in certain periods of Israelite history.

Retaliation as Restoring the Balance: Some Biblical Pronouncements

We speak of the balance of nature as a necessary ecological state, and we are concerned whenever signs of environmental imbalance appear. In many cultures, old and new, it has been similarly thought that there is a balance in the social order that must be maintained, lest the fabric of collective existence come apart. There is the further anxiety that the forces of nature, personified in myth, may turn against humankind if such imbalances, natural and social, are not repaired. As an example, biblical narratives of the primeval flood illustrate how this danger was perceived, and how the human and the natural worlds are interrelated. God's rainbow promise that he would never again destroy the natural world on account of the sins of humankind is a response to this very anxiety (Gen 9:8–17).

We are dealing, therefore, with issues of collective living. Many ancient societies operated on the principle that land belongs to the collective, the tribe or clan or nation, and not to the individual owner alone. On this basis, restrictions were imposed on the alienation of land, with a binding obligation on members of the clan to redeem (Heb. *gāʾal*) land lost to an outsider, however that outsider's status may be defined (Lev 25:47–49; Num 36; the book of Ruth; Jer 32:6–15). In a parallel manner, the "blood," or life, of an individual belongs to the collective, so that we read of the duty to restore the blood of a member of one's clan if it has been shed and thereby lost to the group. The relative who slays the killer in retaliation is appropriately known as *gōʾēl haddām*, "the restorer of the blood," who is, in effect, the one who reestablishes the balance. Forms of the same verb *gāʾal*, "to redeem, restore," are similarly used to describe the retrieval of lost land (Lev 25:49; Ruth 4:8).

In the case of the loss of human life, there are additional factors, as we would expect. To understand the phenomenology of retaliation for homicide, we will examine several biblical texts that reveal what underlies the principle that human blood that has been shed must be replenished through retaliation. We begin with the story of primeval fratricide, as recounted in Gen 4:8b–14:

> It happened when they were in the open field, that Cain assaulted Abel, his brother, and killed him. Then Yahweh said to Cain: "Where is Abel, your brother?" He said: "I do not know. Am I responsible for watching over my brother?" Then he said: "What have you done? Hark! Your brother's blood is crying out to me from the land. Now, then, you will be cursed by the land, which opened its mouth to receive your brother's blood from your hand. When you till the land, it shall no longer yield you its vitality, so that you will become a constant wanderer on the earth." Then Cain said to Yahweh: "My punishment is too great to bear! As of now, you have banished me from the surface of the land, and I must hide myself from your presence. I shall become a constant wanderer on the earth; so that anyone who overtakes me would slay me."

This subtle tale is replete with toned-down, mythic themes. Yahweh surely knew what had happened, if in no other way than by hearing the cry of Abel's lifeblood rising from the earth. The blood of the slain (here expressed by the qualitative plural, Heb. *dāmîm*) seeps into the earth, where it cries out for requital, which is to be realized by slaying the homicide in retaliation. When the blood of the homicide is shed, it likewise seeps into the earth, where it replaces the blood of the victim. In a classic example of substitution, the blood of the manslayer secures the release of the original victim's blood from the chthonic, netherworld deities who had thirsted for it. In the biblical narrative, this mythological projection is toned down and expressed impersonally as *hāʾădāmâ*, "the ground, the earth." The blood of the original victim is thereby restored to the living community. Cain deserved to be put to death, but his punishment was commuted to landlessness, a way of saying that he would no longer be accepted in the agricultural society to which he had previously belonged. Cain realizes that, as a homicide, he is fair game for those who might seek to avenge Abel's blood. The remedy was the mark of Cain, informing all persons who encountered him that his life had been spared by God.

It is surely no coincidence that elsewhere the theme of fratricide also serves to epitomize the dynamic of retaliation. Other fatal assaults likewise occurred in the open field (Heb. *baśśādeh*). Thus, 2 Sam 14 preserves a parable told by a skillful woman from Tekoa, enlisted by Joab, David's general. Joab had noticed how David longed for his son Absalom but could not bring himself to recall Absalom from banishment. So Joab sent in the woman disguised as a grieving widow, to tell the king the following tale:

> "Verily, I am a widowed wife, my husband having died. Your maidservant had two sons, who were fighting, the two of them, in the open field, with none able to tear them apart. Then one struck the other, killing him. Now behold, the entire clan has arisen against your maidservant, saying: "Hand over the one who slew his brother so that we can put him to death in place of the life of his brother, whom he killed." So would *they* destroy the heir, as well, and extinguish the remnant of my ancestral estate, leaving for my husband neither name nor remnant on the face of the earth."
>
> Then the king said to the woman: "Go to your home, and I will issue orders on your behalf." Then the Tekoan woman said to the king: "Upon me, my lord the king, rests the guilt, and upon my patriarchal household. The king, with his throne, is cleared." (2 Sam 14:5–9)

The king gave orders that the remaining son be spared. The implication is obvious: At times, ancient practices must give way before the greater good of the family and community. According to the predicates of the story, the king had the authority to block retaliation by members of the clan. The king responded to the widow's complaint that, in this case, allowing retaliation would have terminated a patriarchal household (Heb. *bêt ʾāb*) in Israel. This would have created an unacceptable imbalance in the social order, comparable to what had resulted from the original homicide. In stating that the king is "cleared" (Heb. *nāqî*) as regards her case, the woman drives home the moral that each family, including the royal family, must act to assure its own survival, and that the king should bring back his heir, Absalom, from imposed exile. Whereas the Cain and Abel story gives voice to mythic themes, the widow's tale highlights the threat to the social order. And yet, the two narratives share an anxiety over continuity: in the primeval story, for the continuity of the human race; and in the widow's tale, for the continuity of a patriarchal family and a royal line in Israel. A third source, legal in its overall formulation, but metalegal in its conception, is to be found in Deut 21:1–9:

> If a slain body is found in the land—which Yahweh, your God, is granting to you, to take possession of it—fallen in the open field, and it is unknown who struck him down: [In that case] your elders and magistrates shall go out to measure [the distances] to those towns that are in the environs of the slain body. It shall be that the town nearest the slain body, [namely,] the elders of that town, shall provide a heifer that has never been worked and has never borne the yoke. The elders of that town shall bring the heifer down to a perennial wadi, which has not been tilled nor has it been sown, and there break the neck of the heifer in the wadi. Then the priests of the Levitical tribe shall approach, for Yahweh, your God, has selected them to serve him, and to pronounce blessings in the name of Yahweh. By their order is every dispute or injury to be adjudged. Then, all of the elders of that town, the one nearest the slain body, shall wash their hands over the heifer whose neck had been broken in the wadi. They shall then make this declaration: "Our hands did not shed this blood, nor did our eyes

see. Grant expiation to your people, Israel, whom you have redeemed, and do not allow blood of the innocent amid your people, Israel." Thus shall the blood of the innocent be expiated on their behalf, and you shall have eradicated the blood of the innocent by doing what is upright in the sight of Yahweh.

In the present case, the relevant unit is the township. Deuteronomy projects a situation where efforts to locate the perpetrator have failed, the crime having occurred outside the usual jurisdictions. As a result, the blood of the slain individual could not be avenged by the township, which generally bore responsibility for crimes committed within its limits. The present circumstances occasioned a special kind of ritual substitution, by which the blood of an animal served to requite the blood of the slain human being. The reason that the ritual, with its statement of disclaimer by the elders, is enacted in a perennial wadi, is to assure that the blood of the animal will flow directly into the earth. The blood of the animal substitutes for the blood of the slain human, thereby releasing it and restoring it to the living community.

The unusual method of slaughter, by which the nape of the animal was broken, thereby severing its head, is elsewhere known from the ritual law applicable to the firstlings of mules, which were unsuitable for sacrificing. According to Exod 13:13 and 34:20, one may either substitute a lamb for the mule, or break the neck of the mule itself. Since Deut 12 forbade all sacrificial activity outside the central sanctuary by the usual method of slaughter, a different method of accessing the blood of the heifer had to be utilized in the present case. Finally, the requirement of slaughtering a heifer that had never been used as a work animal is paralleled in the ritual of purification from corpse contamination, according to Num 19, suggesting that here the prescribed ritual was conceived as purificatory. Expiation of bloodguilt has thus become a matter of cultic purity, and the role of animal sacrifice in attaining expiation, so basic to the biblical system, has been endorsed.

There is one further statement on retaliation that could be classified as legal, but which in immediate context is better understood as metalegal: the blessing of Noah and his family by Elohim, when they emerged from the ark after the flood. In redefining the relationship between man and beast, which allows humans to consume living creatures as food, Elohim has this to say (Gen 9:4–7):

> You must not, however, eat flesh with its lifeblood in it. Moreover, I will demand requital for your lifeblood; from the hand of every beast will I demand it. And from the hand of humans, from the hand of one human for the other, will I demand requital for human life. Whoever sheds the blood of a human, by humans shall his blood be shed. For in the image of God did he fashion the human being. And as for you, be fertile and multiply; swarm over the earth and multiply in it.

The human being is singular in God's creation in form and appearance; only humans look like their creator! But the image of God is not merely a physical feature. It also reflects the role of humankind as God's representatives on earth, the stewards of God's creation, exercising dominion over other living creatures. This theology is spelled out in dramatic fashion in Ps 8. Homicide is, therefore, a most heinous crime, so that God himself will judge a person who kills another; he will demand (Heb. *dāraš*) the blood of the perpetrator.

In summary, the four biblical epitomes cited here share a concept of the role of blood as a potent life force. And yet, Hebrew *dām* (plural, *dāmîm*), is ambiguous, since it also describes death and often connotes a sentence of death (Exod 22:2). This ambiguity makes it difficult to translate the construction *dām nāqî*, which has already appeared in the cited texts. It may connote "blood of the innocent" (= "life of the innocent)," but also "killing, murder of the innocent." (The latter meaning is suggested by comparative usage. In the well-known Ahiqar story, we find the Aramaic construction *qĕṭāl zekî*, "murder of the innocent.")

Application of the principle of retaliation to corporal punishment for lesser crimes often involved bodily mutilation, which seems to derive from deadly retaliation in cases of homicide. Here, too, we are dealing with actions that often lay outside the judicial process and were undertaken on the initiative of injured parties, or by enemies in war. The Hebrew Bible refers to certain forms of bodily mutilation as ways of shaming, most notably gouging out the eye(s) of the perpetrator. This punishment was inflicted on captives, as dramatized by the action of the Philistines in gouging out Samson's eyes (Judg 16:21), and by the blinding of Zedekiah, king of Judah, by his Babylonian captors (2 Kgs 25:7 // Jer 39:7 // 52:11). Then, too, we find taunts that refer to blinding. Thus, Nahash the Ammonite king, when the besieged residents of Jabesh Gilead in Transjordan sought a treaty with him, replied as follows: "I will make a pact with you on this condition; that you gouge out every right eye of yours. I will make this a humiliation for all Israel" (1 Sam 11:2). In a similar vein, Dathan and Abiram taunt Moses for disappointing them by saying that he had intended to gouge out their eyes (Num 16:14). Most revealing is the report of how Adoni-bezek, the Canaanite petty king, was mutilated by his Judean captors after his defeat (Judg 1:6–7):

> Adoni-bezek fled, but they pursued him and seized him. They cut off his thumbs and his big toes. Then Adoni-bezek said, "Seventy kings, with their thumbs and big toes cut off, used to pick up scraps under my table. As I have done, so has God requited me."

At the very least, these sources indicate that mutilation was at home in the biblical ethos and that its imposition as a penalty was accepted practice.

Integrating Initiatory Retaliation within the Judicial Process

Thus far, we have surveyed the background of lex talionis. Biblical law, speaking for a network of communities where initiatory retaliation for homicide was a recognized practice, acted to restrict its exercise by subjecting that practice to judicial norms and procedures. Such restrictions relate both to mitigating circumstances of the original crime, as well as to the unintended consequences of unrestricted retaliation. Of the latter, we have already seen a degree of awareness in the narrative of Cain and Abel and in the parable of the bereaved widow. We can now survey the remedies provided under biblical law.

But first, a word about substitution: Knowing what we do about the workings of clan retaliation in many societies, we are prompted to ask: Was it ever sanctioned in ancient Israel for the avenging clan relative to retaliate against anyone other than the actual killer, such as against his son or other relative? This question cannot be answered conclusively as regards initiatory retaliation. For itself, biblical law is clear on the matter of human substitution. Thus Deut 24:16: "Fathers shall not be put to death [*lōʾ yûmĕtû*] on account of sons, and sons shall not be put to death on account of fathers. Each man on account of his own offense shall be put to death." Yet when we view this law against the background of prevailing attitudes regarding justice, both human and divine, we encounter mixed messages. Thus, Jer 31:29–30:

> In those days they shall no longer say: "The fathers have eaten sour grapes, but the teeth of sons are blunted." Rather, everyone will die for his own sins. Whosoever eats sour grapes, his teeth shall be blunted. (cf. Ezek 18:2–4)

This prophetic statement suggests that people regarded it as unjust for sons to be punished for the sins of their forebears, and that it would be preferable if this were not to persist. In other words, it was something that happened. When we move from human courts to divine judgment, we find the Decalogue admonishing us that the God of Israel will visit punishment for the sins of the fathers on their descendants (Exod 20:5–6; Deut 5:9–10). Ezekiel 18, while rephrasing the proverbial reference to sour grapes in Jer 31, goes on to project a succession of generations, bearing the message that each generation will be judged on its own merits. Ezekiel 18 thus represents a classic example of inner-biblical exegesis. It interprets the dictum of the Decalogue as applying only if coming generations persist in the sins of their forebears, but not if they abandon evil ways. In that case, they would not live under the cloud of punishment for the sins of their fathers. Likewise in the context of divine punishment, we encounter the notion that deferral of punishment by the God of Israel to the next generation is merciful. First Kings 21:28–29 provides an example. After chronicling the sins of Ahab, king of northern Israel, the text states that Yahweh will defer Ahab's punishment until the reign of his son, because Ahab had repented of his sins (see 2 Kgs 9; cf. 2 Kgs 22:20).

In summary, it can be said that as far as the biblical legal system is concerned, substitution was never legitimate, even though that same system acknowledged initiatory retaliation against the perpetrator as being legitimate. Furthermore, the very need to restrict initiatory retaliation in the name of justice probably extended to disavowing substitution, which seems to have been customary.

Now let us consult the legal texts themselves. The Book of the Covenant (roughly Exod 21–23) is the earliest collection of laws in the Torah and contains several pronouncements on imposing the death sentence for homicide. It is followed by the Deuteronomic law code (roughly Deut 12–16), where we observe consecutive institutional developments and legal modifications. The third and final phase of Torah law is represented by priestly collections, which exhibit even further elaboration. In biblical law, the death penalty is also mandated for crimes that do not involve the taking of human life, including religious sins like idolatry and moral sins like adultery. Here we are interested primarily in the taking of human life and its punishment, as well as punishment for the infliction of bodily injury.

An observation is in order regarding the role of kings in the judicial process. Deuteronomy 17 requires that the king govern in accordance with the dictates of the Torah, and from several famous cases, it seems that kings were considered to be bound by law, in principle if not always in actual practice. More important is the recognition that kings possessed judicial authority and were, in effect, the court of last appeal for redress of grievances. We have already seen how the royal role affected the exercise of clan retaliation.

The Book of the Covenant

Exodus 21:12–14

Whoever strikes another person so that he dies, shall surely be put to death. If, however, he did not act with conscious intent, but the deed came his way as an act of God, I will designate a place to which that person may flee. But if a man acts deliberately against his fellow with the intent of killing him treacherously—from my very altar must you apprehend him to face death!

This passage draws a fundamental distinction between intentional, or premeditated, murder and unintended, accidental homicide. As already identified (in Deut 24:16), the Hebrew verb *yûmat*, as conjugated in the *hopʿal* stem (from *mût*), connotes a death sentence imposed under recognized authority, whether court, king, or other. As such, the present statement endorses retaliation in the form of capital punishment, but limits its application to intentional murder. One who claimed that his deadly act had not been intentional would be denied relief, however, if there is evidence of willful intent, in which case the fugitive could be seized even at the sanctuary altar. This refers to the widespread notion that sacred space provides "sanctuary," bringing the person under divine protection. The Hebrew Bible records two incidents where persons fearing retaliation actually clung to the horns of the altar in the Jerusalem temple. In the first case, Adonijah, David's son who had rebelled against Solomon, was torn from the temple altar but was spared after swearing fealty to the king (1 Kgs 1:50–53). In the second instance, Solomon had Joab, David's general, slain at that very altar as punishment for abetting sedition (2:28–35).

Exodus 21:22–25

> When men fight with each other, and shove a pregnant woman, so that her fetuses [or fetus] issued from her, but there was no fatality, the perpetrator shall surely be penalized as the woman's husband may impose on him, and he shall make payment as determined judicially. However, if a fatality occurs, you must exact a life in place of a life; [and in the same way] an eye in place of an eye, a tooth in place of a tooth, a hand in place of a hand, a foot in place of a foot, a burn in place of a burn, a wound in place of a wound, a bruise in place of a bruise.

This is a classic formulation of the principle of retaliation, partially paralleled in Deut 19:21 and Lev 24:19–20. It also establishes the principle of the "unintended consequence," so that, as in this case, the killing of a bystander by one or the other of the fighting men is a crime as severe as the killing of one combatant by the other. That is to say, the killing of a bystander rises to the level of intentional murder, for which the penalty is death, according to Exod 21:12–14. The formulation of the law is problematic, however, because Hebrew *ʾāsôn*, used here, usually connotes a fatality and has been so translated. The problem is that the text quickly shifts from homicide to nonfatal bodily injuries, where the same principle of retaliation applies. Rather than construing the Hebrew to mean something less than a fatality, it would be preferable to deal with the asymmetry of the statement by linking the first case, that of homicide, to the subsequent cases of bodily harm. This has been done by supplying the words "and in the same way." In nonfatal cases it would be an eye for an eye, and so forth.

The syntax is all-important. It is Hebrew *taḥat*, "in place of," that establishes the equivalence of the crime and its punishment. In cases where the woman's life was not lost, compensation for the loss of the fetus(es) is to be negotiated between the perpetrator and the woman's husband. Although the fetuses had value, and their miscarriage represented a loss, they were not living human beings. In antiquity, injuries that we would regard as temporary—burns, wounds, bruises—would often be permanent and beyond remedy.

Exodus 21:18–19

> When men quarrel and one strikes the other with a stone or with his fist, and that person does not die but is laid up—if he should get up and walk about outside on his staff, the assailant is exonerated. He must only compensate the other for his idleness, and surely be liable for his cure.

If one person only injures another in physical combat, but does not kill him, the principle of retaliation does not apply, as we might have expected it to. This is probably so because it would be difficult, if not impossible, to assess the precise retaliation to be inflicted on the body of the perpetrator. Hence, no corporal punishment

196   Lex Talionis

is mandated for him. Instead, "unemployment compensation" is demanded from the man who inflicted the injury, as well as coverage of medical costs.

Laws affecting slaves belonging to Israelites

> Should a man beat his slave, male or female, with the rod, and he dies directly from his blow, he must be avenged. But if he should endure for a day or two, he shall not be avenged, because he is the owner's wealth. (Exod 21:20–21)
>
> Should a man strike the eye of his male slave or the eye of his female slave thereby destroying it, he shall release him to freedom in place of his eye. And if it is the tooth of his male slave or his female slave that he knocks out, he shall release him to freedom in place of his tooth. (Exod 21:26–27)

The two laws are best treated in tandem because they both illustrate an important variable: personal status; in this case, the slave status of the victim relative to that of his Israelite owner. Generally speaking, biblical law, being addressed exclusively to the Israelites, shows little evidence of stratification, since all Israelites enjoyed equality under the law, in principle if not always in actual practice (but see Exod 21:32). It is quite clear, therefore, that reference is to non-Israelite slaves. In the law governing the killing of a slave, the operative Hebrew verb is *yinnāqēm*, "he shall be avenged," or the variant form, *yuqqam*. The verb *nāqam*, "to avenge," often connotes retaliation, and it is significant that the penalty for intentional homicide of a slave is the same, at least in principle, as that for an Israelite. And yet, both the divergent formulation and the stipulation that death must have been instantaneous in order to warrant retaliation—these considerations intimate that compensation may have been allowable in cases where the victim was a slave and considered to be his owner's property. In a case where the owner inflicted bodily injury on his slave, the slave gained his freedom, and there is no retaliation against the slave owner.

Exodus 21:37–22:2

> When a man steals an ox or a sheep and sells it or slaughters it, he must pay five heads of cattle for the ox and four animals from the flock for the sheep. Now, if the thief is overtaken underground and is beaten to death, he [the homeowner] is not to be charged with homicide. But if the sun shone upon him [the thief], he [the homeowner] is to be charged with homicide. He must surely make restitution, and if he lacks the means, he shall be sold on account of his theft.

This law differentiates between (a) accidental homicide, as when the homeowner could not be presumed to know in the dark that the intruder was only a thief, not a killer; and (2) when he should have realized that the threat was not deadly, as in daylight. In the latter case, the homeowner will be charged with accidental homicide, where compensation may be allowable in lieu of retaliation. The Book of the

Covenant goes on to set down procedures for cases where human death is caused indirectly by one's ox or by accidents occurring on one's property.

There can be no doubt that these laws from the Book of the Covenant were to be enforced by judicial authority, although there is no comprehensive statement to that effect. The heading in Exod 21:1 classifies the legalities to follow as *mišpāṭim* "judgments, norms of justice," a term clearly referring to the judicial process, and 21:22 requires that compensation in nonfatal injuries be determined through adjudication. Furthermore, we are told that in the absence of evidence, a victim of theft must take an oath in court that he himself had not misappropriated the lost property (22:7). Then, too, there is the concluding admonition in Exod 23:6–9, which condemns false judgment, the wrongful imposition of the death penalty on the innocent, and also bribery.

The Deuteronomic Laws

Deuteronomy outlines a judicial system with elders and magistrates; it repeatedly speaks of testimony, evidence, and lawsuits. The provisions of Deut 21:1–9 regarding procedures for restoring the balance of blood in cases where the perpetrator of a homicide cannot be identified—these have already been discussed above, in the light of their bearing on the principle of retaliation. We may now review the limits placed on retaliation, as presented in Deuteronomy.

Towns of asylum (Deut 19:1–13). Spelling out the allusive reference to asylum in Exod 21:12–13, the present passage projects a network of "towns of refuge," offering safe haven for those whose homicidal act was unintentional. After settling in the land, the Israelites are to designate three accessible towns in various regions of the land for this purpose. The objective was to prevent the restorer of the blood from seizing the offender before he could reach safe haven. The text then defines unintentional homicide, providing a specific example:

> This is the case of the [alleged] murderer, who would flee there in order to stay alive; the very one who strikes his neighbor unwittingly, without having been his enemy in recent days. [For instance:] One goes with his neighbor into the forest to chop wood, and his arm swings the ax to fell a tree, but the ax-head flies off the handle and strikes the other so that he dies. That man may flee to one of these towns and stay alive. Otherwise, the restorer of the blood, pursuing the [alleged] murderer in the heat of his passions, might overtake him, because the distance [to a town of asylum] is great, and strike him fatally, although he cannot be charged with the death penalty, because he was not his enemy in recent days. For this reason, I am commanding you: Set aside for yourselves three towns. (Deut 19:4–7)

The text goes on to stipulate that in the event the borders of the land were extended, three additional towns of refuge must be designated. The Deuteronomist records compliance with this mandate in Deut 4:41–43, actually naming the three towns of asylum that were designated in Transjordan (see below). It is odd that the unintentional manslayer is called *rōṣēaḥ*, "murderer," since the point of the law is precisely to protect those who are not real murderers. Hence we translate, "the [alleged] murderer." This statement of law tightens the definition of unintentional manslaughter and clarifies the problem of reining in initiatory retaliation by clan relatives, which might result in undue punishment. Most interesting, perhaps, are the provisions that follow in Deut 19:11–13:

> If, however, a person who indeed is his neighbor's enemy ambushes him and assaults him, striking him fatally so that he dies, and then flees to one of these towns, the elders shall have him brought back from there and shall hand him over to the restorer of the blood, and he shall meet death. You must show him no mercy. Thus will you eradicate the blood of the innocent from Israel, and it shall go well for you.

In other words, the elders allow the clan relative himself to execute the murderer once it has been determined, on the basis of testimony and evidence, that his act was intentional. We here observe the institutionalizing of clan retaliation within judicial procedure, as administered by the elders, those same elders who oversaw the ritual of the heifer in Deut 21.

Laws of testimony (Deut 19:15–21). After stipulating that adequate testimony requires a minimum of two, corroborating witnesses, the text takes up the problem of false testimony. One suspected of being a false witness must appear before the authorities:

> The magistrates shall investigate thoroughly, and if the witness is, indeed, a false witness, having testified falsely against his kinsman, you must do to him what he had plotted to do to his kinsman, and thus eradicate the evil from your midst. You must show him no mercy; a life in exchange for a life, an eye in exchange for an eye, a tooth in exchange for a tooth, an arm in exchange for an arm, a foot in exchange for a foot. (Deut 19:18–21)

This text is clearly paraphrasing the statement of the Book of the Covenant (Exod 21:23–25), further applying the principle of retaliation to false testimony. The syntax has changed, however: here, equivalence of one life with another is conveyed by the *bêt* [ב] *pretii* (Latin for "of price"), as in *nepeš běnepeš*, "a life in exchange for a life," rather than by the preposition *taḥat*, which was used in Exodus, but the effect is the same. The difference is that here the mere intent to commit a crime, once confirmed, is sufficient cause for retaliatory punishment, even though the act of false testimony and its consequences had been averted by timely discovery. The decisive power of testimony apparently called for severe punishment of those who sought to undermine the reliability of the process.

Retaliation in corporal punishment (Deut 25:1–4, 11–12). Two statements of law illustrate how the principle of retaliation was adapted to cases of corporal punishment. The first concerns flogging of a person who has been convicted of being the one at fault in a dispute:

> If it happens that the guilty party is to be flogged, the magistrate shall have him lie down, and be given lashes in his presence, by count, to the extent of his guilt. He may administer up to forty lashes but not more, lest he continue to flog him to excess, and your kinsman succumbs in your presence. (Deut 25:2–3)

The specifications of the present law were intended to assure that punishment is commensurate with the crime. Presumably, the number of lashes would vary according to the severity of the crime, and the limit of forty lashes would guard against the possible death of the convicted person under the whip. The second case illustrates an adaptation of the principle of retaliation in corporal punishment:

> If two men engage in physical combat with each other, and the wife of one of them draws near in an effort to rescue her husband from the power of his assailant, and she extends her hand and seizes his genitals, you shall cut off her hand at the palm; show no mercy. (Deut 25:11–12)

Technically speaking, this punishment does not match the crime; the woman in question did not cut off anyone's hand. The "match" relates to that part of the body that was instrumental. It is as though the hand was being held directly accountable for the woman's improper act.

Priestly Laws

The priestly texts of the Torah contain two statements on retaliation. The first is tacked on to a more comprehensive statement on capital crimes, occasioned by a recorded incident of blasphemy. After mandating the death penalty for the blasphemer, to be carried out by the entire community (Lev 24:15–16), the text continues as follows in 24:17–20:

> Whoever fatally strikes another human being shall be put to death, but one who fatally strikes an animal shall make compensation for it; a life in exchange for a life. As for a person who maims his fellow, as he has done shall be done to him: a fracture in place of a fracture, an eye in place of an eye, a tooth in place of a tooth. When one maims another human being, so shall it be inflicted on him.

Once again, we have a paraphrase of the law of retaliatory punishment first stated in the Book of the Covenant, covering both capital and corporal punishment. The participation of the community in meting out punishment, after everyone had heard the blasphemous words of the offender, qualifies as judicial process. In effect, the offender had been convicted; he was damned by the words of his own mouth.

The major, priestly statement on retaliatory punishment for murder is found in Num 35:9–34 and is introduced by a plan for the designation of Levitical towns. These towns were to be specified by the tribes of Israel from their allocated territories, as stipulated in Num 34. The total number of Levitical towns included the six towns of asylum, as ordained in Deut 19:1–10.

Beginning in Num 35:9, the text restates, with considerable elaboration, what had already been set forth in Exodus, Deuteronomy, and Leviticus-Numbers about the right of asylum as protection from clan retaliation. The distinction between intentional and accidental homicide is illustrated by graphic examples, in the spirit of Deut 19. In cases where the slayer claims that his acts were accidental, there shall be a trial:

> The assembly shall judge between the slayer and the restorer of the blood, on the basis of the above judicial principles. The assembly shall rescue the [alleged] murderer from the grasp of the restorer of blood, and the assembly shall return him to his town of asylum, to which he had fled. He shall reside there until the death of the high priest, who has been anointed with the sanctified oil. (Num 35:24–26)

The text goes on to stipulate that if the slayer leaves his safe haven, he is fair game for the avenging clan relative, who will not be held culpable for his death. The release of the slayer comes under the terms of an amnesty, a mechanism for commuting what amounted to town arrest. The chapter provides a summary of the laws of homicide, with reference to testimony, adding an injunction disallowing ransom in cases of intentional murder: "You shall not accept ransom for the life of a murderer, since he is guilty of the death penalty. For he shall surely be put to death" (Num 35:31). Such a person is to be denied asylum. The chapter concludes with an admonition against murder, thoroughly priestly in its diction. It states that the land itself is defiled by unrequited murder. Once again, this statement recalls the need to restore the balance.

Further information on how the network of towns of asylum operated is provided in Josh 20–21, where the names of the three Cisjordanian towns of asylum are listed, thereby complementing Deut 4:41. The fugitive was to present himself at the gate of a town of asylum and declare his innocence of murder before the elders. He would be accepted in residence until one of two things happened: Either he would be exonerated at trial and released, or be freed under amnesty at the death of the high priest. Joshua 20:9 refers to ʿārê hammûʿādâ, "assembly towns," a unique term, derived from the same root as ʿēdâ, "assembly," used in Num 35 (vv. 12, 24–25), which probably refers to the seat of the assembly-court. Finally, 1 Chr 6:42–45 lists thirteen towns of refuge by name (see below).

Asylum and Other Realities of Retaliation

Once we realize that the institution of asylum originated in the cult, important biblical statements assume a greater degree of realism. It was believed that once inside sacred space, a person came under the protection of the patron deity. By adding the stipulation that one who intentionally murdered another human being and fled to asylum may be seized even from the altar, the earliest law of Exod 21:14 is alluding to this very concept. The incidents of attempted asylum related in narratives of the Davidic succession, those of Adonijah and Joab, illustrate how the right of sanctuary operated and how it could be abused and violated (1 Kgs 1–2). We read that David himself sought refuge from Saul in Nob, "the town of priests" (1 Sam 21–22; esp. 22:19). It is likely that Nob was a cult center, a locality that accordingly offered asylum, so that while he was there, David was safe. After he departed, Saul had the priests of Nob executed for giving aid and comfort to his enemy, which was regarded as an atrocity on the part of a king of Israel. Biblical references to asylum regularly use the verb *nûs*, "to flee," and the term for "towns of asylum" is *ʿārê miqlāṭ* (Num 35:11; Josh 20:2), incorporating a rare verb *qālaṭ*, "to draw in, take in." In Josh 20:4, the verb is *ʾāsap*, "to gather in, accept" into the town.

Before the legislation of Deut 12–16, which was aimed at nullifying the sanctity of local and regional cult installations, there was a network of cult installations, large and small, throughout the land of Israel. These sites afforded asylum in addition to serving the cultic needs of the people. Their multiple functions are implied in Exod 21:12–13 by the assurance that a *māqôm* will be provided, to which the manslayer may flee. This northern Israelite term, characteristic of Deuteronomy, is often technical in its usage, and as such means "cult site," not simply "place." The provisions of Deut 19 should be regarded, therefore, as a response to a sea change in the operation of the cult of Yahweh produced by the Deuteronomic reform of the cult. The policy of cult centralization, first voiced in northern Israel shortly before Assyria annexed it in the late eighth century BCE, never reached fruition. Around 622 BCE, Josiah, king of Judah, adopted it in his attempt to reform the cult of the Jerusalem temple.

It is not entirely clear how widespread was compliance with the edicts of Josiah, but on the official level, it became necessary to accommodate practice to the new policy. Access to the central temple in Jerusalem would have been difficult, and its distance would endanger fugitives, who might be overtaken on the way by clan relatives. The concern with distance is characteristic of Deuteronomy and is prominent in Deut 19. It is reasonable to conclude that pursuant to Josianic edicts, which means realistically in the postexilic period, former cult sites became towns of asylum, divested of cultic functions.

The problem is that we first read the names of specific towns of asylum in later sources, beginning in Deut 4 and continuing in Josh 20–21, with some detail as to location provided in Num 35. Long before their composition, both northern Israel and Transjordan had been lost to Israel. How realistic, then, are these later sources? The view adopted here is that although these Torah sources, beginning with Deut 4, do represent retrojections into the early history of Israel, regarding both literary setting and specificity, this does not mean that their contents in substance represent late inventions. For one thing, there was extensive Jewish settlement in Transjordan in the exilic and postexilic periods. What we have are schematized references, which effectively obscure the reforms of Josiah and present a cultic history according to which nothing had changed since earliest times.

As is usual, however, there are giveaways of change. We find that many of the listed towns had temples and cult sites located in them at certain periods. Thus, the towns of Shechem in the Ephraimite hills and Hebron in the Judean hill country are known to have had temples, and one may assume that any town named Kedesh (or Kadesh, for that matter)—since such names incorporate the verbal root *qādaš*, "to be holy"—once hosted a local or regional temple (see Josh 20). The same is probably true of the Transjordanian towns of refuge listed in Deut 4:41–43. Some of the names listed in 1 Chr 6 also belie a cultic presence, such as Beth Shemesh, Debir, and Anathoth, a town of priests. What is particularly telling is the overlap of towns of asylum with Levitical towns in Num 35 and Josh 20–21 (and with priestly towns in 1 Chr 6). What would be more practical than to locate the towns of asylum where cultic personnel resided? In all probability, such communities of priests and Levites assumed welfare functions under the restructured asylum system. Precincts were set aside in the towns, where those who claimed asylum would reside and receive rations of food and other necessities, often for long periods of time. So it is that by reading between the lines, we become aware of what may have really happened: Initiatory retaliation coexisted with the court system and continued to be regulated, with places of asylum provided. All of the varied biblical evidence indicates, however, that initiatory retaliation persisted in antiquity and indeed is still practiced, especially in tribal societies or where family ties are very strong.

Epilogue: Retaliation as *Mentalité*

In addition to providing information on the legal and metalegal dimensions of retaliation, the Hebrew Bible points to a cultural mind-set, *mentalité* in French, in which the theme of retaliation figures strongly. It is evident in many contexts, individual and collective, including in association with the God of Israel. This mind-set is only one of several attitudes toward punishment expressed in biblical literature; but it nonetheless is significant. As we would expect, biblical law shows great concern for justice, which requires control over the acting out of retaliation. Unless it is subordinated to judicial norms, retaliation will tend to exceed the bounds of justice and become vengeful.

This trend can be illustrated rhetorically. Returning to Gen 9, we read how Elohim pledged to Noah and his family, the only survivors of the flood, that he will "demand" (Heb. *dāraš*) requital of human blood. There, the demand for requital is in proportion to the crime, a life for a life. But see how the same theme is taken up in Ps 9, where the speaker, perhaps the king or another leader, is thankful for the victory that Yahweh has given him over his adversaries. He regards the defeat of his enemies as just retaliation for his people's afflictions: "For he who demands requital for blood [*dōrēš dāmîm*] has been mindful of them; he has not ignored the cry of the afflicted" (Ps 9:13; cf. Ezek 33:8).

This statement reflects the truth that the urge to retaliate against enemies and those who have done one harm can be ever so strong. That urge is expressed by still another key verb, Hebrew *nāqam*, "to avenge," which we have also encountered in statements on legal retaliation. Vengeance often exceeds justice, however, and is a function of wrath, so that Israelites are individually admonished to avoid vengeful acts (Lev 19:18). And yet, the God of Israel is often depicted as avenger, a role expressed by forms of the verb *nāqam*. In that role; he retaliates against the enemies of his people, Israel (e.g., Deut 32:35, 41, 43; Isa 35:4; 61:2; 63:4; Mic 5:14 [15 Eng.]; Nah 1:2, 8; Ps 94:1). When God grants victory to Israel, it is presumed to be just, because God is just and because Israel's cause is regarded as just.

We thus observe one way in which the ultimate logic of retaliation plays out in the biblical mentality, and the Hebrew Bible is replete with illustrative examples on the individual level as well. And so, we have come full swing: We began with initiatory retaliation by clan relatives, continued with the imposition of judicial authority in an effort to restrict customary practice, and ended up with an awareness that the urge to retaliate survives. It has often been said that law ordains how people should properly behave, whereas literature reveals how they actually behave and how they think and feel.

17

An Eye for an Eye

Lex Talionis in Talmudic Law

Baruch A. Levine

This section will focus on the principal features of Talmudic law on the subject of lex talionis, against the background of biblical law. In interpreting the relevant biblical dicta, it was argued that the intent of biblical law was literal, and retaliatory. "An eye in place of an eye" (*ʿayin taḥat ʿayin*) meant that one who had intentionally maimed another person would suffer the same mutilation on his person as punishment. This conclusion was based not only on the clear sense of the Torah statements themselves, but also on the observation that mutilation was an acknowledged form of punishment in ancient Israel, as was corporal punishment in general. In this respect, biblical law governing bodily injury inflicted on humans by other humans differed from that applicable in cases involving another's property, or where one's property (such as a "goring ox") had caused injury, or even death to a human. In such circumstances compensation was allowable, in principle.

Talmudic law governing bodily injury inflicted by humans on other humans differs substantively from Torah law, as understood without apologetic. It is, in contrast, based on the principle of monetary compensation, or indemnification for bodily injury. The Talmudic term for such substitution is *māmôn*, "money, monetary compensation," whereas actual retaliation is referred to as *mammāš*, "actual, in actuality." It is the purpose here to show how the rabbinic sages accounted for their reading of Torah law by analyzing the hermeneutic "measures" (Heb. *middôt*) which they employed in the process. The sages attributed to the Torah itself the more humane penalties for bodily injury, which they endorsed, rather than presenting their interpretation as innovation.

It would be best to begin with the fulfillment of the process, namely, the codification of Talmudic law in the Mishnah tractate *Baba Qamma* 8:

> One who causes injury to his fellow becomes liable thereby on five counts: for bodily injury, for pain, for healing, for loss of employment, and for shame [endured]. How [are damages to be assessed] in cases of bodily injury? If one

had blinded another's eye, severed his hand, or fractured his leg—we regard him [the victim] as if he were a slave being sold in the market, and estimate how much he had been worth, and how much he is worth [now]. (8:1)

The Mishnah goes on to deal with multiple variables that come into play, relevant to the identity and status of those who caused the injury as well as those of the victims, and defines in each case how damages are to be calculated. It is clear that the formative term for "injury," Hebrew *nēzeq*, refers both to the injuries themselves and to the damages incurred thereby. We must realize that certain injuries, including fractures and bodily defects, which we are now able to remedy, were untreatable in antiquity. Thus, one whose leg had been fractured might remain disabled all his life and never heal. Only in cases where the death penalty was mandatory for bodily injury, such as for a person who had injured one of his parents, a capital offense according to Exod 21:15, would Talmudic law, like biblical law, disallow monetary compensation. Tosefta *Baba Qamma* 9 adds refinements and specifications to the assignment of damages for injuries, but like the parallel chapter in the Mishnah, never entertains the possibility that the Torah had actually mandated corporal retaliation. If the Mishnah and Tosefta represent the outcome of reinterpretation, how did the sages get there?

It is the structure of the Mishnah and of the Tosefta that accounts in large part for the absence of argument on the issue of retaliation in kind versus compensation. Although these compendia often report arguments on questions of law and record dissenting opinions, they only rarely reveal how they arrived at their determinations. For the hermeneutic process employed to attribute the policy of compensation, not retaliation, to Torah law, we must turn to the Tannaitic midrash collections on the applicable Torah laws, principally the *Mekilta on Exodus*, the *Sipra on Leviticus*, the *Sipre on Numbers*, and the *Sipre on Deuteronomy*—as well as to the Gemara of both the Talmud of Jerusalem and the Babylonian Talmud, *Baba Qamma* 8. In the Babylonian Talmud we find a full-blown *sûgyāʾ*, "course," on the subject of *nēzeq*, which will be reviewed here as the most elaborate collection of Talmudic disputations on this legal category.

Babylonian Talmud *Baba Qamma* 83b–84a

Note: The Talmudic text is both formulaic and laconic, so that a nuanced translation, allowing for interpolation of bracketed informative wording and explanatory comment, serves better than a diplomatic rendition. *On terminology:* The Talmud uses the Aramaic, divine epithet *raḥămānāʾ*, "the Merciful One," to refer to God as author of the Torah.

Pisqāʾ 1

- Q. Why is it so? [On what basis does one who injures another become liable for damages, as the Mishnah states?]
- A. The Merciful One said: "An eye in place of an eye."

Q. But I could say [that this means] an actual eye [ʿayin mammāš]!
A. This should not enter your mind, for it is taught [in a Baraita]: I might conclude that one who blinded another's eye would have his eye blinded, and one who severed another's hand would have his hand severed, and one who fractured another's leg would have his leg broken. Learn to cite [Scripture]: [The form] makkēh [one who strikes] is used with respect to one who injures humans, and [the same form] makkēh is used with respect to one who injures animals. Just as one who strikes an animal [makes amends] by compensation, so does one who strikes another human [make amends] by compensation.

Or, if you prefer you may cite [an alternative scriptural verse]: Behold, He [the Merciful One] states: "You must not accept ransom for the life of a murderer, for he is a criminal condemned to death" [Num 35:31]. It is for the life of a murderer that you do not accept ransom, but you do accept ransom for [loss of] essential parts of limbs, which do not grow back.

Q. Which makkēh [is the referent]? Is he is citing: "One who strikes [makkēh] an animal shall compensate for it, but one who strikes [makkēh] a human shall be put to death" [Lev 24:21], which is written in a case of killing?
A. Rather, from here: "One who fatally strikes [makkēh nepeš] an animal shall pay compensation for it, a life in place of a life" [nepeš taḥat nāpeš, Lev 24:18], and adjoining it: "If anyone inflicts [kî-yittēn] a disability on his fellow, as he has done so shall be done to him" [Lev 24:19].
Q. But this [the latter verse] does not attest [the form] makkēh.
A. We are comparing one act of striking [hakkāʾâ] to another act of striking [hakkāʾâ]. Just as the striking [said] in the case of an animal is remedied by compensation, so is the striking in the case of a human remedied by compensation.
Q. But is it not written: "If a person fatally strikes any human being, he shall be put to death"? [Lev 24:17].
A. It is [nonetheless] a case of māmôn.
Q. On what basis is this a case of māmôn? I could say that it is a case of actual death.
A. This should not enter your mind. For one thing, because it [the case of injury] has been compared to "One who fatally strikes an animal shall compensate for it [a life for a life]" [Lev 24:18], and furthermore, it is written after it: "Just as he maimed another person, so shall be inflicted on him" [Lev 24:19]. Learn from this that it is a case of māmôn.
Q. What, then, is the need for "Or, if you prefer you may cite"? [Why was it necessary for the Tanna[ite] to cite an additional Torah source?]
A. The Tanna[ite] faced a further objection: What prompted you to learn [the law] from one who strikes an animal? Let it be learned from one who strikes a human. They responded: We are to derive the law of damages from damages, and we are not to derive the law of damages from death.
Q. To the contrary: We are to derive the law regarding humans from humans, and we are not to derive the law regarding humans from animals.

A. This is why he taught: "Or if you prefer you may cite 'You must not accept ransom for the life of a murderer, for he is a criminal condemned to death, for he shall surely be put to death' [Num 35:31]. It is for a murderer that you do not accept ransom, but you do accept ransom for parts of limbs that do not grow back."

Q. And as for this very statement: "You must not accept ransom for the life of a murderer" [Num 35:31]: Does it [really] come to exclude [loss of] essential parts of limbs that do not grow back? Is not this statement required [for another purpose, to wit]: The Merciful One said: "Do not subject him to two [penalties]; do not take money from him and kill him as well"?

A. That is derived from "to the extent of his guilt" [Deut 25:2]. You are to hold him culpable for one count of guilt, but you are not to hold him culpable for two counts of guilt. [The context is the administering of stripes, a form of corporal punishment]

Q. But, that verse ["You shall not take ransom for the life of a murderer"] is still required [for another purpose]. The Merciful One said: "Do not take money and release him."

A. If that had been the case, the Merciful One should have written: "You must not accept ransom for one who is condemned to death." Why was it necessary to specify "for the life of a murderer"? Learn from it: It is for the life of a murderer that you do not accept ransom, but you do accept ransom for essential parts of limbs that do not grow back.

Q. Once it was written "You must not accept ransom," what need do I have for [the comparison of] *makkēh* to *makkēh*?

A. They ruled: If [the law was derived] from this verse ["You must not accept ransom"], I might say: If he wishes, he may remit an [actual] eye, or if he wishes, he may remit the monetary value of an eye. And so he teaches us: [Learn the law] from animals: Just as one who strikes an animal makes amends [solely] by compensation, so one who strikes a human makes amends [solely] by compensation.

Commentary

Quoting a Baraita, the Gemara begins its search for Scriptural authority by utilizing *gĕzērâ šāwâ*, one of the thirteen "measures" of legal hermeneutic enumerated in the introduction to the *Sipra*, the halakhic midrash on Leviticus. This term is best rendered "a decision based on equivalence; an analogy," in effect, a legal interpretation of one Torah passage based on the occurrence of the same word form or the same concept in another Torah passage of comparable provenance. If the same word form is used or the same concept expressed in both, we may infer that features of law explicit in one of the two are applicable to the other, even if unstated specifically therein.

In the present case, the form *makkēh*, "one who strikes, injures" is used repeatedly in Lev 24, in laws pertaining to the death and injury of both humans and animals, allowing for potential comparison. Hence, if in the case of fatal injury to animals compensation is prescribed, it should be the intended penalty in cases of injury to humans as well. The Gemara proceeds to search for the appropriate verses that employ the form *makkēh*. It turns out that the most precise parallelism (*makkēh // makkēh*, in 24:21) relates exclusively to *killing* an animal or a human, not at all to injuring humans, which is the case under discussion. That source is consequently ruled out on grounds of provenance. Moving on, the Gemara makes reference to two, sequential statements (24:18–19), one pertaining to fatal injuries sustained by animals and the other to permanent injuries sustained by humans, suggesting that the retaliatory language applied to humans is to be understood as compensation, as is the similar language used with respect to animals.

The objection is then raised that the precise form *makkēh* does not occur in the statement covering injury to humans (in 24:19), but the Gemara responds by qualifying the applicability of *gĕzērâ šāwâ*, explaining that what is required is an equivalent concept, not necessarily an identical word form. Since both of the cited verses deal with the act of "striking" even though they do not employ forms of the same verb, the required inference may be drawn (see Rashi, ad loc.) It is particularly significant that the penalty imposed in cases of a fatal injury to another's animal (24:18) is expressed in retaliatory language as *nepeš taḥat nāpeš*, "a life in place of a life," although it is most surely paid out in compensation. In other words, Lev 24:18 demonstrates that the intent of retaliatory language is not always literal, and that ʿ*ayin taḥat* ʿ*ayin* may indicate compensation. The hidden agenda of the Talmudic dialect lies in the fluidity of the Hebrew verb *hikkâ* (*hipʿil* from *nākâ*), "to strike," which connotes both injury and fatality, depending on immediate context and formulation.

Earlier on, the Gemara, had entertained an alternative derivation of the compensation principle by exclusion, or negative inference, known in Hebrew (and Aramaic) as *miʿûṭ*. It had cited the verse "You may not accept ransom for the life of a murderer" (Num 35:31). Now, it is a basic canon of Talmudic hermeneutic that every affirmation in the formulation of Torah law implies a negation, especially if the affirmation is specific. In the present case, it is inferred that the disallowance of ransom is limited to cases of murder, and that by inference, it excludes cases of loss of limb, for which compensation was rather the remedy. The Gemara then questions the need for this alternative, once a derivation by *gĕzērâ šāwâ* had been validated.

In the give-and-take of the ensuing argument, two variables are introduced with respect to the hermeneutic of analogy: (1) a comparison of humans to humans, versus humans to animals; (2) a comparison of injury to injury, versus injury to death. By offering alternative derivations, the Tannaitic author of the Baraita had provided Scriptural authority on the basis of either hermeneutic preference.

A problem remained, however. Was the exclusionary passage pertaining to the punishment of a murderer in Num 35:31 available for this case, or was it already "taken" for another relevant exclusion, to wit, to prohibit imposing onto the murderer both the death penalty and the need to pay compensation? It is concluded that such a ruling could be derived from another Torah statement, and that nothing encumbered the derivation of the compensation principle for bodily injury from the statement on murder. Underlying the dialectic is the principle that there is not even one superfluous word (even letter!) in the exposition of Torah law, so that what appears as repetitious or elaborate was written for a purpose. It is there to mandate an additional requirement. In Talmudic parlance, such an ostensibly superfluous statement is known qĕraʾ yĕtêrēʾ, "a superfluous biblical statement." As Pisqāʾ I concludes, the Talmudic reading of Torah statements on retaliation for bodily injury has been substantiated. It was demonstrated that in interpreting the Torah, retaliatory language need not be taken literally, and further, that the principled disallowance of compensation is restricted to cases of murder. In the subsequent discussion, the Gemara will introduce other norms and methods, as we shall see presently.

Pisqāʾ II

Q. It has been taught [in a Baraita]: Rabbi Dusta'i son of Judah says: "An eye in place of an eye"—māmôn. Do you say māmôn, or do you say none other than an actual eye [ʿayin mammāš]?

A. [If an actual eye], in a case where one person's eye was large and the other person's eye was small, how would I apply to him the biblical dictum "an eye in place of an eye"? And if you say: In any case of this sort, one would take [commensurate] monetary compensation from him, did not the Torah state: "There shall be one judgment for you" [Lev 24:22a]—a judgment that is equitable for all of you? They responded: What is the objection? Perhaps [it means] that since he had deprived another of sight, the Merciful One decreed that we should deprive him of sight. For if you do not interpret [the verse] in this way, in a case where a short man had killed a tall man, how could we execute him, given that the Torah had stated: "There shall be one rule for you," a rule that is equitable for all of you? Rather: He deprived another of his breath of life, so the Merciful One decreed that we should deprive him of the breath of life. So, too, here: He deprived another of sight, so the Merciful One decreed that we should deprive him of sight.

Commentary

This brief section introduces the principle of equity, stated in the very Torah source that prescribes the penalty for injuries: "There shall be one judgment for you" (Lev 24:22a), which the sages interpret to mean, "a judgment that is equitable to all of you." The question is whether a literal interpretation of "an eye in place of an eye" can be sustained in practice under terms of equity in a case where, for example, the eye of one the parties is large, and that of the other is small. Even if you say that in such cases compensation would be allowable as a concession to disparity, this disposition would also violate the principle of equity, since the remedy would vary for different victims.

This difficulty is addressed in a remarkable way: We are told that the intent of the Torah's statement on equity is functional or qualitative, not necessarily quantitative. If one person deprived the other of sight, he should be deprived of sight. This conclusion is inescapable and is argued once again from the law of murder. In effect, it would be impossible to execute a short man for murdering a tall man if quantitative equity were required. Rather, equity is to be maintained by taking the life of the murderer, who had deprived another of life, just as depriving one who had blinded another of his eyesight is equitable. Ergo: The literal reading of ʿayin taḥat ʿayin as ʿayin mammāš, "an actual eye," which is to say, mutilation, cannot be invalidated on the grounds of equity alone, as matters now stand in the Talmudic discussion. The hermeneutic validation of the compensation principle stands. In Pisqāʾ III the principle of equity under the law will be examined further.

Pisqāʾ III

1. *It has been taught in another source* [a Baraita]: Rabbi Shim'on, son of Yohai said: "An eye in place of an eye"—*māmôn*.

   Q. Do you say *māmôn*, or is it none other than an actual eye? [If an actual eye], in a case where one who is blind blinded another, or one with a severed limb severed another's limb, or one with a crippled leg crippled another's leg—how would I apply to him "an eye in place of an eye," given that the Torah decreed, "There shall be one judgment for you," a judgment that is equitable to all of you?

   A. They responded: What is the objection? Perhaps where it is possible, it is possible, but where it is not possible, it is not possible, and we would release him [altogether]. For if you do not interpret it this way, [in a case where] a terminally wasted man [literally, "one whose flesh had been torn off"] killed a full-bodied man, what would we do to him? Rather: Where it is possible, it is possible, but where it is not possible, it is not possible, and we release him [altogether].

2. *The House of Rabbi Yishmaʿel taught*: Scripture said: "So shall be inflicted on him" [literally, So shall it be "given" to him; Heb. *yinnāten*, Lev 24:20), and "giving" [Heb. *nětînâ*] is none other than payment of money.

   Q. Once this is granted, does "Just as one 'gives' a disability to another" [Lev 24:19] also constitute a case of monetary payment?

   A. They responded: The House of Rabbi Yishmaʿel derives the law by interpreting a superfluous biblical statement. Once it had been written: "Anyone who inflicts a bodily defect on his fellow, just as he has done so shall be done to him" [Lev 24:19], why do I require: "So shall be inflicted on him"? Learn from it [from the superfluous clause] that monetary compensation is intended.

   Q. [If so], why do I require: "Just as he inflicted a bodily defect on another human" [Lev 24:20]?

An Eye for an Eye 211

A. Once he wrote: "So shall be inflicted on him," he also wrote: "Just as he inflicted a bodily defect on another human."

3. *The House of Rabbi Hiyya' taught:* Scripture said: "a hand in place of a hand"; this refers to something that is delivered from one hand to another. And what is that? monetary compensation.

Q. Once this is granted, is "a leg in place of a leg" also to be understood in the same way?

A. The House of Rabbi Hiyya' derives the law from a superfluous biblical statement: "You shall do to him what he conspired to do to his kinsman" [Deut 19:19]. And if it enters your mind that the intent is actual retaliation, why do I require "a hand in place of a hand"? Learn from its inclusion that monetary compensation is intended.

Q. Why, then, do I require "a leg for a leg"?

A. Once it was written, "a hand in place of a hand." He also wrote, "a leg in place of a leg."

4. *Abbaye' said:* It [the law requiring damages instead of actual mutilation] derives from what the House of Hizqiah taught: "an eye in place of an eye, a life in place of a life [Exod 21:23–24], not a life and an eye in place of an eye." And if it enters your mind that [the intent] is actual [retaliation], there are times when it [mutilation] may possibly result in an eye and a life for an eye, since in the course of blinding a person, that person may expire.

Q. What is the objection [to that]?

A. Perhaps [the procedure is] that we diagnose his condition. If he is able to withstand [the mutilation], we carry it out, but if he is not able to withstand it, we do not carry it out.

Q. And [what] if we diagnose his condition as being able to withstand [the mutilation], and we carry it out on him, but he expires, nevertheless?

A. If he dies, let him die! Have we not been taught in the case of stripes: If they diagnosed him [as fit], but he died under his hand, he [the one who administered the stripes] is released?

5. *Rav Zebid in the name of Rabbah said:* Scripture said: "a wound in place of a wound"; one must pay compensation for pain in cases of bodily injury. And if it enters your mind [that the intent] was actual retaliation [for bodily injury], just as this one [the victim] is entitled to [compensation for] pain, so the other [the perpetrator] would be entitled [to compensation] for pain.

Q. What is the objection [to that]?

A. Perhaps there is a person who is very pampered and would experience excessive pain, whereas another person who is not pampered would experience no pain.

Q. What difference results from this [biblical statement]? [What does "a wound in place of a wound" add to the law?]

A. [The difference is] that one must compensate the other for the differential.

6. *Rav Pappa' in the name of Raba' said:* Scripture said: "And he must bear the cost of healing" [to teach us] that he [the perpetrator] must pay for healing in cases of bodily injury. And if it enters your mind [that the intent] was actual retaliation [for bodily injury], just as this one [the victim] is entitled to [compensation for] healing, so would the other [the perpetrator] be entitled to [compensation for] healing.

Q. What is the objection [to that]?

A. Perhaps there is a person whose flesh heals quickly, and another whose flesh does not heal quickly.

Q. What difference results from this [biblical statement]?

A. [The difference is that] one must compensate the other for the differential.

7. *Rav Ashi said:* It [the imposition of damages for bodily injury] derives from a comparison of *taḥat*, "in place of" [in the law of humans] with *taḥat* from [the law of] oxen. Here it is written: "an eye in place of [*taḥat*] an eye," and there it is written: "He shall surely make compensation, one ox in place of [*taḥat*] the other ox" [Exod 21:36]. Just as further on, [the intent is] monetary compensation, so here, too, [the intent is] monetary compensation.

Q. Why do you prefer to learn [the law] from a comparison of *taḥat* to *taḥat* from [the law of] oxen? Let him learn it from a comparison of *taḥat* to *taḥat* from the law of humans? As it is written: "You shall deliver one life in place of [*taḥat*] another life" [Exod 21:23]. Just as further on, the intent is actual retaliation, so here too, the intent would be actual retaliation.

A. They responded: We derive the law of injury from cases of injury, but we do not derive the law of injury from cases of death.

Q. To the contrary. Let us derive the law of humans from cases [involving] humans, and not derive the law of humans from cases [involving] animals.

A. Rather, Rav Ashi said: [We derive the law] from: "in exchange for [Heb. *taḥat*] his having forced her" [Deut 22:29]. He [is able] to learn [both] the law of humans from cases [involving] humans and the law of damages from cases of damages.

8. *It has been taught:* Rabbi Eli'ezer said: "An eye in place of an eye," [which means] actual retaliation. Does it enter your mind that the intent is actual retaliation? Rabbi Eli'ezer does not hold with all of these Tannaim. Rabbah said: This is to say [It is Rabbi Eli'ezer's view] that we do not estimate his worth on the scale of a slave. Abbaye' said to him: What, then is a free man? Since when does a free man have monetary value? Rather, Rav

Ashi said: It [Rabbi Eli'ezer's view] is that we do not estimate his worth on the scale of the injured party, but on the scale of the one who caused the injury.

Commentary

Pisqā' III.1 carries forward the discussion of equity as a principle of Torah law. The equitability of actual retaliation is questioned by adducing a situation where inflicting the same mutilation on the offender would in practice have been impossible. If, for example, the perpetrator was already blind, how would actual retaliation be executed? Does not this practical impossibility, which may be replicated in other circumstances, suggest that the Torah had never intended actual retaliation at all? The response is once again remarkable. We are told that actual retaliation was mandated in the Torah only where it is feasible, but where it cannot be executed, the perpetrator is released entirely. This conclusion is inescapable; otherwise, how could the death penalty, which is inevitably retaliatory, ever be carried out, since it would not be equitable in a case where the perpetrator was, for example, wasting away and near death, and the victim was a full-bodied man? Ergo: Where retaliation can be executed equitably, it is, but where it cannot, the perpetrator is released. (The rule is that one who is liable for the death penalty is freed of any lesser penalties; cf. Babylonian Talmud *Ketubbot* 30a). This being the case, actual retaliation cannot be ruled out as the intent of Torah law on the principle of equity alone, because that principle itself has been accommodated. Whereas *Pisqā' II* had cited a case of quantitative inequity, *Pisqā' III:1* focuses on the feasibility factor.

Pisqā' III:2–3. These two sections revert to the kind of hermeneutic pursued in *Pisqā' I*, with greater emphasis on *qĕra' yĕtêrē'*, "a superfluous biblical statement," explained above in the commentary to *Pisqā' I*. There should be nothing superfluous in Torah law, yet it has been noticed all along that Lev 24:13–23, in which most of the statements of law on the subject of lex talionis are concentrated, is highly repetitious, seemingly paraphrasing the same provisions over and over again. The Gemara cites two Baraitas that invoke textual verbosity, so as to "peg" such paraphrases as confirmation of the compensation principle in cases of bodily injury. The premise is that if literal retaliation had been intended, it would have been possible to state the law more economically. Consequently, some further qualification of the law must have been intended, namely, monetary compensation. And yet, in certain cases, a more rhetorical explanation is offered for seemingly superfluous statements. Once the Torah speaks of certain matters, it may elaborate on the same theme without intending any further inference.

Pisqā' III:4 reverts to the subject of equity, but from a different perspective, that of "unintended consequences." It may happen that corporal punishment causes the death of the perpetrator, so that the loss of an eye would be punished by the loss of an eye and a life! We are informed, however, that the person awaiting punishment is diagnosed for his ability to withstand the strain, and that if he is not considered fit, no corporal punishment or mutilation will be administered. Furthermore, if despite the diagnosis, that person actually expires, there is no responsibility on the part of the one who executed the punishment, just as is the rule in administering stripes, where there is also the danger of death. Once again, the principle of equity alone does not rule out actual retaliation.

Pisqāʾ III:5–6. These sections explore another potential inequity in administering actual retaliation. We are told that one who injures another must compensate him for pain and costs of healing in addition to his liability for the actual injury. Now if the Torah's intent was actual retaliation for the initial bodily injury, a curious situation would emerge whereby the perpetrator could claim damages from the victim for pain and costs of healing arising from his punishment. This would produce an inequity because persons differ in their ability to withstand pain and to heal. The response is that there would be no objection to penalizing the victim in this way so long as provision is made to compensate for any differential that may obtain, as between the two parties.

Pisqāʾ III.7 begins by endorsing the compensation principle on the basis of *gĕzērâ šāwâ*. Rav Ashi compares "an eye in place of an eye," with "He shall surely make compensation, one ox in place of the other ox." As in *Pisqāʾ I*, the use of retaliatory language to connote compensation in the case of animals is adduced as the basis for the same phenomenon in cases involving humans. This is questioned, however, by arguing for the other basis of comparison: from humans to humans. All along, we have been juxtaposing intersecting variables, so as to derive the principle of compensation from Torah statements that project either actual retaliation or compensation: we have been comparing cases of injury to cases of death, and cases involving humans with cases involving death. It has been necessary to sacrifice one or the other "match." In an effort to maintain consistency, Rav Ashi proposes a single verse that satisfies both variables. According to Deut 22:28–29, a man who rapes an unattached young woman must pay her father fifty shekels, *taḥat ʾăšer ʿinnāh*, "in exchange for his having forced her," and he must take her as his lifelong wife. Here we have compensation for injury between humans.

Pisqāʾ III.8. We read that Rabbi Eliʿezer (son of Hyrcanus) dissents, as was often his practice, from the views of the other Tannaim cited above, but it is not clear what is meant by *mammāš* in his statement. It does not seem credible that he would endorse actual mutilation. In a typical exchange, Abbayeʾ and Rabaʾ clarify the issue at hand, as Rashi (ad loc.) explains. By *mammāš*, Rabbi Eliʿezer means that we estimate what the decrease in value resulting from the loss of an eye would be to the one causing the injury (Heb. *mazzîq*), not the loss to the injured party, as we have been assuming in our reading of the Mishnah. In other words, when the Torah states: *ʿayin taḥat ʿayin*, it means "the injurer's eye in place of the eye of the injured," namely, compensation in the precise value of the injurer's eye.

The Semiotics of Talmudic Hermeneutic

The Babylonian Talmud continues to explore further ramifications of its modulation of Torah law in endorsing compensation as the penalty imposed on one who inflicts bodily injury on another person, with reference to actual cases, and by discussion of standards for calculating damages. However, the main thrust of the interpretive process is contained in the three pericopes presented above. It would be well to probe the mentality reflected in the Talmudic discussion. It is both subtle and well reasoned, although transparent in its objective. The following observations come to mind:

1. There can be little doubt that the Tannaim and their successors, the Amoraim, found the Torah laws governing bodily injury to be thoroughly problematic. They realized that a literal reading of the Torah text would normally lead one to conclude that mutilation and severe corporal punishment were intended by the Merciful One, author of the Torah, as the proper penalty for causing permanent bodily injury to another person. In fact, the sages send a mixed message: They never gave up completely on actual retaliation as an acceptable reading of Torah law, while at the same time they repeatedly express wonder that such an interpretation should even "enter your mind!" After all, the Mishnah clearly teaches that one who injures his fellow is liable for damages, not subject to actual retaliation. And so, the sages in several ways try to substantiate a different reading of Torah law, one that endorses the policy of the Mishnah, and they accomplish this in their own ways.

2. One way to do this would be to rule out actual retaliation on grounds of equity, a pervasive principle of Torah law, and this effort is repeatedly pursued. Although it is ultimately unsuccessful, it is nonetheless telling. In practice, it would be more equitable and much less risky, not to speak of being more humane, to impose monetary damages on one who injured another than to harm his body, which could result in unintended consequences, even death. What the complicated discussion of equity produces is a mitigation of actual retaliation by introducing exemptions to its application, while at the same time redefining what is meant by equity under the law. The law of individual difference is invoked, as is the impracticality of retaliation, even the impossibility of its imposition in certain circumstances. It is presupposed that equity must always be maintained, even if hypothetically; if we were to endorse actual retaliation, and if this requires flexibility in the execution of the law, so be it. The substantial effort to sustain actual retaliation as the intent of Torah law leads one to hypothesize that during an earlier stage in the development of rabbinic law, actual retaliation, though somewhat mitigated, was still endorsed.

3. The required modulation from actual retaliation to compensation can only be achieved without challenge on an hermeneutic basis, primarily on the basis of *gĕzērâ šāwâ*, "a decision based on equivalence; an analogy." A less-prominent hermeneutic method, which remains unchallenged, is that of *miʿûṭ*, "exclusion, negative inference," which limits actual retaliation to cases of murder.

It might appear that the prolonged hermeneutic discourse on retaliation versus compensation is merely a method of manipulating the Torah text to make it mean either something different from what it says, or something beyond what it says. And yet, the hermeneutic process has its own logic. As an example, in the case of humans, the sages go to considerable lengths to avoid comparing the legal statements on injury to statements on death; but they tend to allow the comparison of injury in humans to injury that kills animals. This is undoubtedly because laws affecting animals employ the language of retaliation to connote compensation. To be specific, if one fatally injures another's animal, he must pay "a life in place of [*taḥat*] a life." This is monetary compensation expressed as retaliation. Furthermore, a verse from Deuteronomy on the penalty for rape is put forth as additional evidence that retaliatory language can connote monetary damages, even in cases between one human and another.

The effect of Talmudic hermeneutic in the present instance was to alleviate the severity of Torah law by (1) limiting lex talionis to cases of murder, and (2) by comparing damages to damages, even as between humans and animals, while at the same time renouncing a comparison of injury to death in the case of humans. This hermeneutic served to define human injury as categorically different from human death, not merely as less severe than death, and accordingly deserving of a different category of punishment, one that spared physical suffering and at times even human life.

18

The New Testament's Interpretation

Jesus' Lex Talionis

Bruce D. Chilton

The Center of Christian Ethics

The Gospels and the other writings of the New Testament were produced a generation after Jesus' death for people who were about to be baptized (as adults) or had already been baptized. The communities involved were Greek-speaking, predominantly non-Jewish, urban, and culturally different from the Galilee of Jesus time.

Those communities developed ethics appropriate to their own environments.[1] The Gospel according to John, written around 100 CE (after Matthew, Mark, and Luke), provides a good example of that. The last meal of Jesus with his disciples in chapter 13 is a gathering for a Hellenistic symposium, complete with a discourse that continues for several chapters in a philosophical idiom foreign to the earlier Gospels, and that consumes the bulk of John's attention.

The introduction (13:1–12b) has Jesus perform the menial task of washing his disciples' feet, in order to exemplify the sort of mutual service he demands from his followers. The Gospel according to John has Jesus drive the point home directly and categorically in 13:12c–17:

> He said to them, "Do you know what I have done for you? You call me teacher and lord, and you say [well: I am]. If, then, I—lord and teacher—washed your feet, you also ought to wash one another's feet. For I have given you an example, so that just as I have done to you, so you also might do. Truly, truly I say to you, a servant is not greater than his lord, nor an apostle greater than the one who sent him. If you know these things, you are blessed if you do them."

John's placement of the scene, as the formal equivalent of the "Last Supper" in the Synoptics, indicates the importance of the model Jesus is held to convey. By means of this presentation, John's Gospel makes serving others the functional equivalent of Jesus' ministry, the performance of his purpose.

The relative privilege of menial poverty within early Christianity is also reflected in a pivotal section of the earlier Gospels (Matthew, ca. 80 CE; Mark, ca. 73 CE; Luke, ca. 90 CE). The passage concerns a would-be disciple with property and Peter (Jesus' premier disciple, whose name literally means "Rock," as in this translation):

Matt 19:16–30

Look: someone came forward to him and said, "What good should I do so that I might have perpetual life?" But he said to him, "Why do you question me about the good? One is good! But if you want to enter into life, keep the decrees." He says to him, "Which?" But Jesus declared, "do not murder, do not commit adultery, do not steal, do not witness falsely, honor your father and mother, and, love your neighbor as yourself." The young man says to him, "All these things I have kept; what do I still lack?" But Jesus told him, "If you want to be perfect: depart, sell your belongings, and give to the poor, and you will have a store in heavens. And come on, follow me." The young man heard this word and went away grieving, because he had many possessions. Yet Jesus said to his students, "Amen I say to you that a rich person with labor will enter the kingdom of the heavens! Yet again I say to you: It is easier for a camel to enter through a needle's eye than for a rich person to enter into the kingdom of God!" The students heard and were exceedingly overwhelmed, saying, "Therefore: who can

Mark 10:17–31

He was proceeding out on a way and one ran up to him, and kneeling to him, interrogated him, "Good teacher, what should I do so that I might inherit perpetual life?" But Jesus said to him, "Why do you say I am good? No one is good, except one: God! You know the decrees, Do not murder, do not commit adultery, do not steal, do not witness falsely, do not deprive, honor your father and mother." But he told him, "Teacher, I have kept all these things from my youth." Yet Jesus looked at him, loved him, and said to him, "One thing is lacking you: depart, sell as much as you have and give to poor people, and you will have a store in heaven. And come on, follow me." But he was appalled at the word and went away grieving, because he had many effects. Jesus looked around and says to his students, "With what labor will those who have effects enter the kingdom of God!" But his students were astonished at his words; but Jesus replying again says to them, "Children, what labor it is to enter the kingdom of God! It is easier for a camel to pass through a needle's hole than for a rich person

Luke 18:18–30

And some ruler interrogated him, saying, "Good teacher, by doing what shall I inherit perpetual life?" But Jesus said to him, "Why do you call me good? No one is good, except one: God! You know the decrees, Do not commit adultery, do not murder, do not steal, do not witness falsely, honor your father and mother." But he said, "I have kept all these things from youth." Jesus heard and said to him, "One thing escapes for you: everything, as much as you have, sell and distribute to the poor, and you will have a store in heavens. And come on, follow me." He heard and was saddened, because he was exceedingly rich. Jesus saw him and said, "With what labor will those who have effects proceed into the kingdom of God! Because it is easier for a camel to enter through an instrument's eye than for a rich person to enter into the kingdom of God." But those who heard said, "And who can be saved?" Yet he said, "What is impossible with people is possible with God." But Rock said, "Look: we have left our own to follow you." Yet he said to them, "Amen I say to you, that there is no one who

Matt 19:16–30 (cont.)	*Mark 10:17–31 (cont.)*	*Luke 18:18–30 (cont.)*
be saved?" Jesus looked at, and said to, them, "This is impossible with people, but everything is possible with God." Then Rock replied, said to him, "Look: we left everything and followed you. What, then, is for us?" But Jesus said to them, "Amen I say to you, that you who followed me, in the regeneration, when the one like the person sits upon the throne of his glory, you will also sit yourselves upon twelve thrones, judging the twelve clans of Israel. And everyone who has left homes or brothers or sisters or father or mother or children or lands for my name's sake will receive many times over, and inherit perpetual life. But many first shall be last, and last first."	to enter into the kingdom of God." But they were completely overwhelmed, saying to one another, "So who can be saved?" Jesus looked at them and says, "Impossible with people, but not with God: because everything is possible with God." Rock began to say to him, "Look: we left everything, and followed you." Jesus stated, "Amen I say to you, there is no one who has left home or brothers or sisters or mother or father or children or lands for my sake and the sake of the message, except that shall receive a hundred times over—now in this time, homes and brothers and sisters and mothers and children and fields, with persecutions—and in the age that is coming, perpetual life. But many first shall be last, and the last first."	has left home or wife brothers or relatives or children for the sake of the kingdom of God, who shall not receive many times more in this time, and in the age that is coming perpetual life."

The enthusiastic catechumen is told, much to his dismay, to sell up and give to the poor, in order to have treasure in heaven (Matt 19:16–22; Mark 10:17–22; Luke 18:18–23). The normative value of the cautionary story is reinforced by Jesus' statement about rich people and the kingdom of God: a camel would have an easier time wriggling through the eye of a needle than the rich would have getting into the kingdom. Only God's capacity to overcome what is humanly impossible gives them any hope (Matt 19:23–26; Mark 10:23–27; Luke 18:24–27). Peter, speaking for the body of Jesus' peripatetic followers, calls attention to their voluntary poverty and is promised rewards as a consequence (Matt 19:27–30; Mark 10:28–31; Luke 18:28–30).

The message of the passage is trenchant. Those who are poor, simply because they belong to underclasses, enjoy relative proximity to the kingdom, and the rich may enter only by means of the exceptional grace of God. But Peter and his companions, by means of their voluntary poverty for the sake of the movement, are assured of life everlasting. The pericope reflects the stringent practice of Christianity in the circle of Jesus' followers that looked to Peter for leadership.

From that circle, the story of Ananias and Sapphira in the book of Acts also derives. That couple claimed to have sold a property for the benefit of the apostles, but in fact retained some of the profit. Under Peter's interrogation (Acts 5:1–11), each died separately for deceiving the Spirit of God. Within the Petrine group, there seems little question but that voluntary poverty was a principal means of following Jesus, of enacting his ethos. The only evident alternative was death, the obvious alternative to eternal life.

Yet even the Petrine presentation of Jesus' teaching allowed the possibility of rich people wriggling through the needle's eye. The analogy between Jesus' ministry and the voluntary acceptance of conditions typical of underclasses, however much it was recommended, was not taken by itself to be a fulfillment of the imperative to follow Jesus. That analogy was preferred, and even standard, and yet the analogy was not an identity, such that simply accepting poverty made one like Jesus and worthy of eternal life. There was an awareness within the Petrine circle, and within other communities of the New Testament, that the needle's eye was open for those with property, because voluntary poverty was at the service of a more basic means of enacting the ethos of the Christ, a principle that might be realized by programs other than voluntary poverty.

The purest form of the Petrine statement of the larger principle appears in Matthew and Mark:

Matt 22:34-40
The Pharisees heard that he had shut the Zadokites up, and were gathered together in the same place. And one from them, a lawyer, interrogated him, pressing him to the limit: "Teacher, which decree is great in the law?" But he told him, "You shall love the Lord your God with all your heart and with all your life and with all your mind: the great and first decree is this. A second is like this: You shall love your neighbor as yourself. On these two decrees all the law is suspended, and the prophets!"

Mark 12:28-34
One of the scribes came forward—hearing them arguing (seeing that he answered them well)—and interrogated him, "Which is the first decree of all?" Jesus answered that: "First is, Hear, Israel, our God is the Lord; he is one Lord. And you shall love the Lord your God from all your heart and from all your life and from all your mind and from all your strength. This is second: You shall love your neighbor as yourself. There is not another decree greater than these." And the scribe said to him, "Fine, teacher: in truth you have said that he is one and there is not another beside him, and to love him from all the heart and from all the understanding and from all the strength and to love the neighbor as oneself is overflowing all burnt offerings and sacrifices." Jesus saw he answered sensibly and answered, said to him, "You are not far from the kingdom of God." And no one any longer dared to interrogate him.

In both accounts, Jesus is asked by someone outside his group (a Pharisee in Matthew, a scribe in Mark) what is the great (so Matthew) or first (so Mark) commandment. He replies by citing two commandments from the Torah, to love God (drawing from Deut 6:4–5) and love one's neighbor (drawing from Lev 19:18). In Matthew, Jesus concludes that all the law and the prophets hang from those two commandments; and in Mark, that there is no other commandment greater than these.

Matthew and Mark construe the sense of the teaching distinctively. In Matthew, the organic connection among the commandments assures that they all hang together (with the teaching of the prophets) on the principle of love toward God and neighbor (22:40). Mark, on the other hand, has the scribe who initiated the scene conclude that to love is more than all burnt offerings and sacrifices (12:32–33). The construal of Matthew is in the direction of claiming that Jesus represents the fulfillment of the law and the prophets, a thematic concern of the Gospel generally. The construal of Mark takes the tack that Jesus' principle establishes a noncultic means of approval by God.

Both Matthew and Mark find their center of gravity, however, in the conviction that the commandment to love God and love one's neighbor is the action that unites one with Jesus in an approach to God. The emblem of that approach is fulfillment of the law and the prophets in Matthew (22:40), nearness to the kingdom of God in Mark (12:34). The differences between those construals are not to be minimized: they represent the substantive independence of the Gospels as catechetical instruments. But the systemic agreement between Matthew and Mark, that love is the means of access to God after the pattern of Jesus, is an equally striking attribute.

It is a commonplace of critical study to observe that the Jewish teacher Hillel, in a dictum comparable to that of Jesus, is said to have taught that the Torah is a commentary on the injunction not to do what is hateful to one's neighbor (*b. Shabbat* 31a). The centrality of the commandment to love one's neighbor is also asserted by Aqiba, the famous rabbi of the second century (*Sipra on Leviticus* 19:18). Differences of emphasis are detectable and important, but the fact remains that Jesus does not appear to have been exceptional in locating love at the center of the divine commandments. Any rabbi, a teacher in a city or a local village, might have come up with some such principle, although the expressions of the principle attributed to Jesus are especially apt. The principle itself is little more than proverbial: love, after all, is not easily dismissed as a bad idea or beside the point.

Precisely because Jesus' teaching is precedented in the early Judaism of his day, it becomes clear that the tradition presented in aggregate by Matthew and Mark put that teaching in a new light. Jesus' citation of the two biblical passages that demand and define love is, for the two Gospels, concerned no longer simply with a matter of locating a coherent principle within the Torah, the stated terms of reference in the question of the Pharisee or scribe. Rather, the twin commandment of love is now held to be a transcendent principle, which fulfills (so Matthew) or supersedes (so Mark) the Torah. Christ himself, by citing and enacting that principle, is held to offer the ethical key to communion with God.

The Lukan version of the teaching concerning love is quite different from what we find in Matthew and Mark, making it especially apparent that the significance of Jesus' message lies at least as much in who is speaking as in what he says (Luke 10:25–37):

> And look, there arose some lawyer, pressing him to the limit, saying, "Teacher, having done what shall I inherit perpetual life?" But he said to him, "In the law what is written—how do you read?" He answered and said,

"You shall love the Lord your God from all your heart and with all your life and with all your strength and with all your mind, and your neighbor as yourself." Yet he said to him, "You answered rightly: do this, and you will live." He wanted to justify himself and said to Jesus, "And who is my neighbor?" Jesus took up and said, "Some person went down from Jerusalem to Jericho, and thugs fell upon him, who stripped him and inflicted lesions. They went away, leaving him half dead. But by coincidence some priest went down that way; he saw him and passed by opposite. Likewise also a Levite came by the place, but he saw and passed by opposite. Some Samaritan made a way and came by him, saw and felt for him. He came forward and, pouring on oil and wine, wrapped his wounds. He mounted him up on his own animal and led him to a hostel and took care of him. On the next day he put out two denarii and gave them to the hosteler and said, 'Take care of him, and that: Should you spend over, I will repay you when I come back again.' Of these three, who seems to you to have become neighbor to the one who fell among the thugs?" Yet he said, "The one who did mercy with him." But Jesus said to him, "Proceed: and you do likewise."

Here an unidentified "lawyer," rather than the Pharisee of Matthew or the scribe of Mark, asks what to do in order to inherit eternal life. It is not Jesus in Luke who cites the twin principle of love, but the lawyer himself (10:27). At first, Jesus merely confirms what the lawyer already knows (10:28). Jesus' peculiar contribution comes in the response to the lawyer's further question, "Who is my neighbor?" (10:29). The question and the response appear in uniquely Lukan material (10:29–37), the presentation of Jesus' teaching concerning love that was characteristic of the church in Antioch, where the Gospel according Luke seems to have been composed.

The Antiochene transformation of the principle, in distinction from the Petrine transformation, explicitly makes Jesus' application of the commandment, not its formulation, his systemic innovation. The innovation is effected in the parable of the good Samaritan (Luke 10:29–37). Whether Jesus himself told the parable is beside the present point. What concerns us is that (1) the parable informs the commandment to love with a new gist, and that (2) the new gist is the systemic center of Lukan ethics, as distinct from Matthean and/or Markan ethics.

Formally, the parable is designed to answer the question "Who is my neighbor?" And that formal issue is explicitly addressed at the close of the parable, when Jesus tells his questioner to go and do what the Samaritan did, that is: show himself a neighbor to one in obvious need (10:36–37). But the formal issue here is distinct from the systemic issue.

The systemic challenge is not the goodness of the Samaritan, but the fact that he *is* a Samaritan. The victim of the mugging is in no position to complain, but especially as a recent pilgrim to Jerusalem, he might well have objected to contact with a Samaritan, in that Samaritan sacrifice on Mount Gerizim was seen as antagonistic to Judaic sacrifice on Mount Zion. A priest and a Levite have already passed by, motivated by the Torah's teaching that limited their contact with corpses (Lev 21:1–4). In the parable, then, a victim who seemed impure is aided by a Samaritan who was actually impure, and that action nonetheless fulfills the commandment to love one's neighbor as oneself.

The parable of the good Samaritan is a story that formally conveys how to be a neighbor and how to identify a neighbor. It is shaped systemically to insist that one viewed as "impure" may be a neighbor to one who is "pure." The commandment to love is such that, in its application, it creates a new sphere of purity that transcends any other notion of what is clean and what is unclean. The issue of purity was crucial to the church in Antioch. In Gal 2:11–13, Paul describes factional fighting among three groups, classed according to their leaders. On one extreme, Paul himself taught that Gentiles and Jews might freely eat with one another; on the other, James insisted upon the separation of those who were circumcised from those who were not. Peter and Barnabas were caught somewhere in between. Much later, around 90 CE, Luke's Gospel represents how the issue was resolved within Antiochene Christianity: the question of the boundaries established by purity was settled in terms of ethical engagement rather than dietary practice. It is no accident, then, that it is precisely Luke that conveys its unique parable and its peculiar perspective on how Jesus' teaching regarding love was distinctive.

Throughout the literature of the New Testament, Jesus provides a paradigm of loving service; the examples just given could easily be multiplied. Even when one might expect the texts to be straightforwardly historical, the link with catechumens' social situation is strong, and their lives are mirrored in Jesus's as much as his is in theirs. In both Jesus' case and believers' lives, the ethos that goes by the name of love is transformed by distinctive conditions, so that love might be, for example, the integral principle of the Torah (Matthew), or a principle beyond cultic Judaism (Mark), or the single term of reference that determines the purity of one person for another (Luke).

The "Other" and the Throne of God

The argument that love is the systemic center of Christian ethics is easily established; no recent study of New Testament ethics would find much to quarrel with in the first part of this essay, exegetical details apart. This second part is another matter. Here I argue that the attempt to discover a unity in Christian ethics in the general principle of love has obscured its distinctive character.

From most religious perspectives, it is difficult to object to the principle of love. But the target of one's love does differ radically as one moves from Jesus, through Paul, and on to John's Gospel.[2] In my opinion, if we do not consider the target Jesus identifies, we have missed the point of his teaching, however much we might honor his principles.

Jesus commanded his followers to love their enemies:[3]

Matt 5:38–48

You heard that it was said, "Eye for eye and tooth for tooth." Yet I say to you, Not to resist the evil one, but whoever cuffs you on your right cheek, turn to him the other as well. And to the one who wishes to litigate with you, even to take your tunic, leave him the cloak as well! And whoever requisitions you to journey one mile, depart with him two! Give to the one who asks you, and do not withhold from the one who wishes to borrow from you. You have heard that it was said, "You shall love your neighbor and you shall hate your enemy." Yet I say to you, Love your enemies, and pray for those who persecute you, so you might become descendants of your Father in heavens. Because he makes his sun dawn upon evil people and good people, and makes rain upon just and unjust. For if you love those who love you, what reward have you? Do not even the customs agents do the same? And if you greet only your fellows, what do you do that goes beyond? Do not even the Gentiles do the same? You, then, shall be perfect, as your heavenly Father is perfect.

Luke 6:27–36

But I say to you who hear, Love your enemies, act well with those who hate you, bless those who accurse you, pray concerning those who revile you. To the one who hits you on the cheek, furnish the other also. And from the one who takes your garment, do not forbid the tunic! Give to the one who asks you, and do not demand from the one who takes what is yours. And just as you want humanity to do to you, do to them similarly. And if you love those who love you, what sort of grace is that for you? Because even the sinners love those who love them. And if you do good to those who do you good, what sort of grace is that to you? Even the sinners do the same. And if you lend to those from whom you hope to receive, what sort of grace is that to you? Even sinners lend so that they receive the equivalent back. Except: love your enemies and do good and lend, anticipating nothing, and your reward will be great, and you will be descendants of [the] Most High, because he is fine to the ungrateful and evil. Become compassionate, just as your Father is also compassionate.

Christian theologians from Paul to the present day have resisted the simple letter of his directive.

To say, with John (as we saw above), that followers of Jesus should love one another establishes a bond of affection and mutual obligation within the community that defines them. What, however, of those outside the community, or those who are overtly hostile? John's Gospel consigns that group to "the world." In the same discourse that begins in chapter 13, John has Jesus say, "Fear not, for I have overcome the world" (16:33). Although that establishes an attitude of nonaggressive (if not benign) neglect toward outsiders, it is not the same as loving enemies.

On the other hand, John at least represents a distinct improvement on Paul's teaching. Writing to the Romans around 57 CE, Paul clearly refers to Jesus' summary of the Torah (13:8–10), but he also manages to turn the imperative to love into a stratagem of working divine vengeance against one's neighbor (12:18–21):[4]

> If it is possible for you, make peace with all people, without avenging yourselves, beloved, but give place to wrath. Because it is written, "Vengeance is mine, I shall repay, says the Lord." But if your enemy hungers, feed him; if he thirsts, give him drink; for by doing this you will heap coals of fire upon his head. Do not be conquered by evil, but conquer evil with good.

By this point, Paul makes clear that he sees love as a forensic principle, whose power resides in its vindication by divine judgment.

Jesus' view is less abstract in that it calls for love of one's enemies without the expectation of reward. But that pragmatic character is precisely what makes his teaching all the more paradoxical. What is the source of his demand that enemies should be loved?

In this regard, Jesus' teaching came into focus during his last months in Jerusalem. By uncovering those circumstances, we can appreciate the distinctiveness of his ethics.[5] Despite his naïveté concerning the politics of Rome and therefore the growing threat of execution at the hands of Pontius Pilate, Jesus knew that he courted danger during this period. The constant danger took a toll on his followers, as Jesus well knew. They actually had to be ready to give up wealth and family (as we have seen in Mark 10:13–31; Matt 19:13–30; Luke 18:15–30), to ruin their lives if necessary. The message that God's kingdom was to be all-consuming, dissolving even Caesar's power, made it tolerable to bear the Romans' cross if necessary. Jesus speaks of doing that when he refers to his followers as a whole (Mark 8:34–38; Matt 16:24–27; Luke 9:23–26), and not only to his own fate.

Such travails were a small price to pay for being part of the triumph of God's rule over human destructiveness. Jesus' demands were not, as later teaching made them, quasi-Stoic commendations of austerity or materialistic promises of reward later for suffering now. Jesus framed his teaching to make hardship the gateway to the vision of seeing God within the world. The practice of vision was basic to his own experience from the time of his baptism:

Matt 3:13–17	Mark 1:9–11	Luke 3:21–22
Then there came Jesus from Galilee to the Jordan to John to be immersed by him. Yet he prevented him, saying, "I have need to be immersed by you, and do you come to me?" Jesus replied, and said to him, "Permit it now, for so it is proper for us to fulfill all righteousness." Then he permitted him. Yet when Jesus had been immersed, at once he ascended from the water, and look: the heavens were opened, and he saw God's Spirit descending as dove, coming upon him. And look: a voice from the heavens, saying: "This is my Son, the beloved, in whom I take pleasure."	And it happened in those days there came Jesus from Nazareth of Galilee, and he was immersed in the Jordan by John. At once he ascends from the water and saw the heavens split and the Spirit as dove descending into him. And a voice came from the heavens: "You are my Son, the beloved; in you I take pleasure."	But it happened when all the people were immersed, and Jesus was immersed and praying, the heaven opened and the Holy Spirit descended upon him in body, in form as dove, and a voice came from heaven, "You are my Son, the beloved; in you I take pleasure."

Jesus' particular gift as a teacher involved the capacity to convey that visionary experience to his followers, as is attested preeminently in the story of his transfiguration:

Matt 17:1–5	*Mark 9:2–7*	*Luke 9:28–35*
And after six days Jesus takes Rock and James and John his brother and brings them up to a high mountain privately. And he was transmuted before them, and his face shone as the sun, and his clothing became white as the light. And look: there appeared to them Moses and Elijah, speaking together with him. Rock responded and said to Jesus, "Lord, it is good for us to be here; if you wish, I shall build here three lodges: one for you and one for Moses and one for Elijah." While he was still speaking, look: a glowing cloud overshadowed them, and look: a voice from the cloud, saying, "This is my Son, the beloved: in whom I take pleasure. Hear him."	And after six days Jesus takes Rock and James and John and brings them up to a high mountain privately: alone. And he was transmuted before them, and his clothing became gleaming, very white, as a washer on the earth is not able to whiten. And Elijah appeared to them with Moses, and they were speaking together with Jesus. Rock responded and says to Jesus, "Rabbi, it is good for us to be here, and we shall build three lodges: one for you and one for Moses and one for Elijah." For he did not know how he should respond, because they were terrified. And a cloud came overshadowing them, and there came a voice from the cloud, "This is my Son, the beloved: hear him."	Yet it happened after these words (about eight days), taking Rock and John and James, he ascended into the mountain to pray. And it happened while he prayed [that] the appearance of his face was different and his garments flashed out white. And look: two men were speaking together with him, such as were Moses and Elijah, who were seen in glory speaking of his exodus, which he was about to fulfill in Jerusalem. Yet Rock and those with him were weighed down with sleep. But becoming alert, they saw his glory and the two men standing with him. And it happened as they were being separated from him, Rock said to Jesus, "Master, it is good for us to be here, and we shall build three lodges: one yours and one Moses' and one Elijah's" (not knowing what he was saying.) But while he was saying this. there came a cloud and overshadowed them, and they were afraid when they entered into the cloud. And there came a voice from the cloud, saying, "This is my Son, the chosen: him hear."

Relative tranquillity and leisure gave Jesus occasion to refine his own visionary experience and that of his followers. But in the midst of chaotic circumstances of opposition, he also reported (Luke 10:18) that he saw Satan fall like lightening.

The Scriptures of Israel provide ample precedent for visionary practice, and in particular for the conviction that God supports faithful Israelites in the midst of persecution. The classic text of that faith is the book of Daniel, where an angel called "one like a person" appears in the presence of God, before his Throne (Dan 7:13), symbolizing the triumph of God's people. Jesus often spoke of Daniel's "one like a person" (or "son of man," in the traditional rendering) representing the people of Israel before God's Throne.

Near the end of his life, Jesus pursued this insight further: every person possessed the angelic likeness of the "one like a person" and mirrored some of the truth of the divine Throne or Chariot (as it was also called, since it could appear anywhere).[6] God's Throne was there, shining through the eyes of a neighbor, even if that neighbor hated you (Matt 5:43–48; Luke 6:27–36;). While arguing with other teachers in Jerusalem, he had come to the realization that the love one owed the Throne was exactly what one owed one's neighbor (Mark 12:28–34; Matt 22:34–40; Luke 10:25–28). Love of God (Deut 6:5) and love of neighbor (Lev 19:18) were basic principles embedded in the Torah, as we have seen. Jesus' innovation lay in the claim that the two were indivisible: love of God *was* love of neighbor, and vice versa.

Every neighbor belonged within God's presence. That is the basis of Jesus' distinctive and challenging ethics of love in the midst of persecution. He linked his ethics to the transformed society that the prophets had predicted. His words promise that individual suffering can achieve transcendence, provided that the "other" is seen, not as threat or stranger,[7] but as mirroring the presence of God in the world.

Jesus did not innovate by commending a principle of love as the central command of the Torah. Rather, his spirituality of the "other" invested one's neighbor with the attribute of God's presence in the world, so that loving that person was tantamount to the worship of God.

Concluding Remarks

Jesus' distinctive perspective presses us to see altruism in a fresh light, perceiving that care for the other is crucial to the care of oneself.

The Gospel according to Matthew articulates precisely this perception. That refinement comes, in all probability, from a period well after Jesus' death, but it invaluably reflects how earliest Christianity addressed questions of interpretation. In this Gospel, a thematic distinction is made between the public benefit that might come from public prayer and ostentatious worship, and the benefit that comes "in secret" from private devotion, including almsgiving (Matt 6:1–21). That is, concern for the other carries with it a reward from God that cannot be enhanced and is only undermined by the anticipation of benefit in this world.

That emphasis upon how the other determines the value of one's actions is brought home in another Matthean parable, the famous analogy of sheep and goats (Matt 25:31–46). This parable presents the welfare of others as the meaning of behavior: "as much as you did to one of the least of these, my brothers, you did to me" (Matt 25:40).

Jesus asserted that "you always have the poor with yourselves, and whenever you want, you can do them good" (Mark 14:7). He understood that the problem of altruism never has to do with a lack of opportunity. But in this whole passage, Jesus also refuses to make categorical assertions of what, precisely, his disciples should do for others, and that feeds the impression of Jesus' insouciance in regard to poverty. His attitude, however, proceeds from the fact that the other person *is* the primordial fact, not a preconception of how God should be honored in that person. What endures is Jesus' insight that, once action is undertaken on behalf of any person who is in God's image, that demands—as Ananias and Sapphira discovered—the same commitment that one owes God.

Notes

3. Early Christian Interpretation: The Case of Justin Martyr

1. See Ben Witherington III, "Not so Idle Thoughts about *EIDOLUTHUTON*," *Tyndale Bulletin* 44, no. 2 (1993): 237-54.

2. See Graham Keith, "Justin Martyr and Religious Exclusivism," *Tyndale Bulletin* 43, no. 1 (1992): 57-80.

3. See the chronology of Miroslav Marcovich, *Iustini Martyris Dialogs cum Tryphone*, Patristische Texte und Studien (Berlin: de Gruyter, 1997), 1. He places the *Dialogue* during the period 155-160 CE, after the *First Apology*, ca. 150-155. I follow his Greek text of the *Dialogue* as well as the two volumes of Philippe Bobichon, *Justin Martyr: Dialogue avec Tryphon*, édition critique, 2 vols., Paradosis 47.1-2 (Fribourg: Academic Press, 2003). For the *Apology*, I follow André Wartelle, *Saint Justin: Apologies; Introduction, texte critique, traduction, commentaire et index* (Paris: Études Augustiniennes, 1987), who places the *First Apology* in 153-154 (p. 35), and the *Second Apology* (which will briefly take up our attention) shortly thereafter.

4. Oskar Skarsaune, "Judaism and Hellenism in Justin Martyr, Elucidated from His Portrait of Socrates," *Geschichte—Tradition—Reflexion: Festschrift für Martin Hengel zum 70. Geburtstag*, vol. 3, *Frühes Christentum*, ed. Hermann Lichtenberger (Tübingen: Mohr, 1996), 585-611, esp. 608.

5. See esp. *Dial.* 44.2: "Because no one of them by any means was able to receive [the good promised to Abraham], apart from those likened by thought [*gnōmē*] to the faith of Abraham who recognize all the mysteries: I mean that one command was appointed for piety and the practice of righteousness, and another command and action was in the same way spoken either as referring to the mystery of Christ or on account of the hardness of your people's heart"; and *Dial.* 92.1: "So if someone undertakes, without the help of an immense grace received of God, to appreciate what was done, said, or accomplished by the Prophets, it will not help him to wish to relate words or events, if he is not in a position to render their reason [*logos*] also."

6. Oskar Skarsaune, *The Proof from Prophecy: A Study in Justin Martyr's Proof-Text Tradition: Text Type, Provenance, Theological Profile*, Supplements to Novum Testamentum 56 (Leiden: Brill, 1987).

7. Dominique Barthélemy, *Les devanciers d'Aquila: Première publication intégrale du texte des fragments du Dodécaprophéton trouvés dans le désert de Juda*, Supplements to Vetus Testamentum 10 (Leiden: Brill, 1963). For a more recent discussion, see George J. Brooke, "The Twelve Minor Prophets and the Dead Sea Scrolls," in *Congress Volume: Leiden, 2004*, ed. André Lemaire (Leiden: Brill, 2006), 19-43.

8. Skarsaune, *Proof from Prophecy*, 432.

9. Ibid., 46.

10. See Judith M. Lieu, "Justin Martyr and the Transformation of Psalm 22," *Biblical Traditions in Transmission: Essays in Honour of Michael A. Knibb*, ed. Charlotte Hempel and Judith M. Lieu, Supplements to the Journal for the Study of Judaism 111 (Leiden: Brill, 2006), 195-211. Lieu nonetheless find it "hard to resist the 'school' model that many have used to understand the development of early Christian scriptural interpretation," and she speaks of a "testimonia-tradition." See also Judith M. Lieu, "Accusations of Jewish Persecution in Early Christian Sources, with Particular Reference to Justin Martyr and the *Martyrdom of Polycarp*," in *Tolerance and Intolerance in Early Judaism and Christianity*, ed. Graham N. Stanton and Guy G. Stroumsa (Cambridge: Cambridge University Press, 1998), 279-95. The entire perspective relies upon Pierre Prigent, *Justin et l'Ancien Testament: L'argumentation*

scripturaire du traité de Justin Contre toutes les hérésies comme source principale du Dialogue avec Tryphon et de la Première Apologie (Paris: Gabalda 1964), who together with Barthélemy offered a new perspective for the study of Justin that Skarsaune and those who have followed him have pursued.

11. J. R. Harris and V. Burch, *Testimonies* (Cambridge: Cambridge University Press, 1920). It is noteworthy that when Barnabas Lindars took this model up in *New Testament Apologetic* (London: SCM, 1961), he decisively distanced himself from conceiving of apologetic as mere *Auseinandersetzung* and explored the category of *pesher*. Cf. Bruce D. Chilton, "Commenting on the Old Testament (with Particular Reference to the Pesharim, Philo, and the Mekhilta)," in *It Is Written: Scripture Citing Scripture; Essays in Honour of Barnabas Lindars*, ed. D. A. Carson and H. G. M. Williamson (Cambridge: Cambridge University Press, 1988), 122-40.

12. Tessa Rajak, "Talking at Trypho: Christian Apologetic as Anti-Judaism in Justin's *Dialogue with Trypho the Jew*," in *The Jewish Dialogue with Greece and Rome: Studies in Cultural and Social Interaction*, Arbeiten zur Geschichte des antiken Judentums und des Urchristentums 48 (Leiden: Brill, 2001), 511-33, esp. 531.

13. See Theodore Stylianopoulos, *Justin Martyr and the Mosaic Law*, Society of Biblical Literature Dissertation Series 20 (Missoula, MT: Scholars Press, 1975), 50, who thinks that, because Justin was a Samaritan, he believed tassels were scarlet rather than blue (*Dial*. 46.5) and that hot water should not be drunk on the Sabbath (19.3 [sic]; but see 29.3). It seems risky, however, to base an argument about Justin's thought on his Samaritan background, both because second-century Samaritanism is not a known quantity (see Reinhard Pummer, *The Samaritans*, Iconography of Religions 23.5 [Brill: Leiden, 1987]) and because it is not even clear that Justin had been a Samaritan by anything but race. Tessa Rajak reads *Dial*. 29 to mean that Justin had been a pagan, so that the term *genos* should be understood only of his people (120), not his thought; Tessa Rajak, "Talking at Trypho," 511-33, esp. 512. In a brief but helpful treatment, Peter Philhofer, "Von Jakobus zu Justin: Lernen in den spätschriften des Neuen Testaments und bei den Apologeten," in *Religiöses Lernen in der biblischen, frühjüdischen und frühchristlichen Überlieferung*, ed. Beate Ego and Helmut Merkel, Wissenschaftliche Untersuchungen zum Neuen Testament 180 (Tübingen: Mohr Siebeck, 2005), 253-69, 265, says: "Justin sieht sich in einer Schultradition: Er hat eine Lehre empfangen, die er seinerseits nun weitergibt."

14. See Bernard Grossfeld and Moses Aberbach, *Targum Onqelos on Genesis 49: Translation and Analytic Commentary*, SBL Aramaic Studies 1 (Missoula, MT: Scholars Press, 1976). Grossfeld was an early advocate of what has since become a consensus, that the earliest *Targumim* represent Judaism during the second century, not only within rabbinic discussion, but also as that discussion was intended to influence popular practice and belief; see Bruce D. Chilton, "The Targumim and Judaism of the First Century," in *Judaism in Late Antiquity*, part 3, *Where We Stand: Issues and Debates in Ancient Judaism*, ed. J. Neusner and A. J. Avery-Peck, vol. 2, Handbuch der Orientalistik 41 (Leiden: Brill, 1999), 115-50.

15. Justin also uses this argument as a weapon in his dispute with Marcion. The theme as a whole is explored in J. C. M. van Winden, *An Early Christian Philosopher: Justin Martyr's Dialogue with Trypho, Chapters One to Nine; Introduction, Text and Commentary*, Philosophia partum (Leiden: Brill, 1971).

16. Bobichon, *Justin Martyr: Dialogue avec Tryphon*, 1:81-82.

17. Wartelle, *Saint Justin*, 246, cites the same theme among other apologists, as well as writers in the classical tradition.

18. See Bruce D. Chilton and Jacob Neusner, *Judaism in the New Testament: Practices and Beliefs* (London and New York: Routledge, 1995).

19. To this extent, the rabbinic project is more Aristotelian than Platonic; see Jacob Neusner, *The Theology of the Oral Torah: Revealing the Justice of God* (Montreal: McGill-Queen's University Press, 1999).

20. Edward Kessler, *Bound by the Bible: Jews, Christians and the Sacrifice of Isaac* (Cambridge: Cambridge University Press, 2004), 19.

21. On the necessary element of supersessionism in Paul, see Bruce D. Chilton, *Rabbi Paul: An Intellectual Biography* (New York: Doubleday, 2004).

22. Philippe Bobichon, *Justin Martyr: Dialogue avec Tryphon*. On the phrase "la race israélite (*israèlitikon genos*) véritable, spirituelle," see Bernard Meunier, "Le clivage entre Juifs et chrétiens vu part Justin (vers 150)," in *Le judaïsme à l'aube de l'ère chrétienne: XVIIIe congrès de l'ACFEB (Lyon,*

Septembre 1999), ed. Philippe Abadie and Jean-Pierre Lémonon, Lectio Divina 186 (Paris: du Cerf, 2001), 333-44, esp. 336. This leads to his conclusion (344): "Le judaïsme est à la rigueur hébergé par le chrétiens, ce n'est en aucun cas l'inverse."

23. See Philippe Bobichon, "Préceptes éternels de la loi mosaïque et le *Dialogue avec Tryphon* de Justin Martyr," *Revue Biblique* 111, no. 2 (2004): 238-54, esp. 238.

24. Theodore Stylianopoulos, *Justin Martyr and the Mosaic Law*, 55.

25. Peter Schäfer, *Die Vorstellung vom heiligen Geist in der rabbinischen Literatur*, Studien zum Alten und Neuen Testament 28 (Munich: Kösel, 1972).

26. A probable awareness of the Birkhat ha-Minim causes him to reinterpret Gal 3:10 in *Dial*. 95-96. As Lieu, "Accusations of Jewish Persecution," 291, says: "On the one hand, the scriptural 'cursed be everyone who hangs on a tree' anticipates how the Jews would treat both Christ and Christians, yet, on the other, it also sets into sharp relief the Christian response of steadfastness and forgiveness."

27. Rodney Werline, "The Transformation of Pauline Arguments in Justin Martyr's *Dialogue with Trypho*," *Harvard Theological Review* 92, no. 1 (1999): 79-93, esp. 90.

28. See Bruce D. Chilton, "Prophecy in the Targumim," *Mediators of the Divine: Horizons of Prophecy, Divination, Dreams, and Theurgy in Mediterranean Antiquity*, ed. R. M. Berchman, South Florida Studies in the History of Judaism 163 (Atlanta: Scholars Press, 1998), 185-201.

29. Sylvain Jean Gabriel Sanchez, *Justin, apologiste chrétien*, Cahier de la Revue Biblique 50 (Paris: Gabalda, 2000), 253.

30. Eric Francis Osborn, *Justin Martyr*, Beiträge zur historischen Theologie 47 (Tübingen: Mohr, 1973), 88, 89.

31. See Sanchez, *Justin, apologiste chrétien*, 185-94.

32. Cf. Laura Nasrallah, "Mapping the World: Justin, Tatian, Lucian, and the Second Sophistic," *Harvard Theological Review* 98, no. 3 (2005): 283-314.

33. Skarsaune, "Judaism and Hellenism in Justin Martyr," 585-611, esp. 599, 606.

34. See Bruce D. Chilton, "Typologies of Memra and the Fourth Gospel," *Targum Studies* 1 (1992): 89-100; idem, *Judaic Approaches to the Gospels*, International Studies in Formative Christianity and Judaism 2 (Atlanta: Scholars Press, 1994), 177-201.

35. See van Winden, An Early Christian Philosopher, 118.

36. Bobichon, *Justin Martyr: Dialogue avec Tryphon*, 1:500.

37. See Bruce D. Chilton, *A Feast of Meanings: Eucharistic Theologies from Jesus through Johannine Circles*, Supplements to Novum Testamentum 72 (Leiden: Brill, 1994).

6. The New Testament's Interpretation: The Nazirite Vow and the Brother of Jesus

1. See Richard Bauckham, "James and the Jerusalem Church," in *The Book of Acts in Its Palestinian Setting*, ed. R. Bauckham (Grand Rapids: Eerdmans, 1995), 415-80.

2. On the influence of "the Tübingen school," see Ernst Haenchen, *The Acts of the Apostles*, trans. B. Noble et al. (Philadelphia: Westminster, 1971), 15-24. In view of Professor Hengel's association with Tübingen during the intervening period, we may have to think again about this designation!

3. See Bruce D. Chilton, *Rabbi Paul: An Intellectual Biography* (New York: Doubleday, 2004), 168-70.

4. For the roots of the practice, see Eliezer Diamond, "An Israelite Self-Offering in the Priestly Code: A New Perspective on the Nazirite," *Jewish Quarterly Review* 88, nos. 1-2 (1997): 1-18.

5. See Bruce D. Chilton, *Rabbi Jesus: An Intimate Biography* (New York: Doubleday, 2000), 213-30.

6. As a matter of fact, Hegesippus accepts that this signification is Greek; James seems to be so named here because after his death the Roman siege of Jerusalem was successful.

7. See Joseph A. Fitzmyer and Daniel J. Harrington, *A Manual of Palestinian Aramaic Texts*, Biblica et orientalia 34 (Rome: Biblical Institute Press, 1978).

8. See Martin Hengel, "Jakobus der Herrenbruder—der erste 'Papst'?" in *Glaube und Eschatologie: Festschrift für Werner Georg Kümmel zum 80. Geburtstag*, ed. E. Grässer and O. Merk (Tübingen:

Notes to Chapter 6

Mohr, 1985), 71–104, esp. 81. The ordering of Peter under James is clearly a part of that perspective, as Hengel shows, and much earlier Joseph Lightfoot found that the alleged correspondence between Clement and James was a later addition to the Pseudo-Clementine corpus (see J. B. Lightfoot, *The Apostolic Fathers* 1 [London: Macmillan, 1890], 414–20). But even if the Pseudo-Clementines are taken at face value, they undermine the view of Eisenman (or of the "Tübingen school," which, as Hengel ["Jakobus der Herrenbruder," 92] points out, is the source of such contentions): the Pseudo-Clementines portray James (rather than Paul, as claimed by Eisenman) as the standard for how Hellenistic Christians are to teach (see the Pseudo-Clementine *Recognitions* 11.35.3). Cf. Robert Eisenman, *James, the Brother of Jesus* (New York: Viking, 1997).

9. See Markus Bockmuehl, "The Noachide Commandments and New Testament Ethics," in *Jewish Law in Gentile Churches: Halakhah and the Beginning of Christian Public Ethics* (Edinburgh: T&T Clark, 2000), 145–73.

10. See Ethelbert Stauffer, *Jesus and His Story*, trans. R. and C. Winston (New York: Knopf, 1960), 13–15.

11. See Wayne Meeks, *The First Urban Christians: The Social World of the Apostle Paul* (New Haven: Yale University Press, 1983).

12. See Abraham Malherbe, *Social Aspects of Early Christianity* (Philadelphia: Fortress, 1983).

13. See Dennis E. Smith and Hal Taussig, *Many Tables: The Eucharist in the New Testament and Liturgy Today* (Philadelphia: Trinity Press International; London: SCM, 1990).

14. For the situation of this vow within Paul's biography, see Chilton, *Rabbi Paul*, 237–40.

15. The discussion appears in Maas Boertien, *Nazir (Nasiräer): Text, Übersetzung und Erklärung nebst einem textkritischen Anhang*, vol. 3.4 of *Die Mischna* (Berlin: de Gruyter, 1971), 28–29, 71–72, 90–95.

16. Ibid., 90–91.

17. Ibid., 93.

18. Ibid., 72.

19. So ibid., 92, citing *Nazir* 7:3.

20. The Mishnah envisages a man saying, "Qorban [Korban] be any benefit my wife gets from me, for she stole my purse" (*Nedarim* 3:2).

21. See Pierre Benoit, *La Bible de Jérusalem* (Paris: Éditions du Cerf, 1977), 1619–1620.

22. Florence Morgan Gillman suggests that Hegesippus's source is the *Acts of the Apostles* used among the Ebionites, a Christian group that sought also to follow the Torah; "James, Brother of Jesus," The *Anchor Bible Dictionary* (ed. D. N. Freedman; New York: Doubleday, 1992), III., 620–21. She connects their veneration of James to the praise given him in *The Gospel according to Thomas* 12.

23. See Josephus, *Jewish War* 2 §§590–594; Mishnah *Menaḥoth* 8:3–5 and the whole of *Makširin*. The point of departure for the concern is Lev 11:34.

24. See Bruce D. Chilton, "Exorcism and History: Mark 1:21–28," *Gospel Perspectives* 6 (1986): 253–71.

25. This geographical meaning is also expressed in the Gospels by another term, "Nazorean" (Greek *Nazoraios*), which does not rhyme with "Magdalene." "Nazorean" predominates in the Gospels according to Matthew, Luke, and John, while Mark uses only "Nazarene." See the still-worthwhile article by Hans Heinrich Schaeder in *Theological Dictionary of the New Testament*, ed. G. Kittel, trans. G. W. Bromiley, vol. 4 (Grand Rapids: Eerdmans, 1967), 874–79. In the Talmud and other rabbinic sources, Jesus is called the *Notsri*, an evident play on *Nazaraya* and *Nazoraya*. The term *Notsri* means someone who keeps or hinders: Jesus and his followers keep their own traditions, and therefore hinder other Israelites. See, for example, *Avodah Zarah* 166–17a and Sanhedrin 43a in The Babylonian Talmud.

26. See Bruce D. Chilton, "Friends and Enemies," in *The Cambridge Companion to Jesus*, ed. M. Bockmuehl (Cambridge: Cambridge University Press, 2001), 72–86; idem, *Rabbi Jesus*, 168–73, where the context of the events, in the deadly threat to Jesus from Herod Antipas, explains the political symbolism of this exorcism. The sequel to the exorcism (Mark 5:14–17) is also discussed in those pages of *Rabbi Jesus*.

27. For the recovery of this source, see Bruce D. Chilton, *Mary Magdalene: A Biography* (New York: Doubleday, 2005), 33–46, 203–6.

28. This is the position of Marcus Bockmuehl, given at the meeting of the Studiorum Novi Testamenti Societas in Birmingham in 1997. Of all the arguments adduced, the most attractive is that

Jesus' statement concerning wine and the kingdom involves his accepting Nazirite vows. See P. Lebeau, *Le vin nouveau du Royaume: Étude exégétique et patristique sur la parole eschatologique de Jésus à la Cène* (Paris: Desclée, 1966); Michal Wojciechowski, "Le naziréat et la Passion (Mc 14,25a; 15,23)," *Biblica* 65 (1984): 94-96. But the form of Jesus' statement has not been rightly understood, owing to its Semitic syntax. He is not promising never to drink wine, but only to drink wine in association with his celebration of the kingdom. See Bruce D. Chilton, *A Feast of Meanings: Eucharistic Theologies from Jesus through Johannine Circles*, Supplements to Novum Testamentum 72 (Leiden: Brill, 1994), 169-71.

9. Early Christian Interpretation: Sunday in the New Testament

1. So C. K. Barrett, *The Acts of the Apostles*, vol. 1, International Critical Commentary (Edinburgh: T&T Clark, 1994), 108. See also Lars Hartman, *"Into the Name of the Lord Jesus": Baptism in the Early Church*, Studies of the New Testament and Its World (Edinburgh: T&T Clark, 1997), 131-33, who observes the coherence with Luke 24:44-49. That is a telling remark, because it shows, together with the preaching attributed to Peter in the house of Cornelius, that from a primitive stage, the narrative of Jesus' passion was connected with the catechesis that lead to baptism.

2. Barrett, *Acts of the Apostles*, 1:129-57, presents a fine analysis on how deeply influential the text of Joel is on the speech of Peter as a whole.

3. See Hartman, *Baptism in the Early Church*, 133-36.

4. For a discussion, see Bruce D. Chilton and Jacob Neusner, *Judaism in the New Testament: Practices and Beliefs* (London: Routledge, 1995), 99-104, 108-11.

5. Hartman, *Baptism in the Early Church*, 140, citing Acts 8:37; 22:16.

6. See Jöram Friberg, "Numbers and Counting," *Anchor Bible Dictionary*, ed. D. N. Freedman (New York: Doubleday, 1992), 4:1139-46.

7. Kirsopp Lake, "The Apostolic Council of Jerusalem," in *The Beginnings of Christianity*, ed. F. J. Foakes-Jackson and Kirsopp Lake, vol. 5 (1933; repr., Grand Rapids: Baker, 1979), 195-212, 208-9, with a citation of the Greek text. For an English rendering and fine introductions and explanations, see John J. Collins, "Sibylline Oracles: A New Translation and Introduction," in *The Old Testament Pseudepigrapha*, vol. 1 (Garden City, NY: Doubleday, 1983). Collins (381-82) dates book 4 within the first century, but after the eruption of Vesuvius in 79 CE. With due caution, he assigns book 4 a Syrian provenance.

8. See John T. Squires, *The Plan of God in Luke-Acts*, Society for New Testament Studies Monograph Series 76 (Cambridge: Cambridge University Press, 1993), 121-54.

9. See Collins, "Sibylline Oracles," 317.

10. See Bruce D. Chilton and Jacob Neusner, *Types of Authority in Formative Judaism and Christianity* (London: Routledge, 1999), 116-19.

11. Lake, "The Apostolic Council," 108-9, also cites *Sib. Or.* 4:162-70.

12. Collins, "Sibylline Oracles," 355.

13. Ibid., 331.

14. This idiomatic translation and its explanatory insertions (in square brackets) are Jacob Neusner's in *The Talmud of Babylonia: An Academic Commentary*, vol. 29, *Bavli Tractate Menahoth*, part A, South Florida Academic Commentary Series 23 (Atlanta: Scholars Press, 1996). The term "schmuck" is usually rendered "fool," and the Talmud refers to "the day after Sabbath," rather than to "Sunday"; but this remains a most vivid and apt translation. Cf. *Menachoth min Talmud Bavli* (Jerusalem: Vagshal, 1980).

15. Hartman, *Baptism in the Early Church*, 37-50.

16. That is precisely the translation in Jacob Neusner, *The Mishnah: A New Translation* (New Haven: Yale University Press, 1988), 707. See also *Pesaḥim* 60a, cited by Hartman, *Baptism in the Early Church*, 49n53.

17. Hartman, *Baptism in the Early Church*, 47.

18. See Bruce D. Chilton, *A Feast of Meanings: Eucharistic Theologies from Jesus through Johannine Circles*, Supplements to Novum Testamentum 72 (Leiden: Brill, 1994), 75-92. Hartman, *Baptism in the Early Church*, 61, also approaches this idea.

19. Hartman, *Baptism in the Early Church*, 67-68.

234   Notes to Chapters 9 and 12

20. Paul's insistence here that the "rock" was Christ might be intended to qualify the claims of the Petrine circle.

21. See Charles Gore, *The Holy Spirit and the Church: The Reconstruction of Belief*, vol. 3 (New York: Scribner's Sons, 1924), 112.

22. Gore (ibid.) here is referring to the baptism in Acts 19:1-7. It would be more accurate to say that they were followers of Jesus who had formerly practiced immersion only as taught by John (and Jesus himself, at first). But their baptism at Paul's hands brings with it the Holy Spirit.

23. Here Gore (ibid.) cites Acts 4:31; 6:3, 5; 11:24.

24. Clarke Garrett, *Spirit Possession and Popular Religion: From the Camisards to the Shakers* (Baltimore: Johns Hopkins University Press, 1987), 8.

12. The New Testament's Interpretation: Eucharist as Holy Food, Mimesis of Sacrifice

1. Bruce D. Chilton, *The Temple of Jesus: His Sacrificial Program within a Cultural History of Sacrifice* (University Park: Pennsylvania State University Press, 1992).

2. Bruce D. Chilton, *A Feast of Meanings: Eucharistic Theologies from Jesus through Johannine Circles*, Supplements to Novum Testamentum 72 (Leiden: Brill, 1994).

3. Because my interest here is in the traditional form of the saying, before changes introduced in Matthew and Luke, I give a reconstructed form; see Bruce D. Chilton, *God in Strength: Jesus' Announcement of the Kingdom*, Studien zum Neuen Testament und seiner Umwelt, series B, vol. 1 (Freistadt: Plöchl, 1979; repr., Biblical Seminar 8, Sheffield: JSOT Press, 1987), 179-201. More recently, see idem, *Pure Kingdom: Jesus' Vision of God*, Studying the Historical Jesus 1 (Eerdmans: Grand Rapids; London: SPCK, 1996), 12-14.

4. When I participated in the Jesus Seminar, I noticed that the enthusiasm of the fellows for the authenticity of this saying was surpassed only by their refusal to see its implications for Jesus' conception of purity. See Robert W. Funk, Roy W. Hoover, and The Jesus Seminar, *The Five Gospels: The Search for the Authentic Words of Jesus* (San Francisco: HarperSanFrancisco, 1997), ad loc.

5. See the order of wine followed by bread in 1 Cor 10:16; Luke 22:17-20; *Didache* 9:1-5, and the particular significance accorded the wine in Mark 14:25; Matt 26:29; Luke 22:18.

6. Professor Albert Baumgarten has pointed out to me that a rabbinic tradition in the name of R. Nehemiah supports this analysis. In the Tosefta (*Hagigah* 3:19), as Baumgarten says in a personal letter written in 1999, Nehemiah "explains the willingness of temple authorities to be flexible, understanding, and willing to trust all Jews at the time of pilgrimage festivals as motivated by the fear lest someone set up his own altar or offer his own red heifers. Erecting one's own altar or offering one's own red heifers were intolerable assaults on the legitimacy of the Jerusalem temple. Accordingly the law was to be stretched as much as possible to avoid that outcome."

7. I would not deny for a moment that a sense of impending martyrdom might well have suffused Jesus' last meals with his disciples; see Bruce D. Chilton, *Rabbi Jesus: An Intimate Biography* (New York: Doubleday, 2000), 253-68. The elevation of that sense to the predominant meaning, however, seems to me to be a later development.

8. See Günther Bornkamm, "Mystērion, myeō," *Theological Dictionary of the New Testament*, ed. G. Kittel, trans. G. W. Bromiley, vol. 4 (Grand Rapids: Eerdmans, 1967), 802-28. More recently, see Marvin W. Meyer, ed., *The Ancient Mysteries: A Sourcebook; Sacred Texts of the Mystery Religions of the Ancient Mediterranean World* (San Francisco: HarperSanFrancisco, 1987); Walter Burkert, *Ancient Mystery Cults* (Cambridge, MA: Harvard University Press, 1987); David Ulansey, *The Origins of the Mithraic Mysteries: Cosmology and Salvation in the Ancient World* (New York: Oxford University Press, 1989).

9. In this regard, see Reimund Bieringer, Didier Pollefeyt, Frederique Vandecasteele-Vanneuville, eds., *Anti-Judaism and the Fourth Gospel* (Louisville: Westminster John Knox, 2001).

10. See Morton Smith, *The Secret Gospel* (New York: Harper & Row, 1973); idem, *Jesus the Magician* (New York: Harper & Row, 1977). Throughout, the influence of Hans Lewy, *Chaldean Oracles and Theurgy* (Cairo: Institut français d'archéologie orientale, 1956), is apparent. It may be that some

of Smith's other assertions about Jesus have obscured this well-documented and incisive aspect of his contributions.

11. See Ralph Schroeder, *Max Weber and the Sociology of Culture* (London: Sage, 1992), 33-71, a chapter titled "The Uniqueness of the East." For further discussion, see Bruce D. Chilton, "Eucharist: Surrogate, Metaphor, Sacrament of Sacrifice," in *Sacrifice in Religious Experience*, ed. A. I. Baumgarten, Numen Book Series 93 (Leiden: Brill, 2002), 175-88.

12. Schroeder, *Max Weber and the Sociology of Culture*, 37; citing Max Weber, *Wirtschaftgeschichte: Abriss der universalen Sozial- und Wirtschaftsgeschichte*, ed. S. Hellmann and M. Palyi, rev. J. F. Winckelmann, 3rd ed. (Berlin: Duncker & Humblot, 1981); and idem, *Economy and Society*, 3 vols. (New York: Bedminster, 1968).

13. Schroeder, *Max Weber and the Sociology of Culture*, 40.

14. According to Colin Brown, Theudas was inspired by John the Baptist, whose program was not purification but a recrossing of the Jordan; see Brown, "What Was John the Baptist Doing?" *Bulletin for Biblical Research* 7 (1997): 37-49, esp. 48. That seems to be a desperate expedient to avoid the obvious connection with purification. In this avoidance, many conservative evangelical scholars are at one with the Jesus Seminar. The equally obvious obstacles are that crossing the Jordan is not a part of any characterization of John's message in the primary sources, and that Josephus does not associate John with the "false prophets." For the context of John's immersion (and Jesus'), see Bruce D. Chilton, *Jesus' Baptism and Jesus' Healing: His Personal Practice of Spirituality* (Harrisburg: Trinity Press International, 1998).

15. Christian Interpretation: Sexuality and Family

1. See Bruce D. Chilton, *Pure Kingdom: Jesus' Vision of God*, Studying the Historical Jesus 1 (Eerdmans: Grand Rapids; London: SPCK, 1996).

2. See Bruce D. Chilton and Jacob Neusner, *The Intellectual Foundations of Christian and Jewish Discourse: The Philosophy of Religious Argument* (London: Routledge, 1997).

3. Jaroslav Pelikan, *The Emergence of the Catholic Tradition (100-600)*, vol. 1 of *The Christian Tradition: A History of the Development of Doctrine* (Chicago: University of Chicago Press, 1971), 126.

4. See Jean Daniélou and Henri Marrou, *The First Six Hundred Years*, trans. V. Cronin, The Christian Centuries 1 (New York: McGraw-Hill, 1964), 86-90.

5. Cited in Augustine, *City of God* 16.6.

6. See the translation by Hans-Gebhard Bethge and Orval S. Wintermute in *The Nag Hammadi Library*, ed. J. M. Robinson (San Francisco: Harper & Row, 1978), 161-79.

7. Elisabeth Schüssler Fiorenza et al., eds., *Searching the Scriptures*, vol. 2, *A Feminist Commentary* (New York: Crossroad, 1994), 4.

8. Ibid., 745-46.

9. Ibid., 748.

18. The New Testament's Interpretation: Jesus' Lex Talionis

1. See Richard B. Hays, *The Moral Vision of the New Testament: Community, Cross, New Creation; A Contemporary Introduction to New Testament Ethics* (San Francisco: HarperSanFrancisco, 1996; Bruce D. Chilton and J. I. H. McDonald, *Jesus and the Ethics of the Kingdom*, Biblical Foundations in Theology (London: SPCK, 1987; also published outside the series, Grand Rapids: Eerdmans, 1988).

2. I take these differences to be exemplary, because they have been traced in other documents within the New Testament and early Christian literature. See Robin Gill, ed., *The Cambridge Companion to Christian Ethics* (Cambridge: Cambridge University Press, 2001).

3. For a consideration of the social conditions in Jesus' experience that this teaching reflects, see Bruce D. Chilton, *Rabbi Jesus: An Intimate Biography* (New York: Doubleday, 2000), 46.

4. Paul works out his position by splicing together passages from the Scriptures of Israel: Deut

32:35; Prov 25:21-22. See Joseph A. Fitzmyer, *Romans: A New Translation with Introduction and Commentary*, Anchor Bible 33 (New York: Doubleday, 1993), 656-59. For Paul's characteristic combination of Judaism and philosophical thought, see Bruce D. Chilton, *Rabbi Paul: An Intellectual Biography* (New York: Doubleday, 2004).

5. A more detailed analysis of the historical circumstances appears in Chilton, *Rabbi Jesus*, 197-289. Here my concern is the impact of those circumstances in shaping Jesus' distinctive ethics.

6. See ibid. for a full discussion of the relevant texts, interwoven with narrative together with bibliography.

7. See Christopher D. Marshall, *Beyond Retribution: A New Testament Vision for Justice, Crime, and Punishment* (Grand Rapids: Eerdmans, 2001); Robin W. Lovin, *Christian Ethics: An Essential Guide* (Nashville: Abingdon, 2001).

Index

Abel, 189, 190, 193
Abodah Zarah, 25–30
abomination, 20, 116
Abraham, 169–171
Absalom, 189
activity, 95–96
Acts, 63, 69, 106
Adam, 165, 168
adultery, 147–149, 153, 160–164
Ahaz, 80
altruism, 227–228
Amos, 13, 36, 51, 78
Ananias, 219–220
angels, 180
aniconism, 6, 23–24
animals
    pure and impure, 116–122, 129–130
    slaughter methods, 122–123, 126–128, 130
anthromorphisms, 18
Apology (Justin Martyr), 33–36
Apostolic Council, 107
Apostolic Decree, 37
Asherah (diety), 11, 12
asylum, 193–194, 200–202
Aten cult, 6, 18, 24
attitudinal terms, 20
Augustine of Hippo, 179–181, 183–184
autogenesis, 18
avenge slayings, 188–189, 193

Baal (diety), 10, 11, 12
Baba Qamma, 205–214
Babylonia, 14, 16
Babylonian Talmud, 205–214
balance of nature, 188–192
baptism, 105–106, 109
Bar Kokhba, 35
Benoit, Pierre, 69
bestiality, 154–155
betrothal, 148

biblical law, 188–194, 204. *See also lex talionis*
biblical narratives, related to northern Israelite cults, 8–9
Binding of Isaac, 38
Bobichon, Philippe, 39
Boertien, Maas, 67, 68
Book of the Covenant, 81, 193–197
bread, blessing of, 136
bull cults, 8, 11, 18, 23

Cain, 189, 190, 193
Canaan, 155
capital punishment, 187, 194
causality, 90–91
childbirth, 144, 156, 158
children, legitimacy of, 143
Christ. *See also* Jesus, coming of, 40
Christian ethics, 217–223
Christianity, sexuality and family in, 173–184
Chronicles, 12, 88
circumcision, 63–64, 69
City of God (Augustine), 179–181, 184
clan retaliation, 188–189, 193
Cleansing of the Temple, 134
cloud tradition, 18
collective living, 188–189
compensation principle, 214, 215–216
constitution rituals, 18
contagion, 144
corporal punishment, 187, 192, 195–196, 199
corpses
    idolatry and paganism, 25
    prohibition of contact with, 47, 53–56
creation, 19, 100
criminal justice
    corporal punishment, 187, 192, 195–196, 199
    homicide, 188–192, 194–197, 200

integration of retaliation in, 192–202
personal status and, 196
to restore natural order, 188–192
cult centralization, 12
cultic activity, in northern Israel, 8–9
cultic purity, 113, 114
cult images, 3–5. *See also* idolatry and paganism
ban on, 5–7, 9–12
degrees of pictorial representation, 23–24
golden bull-calf, 8
meaning of, 17–19
terminology of, 19–24
cult installations, 201

Daniel, 226–227
Danites, 9
David, 189–190
day, 78
Day of Atonement, 78
dead bodies, prohibition of contact with, 47, 53–56
Decalogue, 3, 4, 12, 77, 82
defilement, 143
demons, 70–71, 72
Deutero-Isaiah, 15–17
Deuteronomic Code, 6–7
Deuteronomic laws, 197–199
Deuteronomist, 4, 5–6, 18
Deuteronomy, 4, 83, 190–191, 201
Deuteronomy 14, on dietary purity, 116–119
devotion, Nazirite, 45–55
Dialogue with Trypho (Justin Martyr), 33–34, 35–37, 38–40
dietary purity
clean and unclean foods, 124–130
Deuteronomy 14, 116–119
Eucharist and, 131–140
Leviticus 11, 119–123
rabbinic reading, 124–130
Scripture's account, 113–123
direct consequences, 91–92
distributive reward, 169
divine judgment, 193
divine justice, 160–167
divine vengeance, 224–225
divorce, 151–152, 153–154
doctrine of replacement theology, 38

Eden, 101, 103
Edomite cult, 4
El (deity), 8, 10, 23
enemies, love for, 223–225
epic traditions, 18
equity, 209–211, 213–214
eschatology, 179
ethics
Christian, 217–223
of love, 220–227
Eucharist, 42, 109–110, 131–140
as blessing of bread at home, 136
as mimetic surrogate of sacrifice, 134–136, 138–140
as sacrament, 137
as sacrifice for sin, 136–137
as sanctification of the kingdom, 133–134
as Seder, 136
types of, 132–138
Eve, 168
evil, 180
Exodus, 77, 83, 84–85, 106
exorcism, 70–71, 73
Ezekiel, 17, 86, 123, 154, 193
Ezra-Nehemiah, 12

fairs, 26–27
false prophecy, 40
false prophets, 139
false testimony, 198
family
in Christianity, 173–184
embrace of, 175–179
opposition to conventional, 174–175
feminism, 181–183
fetishism, 17
Fiorenza, Elisabeth Schüssler, 182
first commandment, 3
food. *See also* dietary purity
clean and unclean, 124–130
Eucharist as holy, 131–140
fratricide, 189

Gemara, 207–209
gender, 183–184
contention over, 181–183
transformation of sexuality into, 179–181
Gentiles, 25–32, 106–107
Gideon, 11

God. *See also* Yahew
   alienation from, 28
   as avenger, 203
   enemies of, 28–29
   human cognition of, 41–42
   kingdom of, 133–134, 174–175
   love for, 220–221
   mercy of, 165, 167
   worship of, 3
goddesses, 10
God's Thone, 227
golden bull-calf, 8, 18
good Samaritan, 222–223
Gore, Charles, 110
Gospels, 217–219, 220–221
Greek philosophy, 35, 37–38
group continuity, 143

Habakkuk, 14
Haggadah, 162–163
hair cutting, 47–51, 56, 67–68
Halakhah
   clean and unclean foods, 128–130
   idolatry, 25–29
   intentionality, 90–91
   Sabbath, 89–90, 96–103
   sexual purity, 160–162
   vows, 57–62
Hannah, 52
harlotry, 149–151, 153–154
Harris, Rendell, 35
Hartman, Lars, 109–110
head shaving, 47–51, 56
Hegesippus, 63–64
heirs, 143
henotheism, 3
heterosexual intercourse, 155–159
holiness, attainment of, 45
Holiness Code of Leviticus, 7, 83–84, 150
Holy Spirit. *See* Spirit
homicide, 188–192, 194–197, 200
homosexuality, 154–155
Hos, 13, 14
Hosea, 12–13
human-divine contract, 45
humankind, as God's representatives on Earth, 191–192
human reproduction, 144

iconclasm, 5–7, 11–12
iconography, terminology of, 19–24
idolatry and paganism
   case of Justin Martyr and, 33–42
   Halakhah of, 25–29
   meaning of, 17–19
   as phenomenon, 17–24
   polytheism and, 5
   prohibition on, 3–7
   rabbinic reading, 25–32
   Scripture's account, 3–24
   as target of prophetic movement, 12–17
idols, as corpses, 25
image ban, role of, in advancing Yahwist movement, 9–12
impurity, 113–114, 143–144. *See also* purity
incest, 144–147
indirect consequences, 91–92
initiatory retaliation, 187–188, 192–202
intentionality, 90–91
Isaiah, 13–14, 36, 79
Israel
   enemies of, 28–29
   infidelity of, in relationship with Yahweh, 153–154
Israelites, coexistence of, with idolatry, 25–32

James, 107
   Nazirite vow and, 63–73
   temple and, 65–66
Jeremiah, 14, 14–15
Jeroboam I, 8, 11
Jerubbaal, 11
Jesus, 64
   ethics of, 220–228
   Eucharist and, 131–140
   family of, 174–175
   Last Supper, 132–135, 137–138
   lex talionis and, 217–228
   magical surrogacy, 138–140
   mimetic surrogacy of sacrifice, 134–136, 138–140
   as Nazirite, 70–73
   resurrection of, 104
   visionary experience, 225–227
Joash, 79
John the Baptist, 39–40, 139
Josephus, 139

Josiah, 11–12, 54–55
Judah, 149
judicial system. *See also* criminal justice
    Book of the Covenant, 193–197
    Deuteronomic laws, 193–197
    priestly laws, 199–200
justice. *See also* retaliation
    distributive, 169–172
    divine, 160–167
    retributive, 169
Justin Martyr, 33–42

kabôd (glory) theology, 18
Kessler, Edward, 38
kingdom of God, 133–134, 174–175

labor
    defining, 96–103
    on Sabbath, 95–103
Lamentations, 80
language
    power of, 57–61
    of purity, 114–115
Last Supper, 132–135, 137–138
law of retaliation, 187. *See also* lex talionis
laws
    biblical, 188–194, 204
    Book of the Covenant, 194–197
    Deuteronomic, 193–197
    priestly, 199–200
    Talmudic, 204–216
    of testimony, 198
    Torah, 204
legal system, 187. *See also* judicial system
lesbians, 155
Levites, 202
Leviticus 11, 119–123
lex talionis. *See also* retaliation
    background of, 188–192
    Book of the Covenant, 193–197
    Deuteronomic laws, 193–197
    Jesus', 217–228
    judicial process and, 192–202
    priestly laws, 199–200
    Scripture's account, 187–203
    in Talmudic law, 204–216
literary references, to the Sabbath, 78–81
Logos, 41–42
love, 220–227

Luke, 182–183, 219, 224
Luke-Acts, 107, 183

Magdalene, 71–72
magical acts, 143
magical surrogacy, 138–140
Manicheanism, 180–181
manufacture, terms of, 20–21
marital fidelity, 147–149. *See also* adultery
Mark, 219, 220–221
marriage
    among relatives, 146–147
    stages of, 148–149
    valid, 161
Martyr, Justin, 33–42
Mary, 182–183
Mary Magdalene, 71–72
masturbation, 144
Matthew, 219, 220–221, 224
meals, 133
memra, 42
menstruation, 144, 155–159
mentalité, 202–203
mercy, 165, 167
Micah, 8–9, 13
Micaiah, 8–9
mimetic surrogacy, 134–136, 138–140
Mishnah, 26–27, 38, 204–205
monotheism, 3
morphic terms, 21
Mosaic law, 35–36
Moses, 18–19, 23, 35–37, 47, 106
murder. *See* homicide

Nazarene, 70–73
na-zîr, meaning of, 46–47
Nazir, metaphorical, 70–73
Nazirite
    hair cutting and, 47–51, 56, 67–68
    New Testament interpretation, 63–73
    Numbers 6, 45, 47–55
    practical, 66–70
    prohibition on contact with corpses, 47, 53–55
    rabbinic reading, 56–62
    Scripture's account, 45–55
    vows, 56–62, 63–73
    wine prohibition, 47, 48, 51, 56, 58, 123
Nebuchadnezar, 12

Nehemiah, 87–88
neighbor, love for, 220–221, 223–224
New Testament
  Eucharist in, 131–140
  Sunday in, 104–110
Noah, 106, 107–108, 191, 202
northern Israelite cults, 8–9
Num 6, 45
Numbers 6, 47–48
  background of, 48–52
  priestly agenda, 52–55

oaths, 53
Omride dynasty, 11
Osborn, Eric, 41

paganism. *See* idolatry and paganism
parturition, 144, 155–159
Passover, 108, 137
Paul, 67–70, 108, 136–137
Pelikan, Jaroslav, 176
Pentacostalism, 110
Pentecost, 104–110
periodization, 39
Persians, 30–31
Peter, 104–105, 107
Petrine theology, 107, 109, 136
Philo, 37, 41
pictorial representation, degrees of, 23–24
Plato, 37, 179
Platonism, 33–34, 37–38
polytheism
  idolatry and, 5, 12–17
  negation of, 3
  prohibition of, 4–5, 6
poverty, 218–220
priestly laws, 199–200
priestly towns, 202
private domain, 92–93, 97–99
private property, 101
private religion, 45
private vow, 45
prophecy, 38–40, 106–107
prophetic movement, idolatry as target of, 12–17
Prophets, 35–37
  divine *Logos* and, 41–42
  false, 139
  Greek philosophy and, 37–38
  transfer of prophetic spirit from Israel to Christians, 38–40
prostitution, 149–151
Proverbs, 41
public domains, 92–93
punishment. *See also* retaliation
  corporal, 187, 192, 195–196, 199
  divine, 160–167, 193
  retaliatory, 187–203
  of sin, 160–167
purification, 53–54
purity. *See also* dietary purity; sexual purity
  cultic, 113, 114
  in general, 113–114
  language of, 114–115

Quartodeciman controversy, 136

Ra (diety), 6, 18
Rajak, Tessa, 36
rape, 148, 152
renunciation, 45
repentance, 13
replacement theology, 38
resurrection, 180–181
retaliation, 187. *See also* lex talionis
  asylum and, 200–202
  biblical pronouncements on, 188–192
  Book of the Covenant, 193–197
  corporal punishment, 199
  fratricide and, 189
  initiatory, 187–188, 192–202
  integration of, within judicial process, 192–202
  killing of relative's killer, 188–189
  as *mentalité*, 202–203
  substitution and, 193
retributive justice, 169
ritual acts, 114, 143
ritual character, 63
Roman Empire, 175
Romans, 30–31

Sabbath
  activity, 95–96
  of creation, 100
  direct and indirect consequences, 91–92
  early Christian interpretation, 104–110
  intentionality, 90–91

labor on, 95–103
in late biblical times, 86–88
literary references to, 78–81
rabbinic reading, 89–103
scripture's account, 77–88
space, 92–94
time, 94–95
in Torah sources, 81–85
sacrament, 137
sacrifice
mimetic surrogate of, 134–136, 138–140
for sin, 136–137
sages, 59
salvation, 178–179
Samaritan, 222–223
Samson, 51
Samuel, 52
Sanchez, Sylvan, 40
sanctification, 124–130, 133–134, 139, 160
Saphhira, 219–220
Saturn emblems, 23
Schroeder, Ralph, 138–139
Scripture, periodization of, 39
second commandment, 3–4, 4–5, 12
Seder, 136
Seim, Turid Karlsen, 182–183
self-denial, 53
seminal emissions, 159
sexuality
in Christianity, 173–184
transformation of, into gender, 179–181
sexual purity, 113
adultery, 147–149, 153, 160–164
bestiality, 154–155
Christian interpretation, 173–184
divorce, 151–154
harlotry, 149–151, 153–154
heterosexual intercourse, 155–159
homosexuality, 154–155
incest, 144–147
justice for accused wife, 160–164
menstruation, 155–159
parturition, 155–159
rabbinic reading, 160–172
rape, 148, 152
Scripture's account, 143–159
seminal emissions, 159
transvestism, 154–155
virginity, 152–153

Shepherd of Hermas, 176–179, 184
sin
Eucharist as sacrifice for, 136–137
punishment of, 160–167
Sipre on Numbers, 164–165
Skarsuane, Oskar, 33–34, 41
slaves, 196
Smith, Morton, 138
Socrates, 33–34, 37
space, 92–94
Spirit, 34, 104–105
baptism in, 105–106, 109
Eucharist and, 109–110
vs. *Logos*, 41
Spirot of prophecy, 40
Subylline Oracles, 107–108
Sunday, 104–110
supersessionism, 38–39
surrender, 45

Talmudic hermeneutic, 214–216
Talmudic law, *lex talionis* in, 204–216
Targumim, 37
temple, 63, 65–66, 80, 124–125, 134
temple of Jerusalem, 81
Ten Commandments, 31
testimony, 198
Throne, God's, 227
time, 94–95
Torah
prohibition of cult images in, 5–7
Sabbath in, 81–85
Torah law, 204
Tosefta, 166–171, 205
transvestism, 154–155
Trito-Isaiah, 86–87
Trypho, 39, 41

Ugaritic mythology, 8
uncleanness, 25
universal monotheism, 3
utensils, 120–121

virginity, 152–153
visionary experience, 225–227
vows, 53, 56
James and, 63–73
Nazirite, 57–73

Weber, Max, 139
week, 77
Werline, Rodney, 40
wife, law of accused, 160–164, 172
wine, 27, 47, 48, 51, 56, 58, 123
women
　legal status of, 148
　participation of, in religious life, 45
　recognition of, 174–175
　sexuality and, 180–181
　silence of, 175–179
working day, 78

worship, of God, 3

Yahew, 3. *See also* God
　human form, 18–19
　images of, 4, 5–7, 8–9
　infidelity of Israel to, 153–154
Yahwist movement, role of image ban in advancing, 9–12

Zechariah, 17
Zechariah's prophecy, 64

WITHDRAWN